EXPLORING INTIMACY

EXPLORING INTIMACY

Cultivating Healthy Relationships through Insight and Intuition

Suzann Panek Robins

Rowman & Littlefield Publishers, Inc.
Lanham • Boulder • New York • Toronto • Plymouth, UK

Source of Illustrations

Figure 1.1. Based on an illustration from *Mind Matters*. Jock Millenson. Vista, CA: Eastland Press, 1995 and www.bodynamicusa.com
Figure 1.2. credit: Nancy Moore
Figure 2.2. Copyright © 2008. The Nutrition Source, Department of Nutrition, Harvard School of Public Health, http://www.thenutritionsource.org, and Eat, Drink, and Be Healthy, by Walter C. Willett, M.D. and Patrick J. Skerrett (2005), Free Press/Simon & Schuster Inc.
Figure 3.2. credit: Nancy Moore
Figure 4.1. credit: Gary Stroup and Nancy Moore
Figure 5.1. credit: Gary Stroup and Jeff Panek
Figure 9.2. credit: Gary Stroup and Nancy Moore
Figure 10.1. credit: Nancy Moore
Figure 10.2. credit: Gina Ogden and Gary Stroup
Figure 10.3. credit: Nancy Moore and Gary Stroup

Published by Rowman & Littlefield Publishers, Inc.
A wholly owned subsidiary of The Rowman & Littlefield Publishing Group, Inc.
4501 Forbes Boulevard, Suite 200, Lanham, Maryland 20706
http://www.rowmanlittlefield.com

Estover Road, Plymouth PL6 7PY, United Kingdom

Copyright © 2010 by Rowman & Littlefield Publishers, Inc.

British Library Cataloguing in Publication Information Available

Library of Congress Cataloging-in-Publication Data

Robins, Suzann Panek, 1947–
  Exploring intimacy : cultivating healthy relationships through insight and intuition / Suzann Panek Robins.
     p. cm.
  Includes bibliographical references and index.
  ISBN 978-1-4422-0090-6 (cloth : alk. paper)—ISBN 978-1-4422-0092-0 (electronic)
  1. Intimacy (Psychology) 2. Insight. 3. Intuition. 4. Interpersonal relations. I. Title.
  BF575.I5R64 2010
  158.2—dc22   2009025387

∞™ The paper used in this publication meets the minimum requirements of American National Standard for Information Sciences—Permanence of Paper for Printed Library Materials, ANSI/NISO Z39.48-1992.

Printed in the United States of America

This book is dedicated to my children and their children's
children onward for the next many generations,
so that we can learn from the past to create a more pleasurable
and sustainable future. It is my wish that we all learn
to ask for 100% of what we want, 100% of the time.
To be successful in doing this, we must be willing
to hear NO for an answer and negotiate from there.

CONTENTS

FOREWORD

Humans have traveled a long journey to discover what is most basic: the ability to love and be loved, to know ourselves, and in this way to know one another. As simple as this sounds, most who have attempted it have found themselves either at loose ends or tangled in complexities. As we grow and mature, our understanding gets more sophisticated, yet the simplest things may still elude us. Shelves of books tell us how to find ourselves, how to relate to another, how to do life right, and how to be a good, upstanding person. But what do we make of it all when we come home and reach for the arms of another after a hard day's work?

Through the ages, theories of the human personality have changed many times depending on the styles and beliefs of the day. Freud discovered we had an unconscious; that was news only a century ago, taken for granted today. Jung showed us that we had a shadow, and we are still grappling to come to terms with it. Children are born and raised according to the fashion of the day, and each generation tries to figure out what went wrong or right in the process.

No one can live a life without the need to understand psychology. Even the most introverted hermit has to deal in some way with the world around him. Most everyone wants love, and the world itself is trying to learn how to love on a grand scale and create a new paradigm of the heart. This is the lesson of our day and the only thing that will save our planet from ravage and destruction.

Never has there been more need for weaving the many threads of life into a web strong enough to hold us all. Never has there been such a need for theories that integrate rather than separate, that show how things are related rather than just make distinctions.

Our future destination is not some kind of mystical high but a state of deep integration and healing. The vehicle that takes us there is the body. The driver is the mind. But the passenger is the soul itself, on its journey to the heart of the world.

It is time to integrate the physical, the mental, the emotional, and the spiritual into one comprehensive whole. This is our true psychology—the study of the whole being and the study of a being trying to become whole. We cannot leave the body out of it, for the body is the only constant through life: the one thing we know we will have as long as we live. We can't leave the mind out of it, because the mind needs to learn, to understand, and thereby become a more intelligent driver of the vehicle. We can't leave the emotions out of it, for they are the engine of the vehicle, which we hope is gently guided by the mind. And we can't leave the spiritual realm out of it, because that is the field in which we are traveling—the ultimate realization.

Where do we find models that address each of these important aspects and put them together in the spirit of true integration? Many disciplines are trying to address various parts. Transpersonal psychology combines the psyche with its spiritual dimensions but tends to leave out the importance of the body. Somatic therapies combine body and psyche but tend to leave out the spiritual dimension. Yoga beautifully holds the body within a spiritual context, but it tends to be weak in the area of addressing the wounds of the psyche.

It is this call for wholeness and integration that first brought me into the chakra system. I see it as a profound formula for wholeness, a template for transformation, a map to the human journey. It puts body, emotion, action, relationship, creativity, vision, and spiritual understanding all on a logical continuum, like any map, complete with the highways and byways to get you where you want to go.

We also need maps for the human journey through time, the miraculous development of the infant into a fully functioning—and thriving—

adult. Erik Erikson was one of the first developmental theorists to take us beyond childhood and outline the stages of a full life, all the way into our elder years. These are stages of spiritual development that map onto the chakras as easily as correlating the seasons to months of the year, for they are the seasons of life and the chakras are the wheels of life that take us through each season from birth to death.

It is high time that someone wrote a book drawing these concepts into a dynamic whole, and Suzann Robins has done just that. Not only has she woven the wisdom of the past with the spiritualities of the future, she has taken us beyond the realm of the isolated individual and examined the complex psyche of relational intimacy. We can only be intimate with another through intimacy with ourselves. But only another can take us to the deepest parts of ourselves and bring those parts together.

I first met Suzann Robins in one of those odd circumstances that only happens when there is a higher purpose at work. I was on my way to Hollyhock, a delightful retreat center on a remote island in British Columbia. It was a long drive from Vancouver that took us several days. We stopped midway at a lovely seaside resort late in the afternoon. The place was almost deserted and walking through the eerie silence of an empty dining hall, looking for someone to help me, I heard in the corner the soft tap-tapping of fingers on a keyboard. A fuzzy gray head buried behind the laptop screen suddenly looked up at me and said, "Hi, You're Anodea Judith. I was just writing about you in my book, and I'm on my way to your workshop."

Needless to say this is not an everyday experience. I stood speechless, an uncommon state for a wordswoman like myself, but then began the first of many conversations over the years. The workshop in Hollyhock was on the use of the chakra system for manifesting your dreams from conception to reality, and Suzann's dream was to finish and publish this book. What you hold in your hands is obvious proof that she did. May you learn from its pages something that helps you become a better lover to yourself and to the world around you. And may we all awaken to the wonders within and around us.

Anodea Judith, PhD

ACKNOWLEDGMENTS

A book is never written alone. Many people come together to discuss ideas and make the actual writing possible. I want to acknowledge the many teachers quoted throughout this book for the pioneering work they did. I have merely synthesized their ideas and added my own.

First, I would like to thank Cheryl Marinoff who provided the time and space for me to begin. Next, I want to thank Jack Cargill, Len Daly, Francesca Moscatelli, Tam Ropp, Marie Rowe, and Edi Weinstein-Moser for reading an early draft and providing valuable feedback.

Special applause goes to Bill Nathan, Carolyn Elderberry, and Ani Colt, who all worked very hard to help me think in a more logical fashion. I could not have completed this work without the aid of Bari Falese and Liz and David Caukins, who hung in with me at the very end, and my friends Kyle Applegate, Jacqueline Carleton, Linda Ferguson, Jack Eagan, Taj Jones, Alice Ladas, Sameon, Brian Saper, David Savage, Dell Williams and others who read bits and pieces along the way. I appreciate their contributions and encouragement.

Serendipity and synchronicity dropped Nikki Hayes into my life just as I was struggling with final endnotes and references. She reminded me that if we take information from one person and call it our own, it is plagiarism, taking from two or more sources becomes research, and quoting from many becomes a book. If I have misrepresented anyone of the many I have quoted it is my responsibility alone.

Nancy Moore and Jeff Panek made the book what it is with their art expertise. Big hugs and kisses go to Gary Stroup who provided the time and space for me to finish. I offer my apologies to anyone else I have forgotten or for any errors that I have made. Thanks to my editors Suzanne Staszak-Silva, Elaine McGarraugh, and Julie Blackburn. None of this would have been possible without them believing it is a worthwhile project. Lastly, I would like to acknowledge the love I developed for myself over this process of writing about intimacy.

Oscar Wilde once said: To love one's self is the beginning of a life-long romance.

INTRODUCTION

Writing a book is a labor of love.

First, I love topics of integration and synthesis; second, I love thinking deeply and talking to many people about how to communicate that love. Next, I loved sitting still long enough to actually write. This process began many years ago when I questioned my strict Catholic background in parochial school. I knew then there was more I wanted to learn. I married when I turned twenty-one and had three children before I was twenty-six. In the early 1970s, I sought out the practice of yoga and meditation to help me cope with the stress of motherhood. In 1979, I discovered Unity, Buddhism and Science of Mind, and these new ways of thinking changed my life. I began my college education and fell in love with psychology classes. But something was missing.

Psychology and health education addressed the mental and physical expressions of life; religion and science both questioned the reality of god. None of it helped me understand what was happening in my own body. Intimate aspects of healthy relationships remain emotional topics that are too often avoided. Human sexuality is still a taboo subject in many circles, or it is glossed over without acknowledging its importance. Health is discussed, but seldom as it contributes to healthy relationships.

I dropped out of academics for another fifteen years and read books that looked at life from an Eastern perspective. One phrase that resonates with me is the reminder that "we are human beings, not human doings." I spent several years just "being" while traveling, gold mining, attending women's workshops, and experimenting with tantric sexuality and Taoist practices. I lived in retreat centers where I had the opportunity to directly experience several authors mentioned in my lengthy suggested reading list. Eventually, I realized what was missing. My education lacked a *metaphysical interpretation*, which would provide a means of thinking beyond mental concepts into intuitive, emotional aspects of life.

When I discovered the idea of "energy in motion" this also resonated in me and I wanted to know more about my own e-motions. In the early 1990s, I began to research, teach, and write about interpreting the world through mental, emotional, and spiritual portals, and especially through the physical. I learned to be centered and still have my energy in motion; soon I was ready to be doing again.

In 1999, I earned a Masters of Arts in Liberal Studies. This time, I was fascinated with Freud, and came to a deeper appreciation of Erikson's theories of childhood and adult development as I continued to face my own emotional and sexual curiosity. I fell in love with the teachings of Karl Gustav Jung, and began to publish in spurts and starts about hypnosis and wholistic medicine. My experiential work through yoga and tai chi led me to recognize how using my sixth sense brings psychology, sexuality, physical well-being, intimacy, and intuition together. While presenting a wide variety of health-related classes in various college and adult education settings, I found several themes that provided a firm foundation to understand how the underpinnings of developmental and depth psychology contributed to personal growth and healthy relationships.

I want you, the reader, to know what I have learned about some strange bedfellows as I synthesize the divergent topics of intimacy and intuition in this small book. Although I am passionate about the field of social science, I find that many of the connections that need to be made are not found in the classroom. Psychological theory helps us rethink childhood conditioning, and Sociology contributes to understanding society, but what many college students learn is often irrelevant to real life. I have attempted to bridge this gap by introducing a more symbolic way of thinking. My dream is that this book will be used as a basis for discussion in many diverse settings. It is a name-dropping book and I trust the reader will look back or forward at what these teachers have accomplished. For each subject introduced, there is more to learn and much is readily accessible on the Internet. Arthur Schopenhauer (1788–1860) once noted that all truth goes through three stages: first, it is ridiculed; second, it is violently opposed; third, it is eventually accepted as self-evident.

The history of holism is traced throughout the book as a background for the cultural revolution that is occurring in present time. The first chapter, "Birthing Integration," defines conscious awareness and introduces the yogic concepts of the aura and chakra systems in regard to knowing ourselves better. "Evolving Definitions" expands ideas of love and intimacy as we learn about self-actualization and better self-care through healthier eating habits and meridian-based therapies. "Understanding Life Force" addresses libido and vitality through the eyes of Sigmund Freud and his student Karl Jung. "Discerning Systems" illuminates life force as some witness it flowing throughout the body, and "Sensing Perception" draws another model for understanding the conscious and unconscious influences that affect all partnerships.

The sixth chapter, "Connecting Tensions," spells out defense mechanisms and introduces the concept of projection. Erik Erikson is highlighted in the seventh chapter, "Developing Stages," and his social theories of age-related tensions are compared with Freud's sexual stages. "Maintaining Balance" presents various Levels of Being and ways of thinking that provide the freedom of "Activating Energy" as described in chapter 9. In "Overflowing Pleasure" I invite you to experiment with creative visualizations, the idea of integrating spirituality into sexuality (ISIS) and an exploration of Kundalini energy.

Chapter 11 addresses "Changing Roles" through the myth of Eros and Psyche, and chapter 12 is about "Opening Connections" between men and women as we overcome past conditioning. "Blending Genders" begins to offer possibilities about how things might change when we are "Embracing Shadow" to learn more about our own personalities. The final chapter strives to help with "Creating Focus" through dream analysis and consciously imaging the future.

Many of us, young and old, are "cultural creatives" caught in the midst of a global shift in consciousness and failing economic structures, while educational approaches lag behind. Here at the threshold of the twenty-first century, many struggle to catch up as the divorce rate and the dominance of blended families attest to the fact that lifelong monogamy has worked for only a small portion of society. We have new means of living longer, which means we must find ways of relating beyond old gender roles and across generations. We all desire more richness and a depth of true intimacy in the many varied partnerships we form.

As we enter the second decade of this new millennium, this book highlights the seeds, the gems, and the brilliance of some great teachers and thinkers. I have done my best to give credit to the original source; however, thinking about conscious awareness has become accepted knowledge for many and much information is readily available from varied references. Hopefully I have provided an opportunity to look back over what we have learned about being conscious in relationships and how we can apply that learning in the future. To participate in healthy relationships, we must be healthy. One way to do this is through complementary and alternative medicine (CAM), which is a combination of ancient and new modialities that are merging into a more holistic synthesis. Integrative medicine is a hot topic as America struggles to provide efficient healthcare for all of its citizens. It is my hope that the diverse topics outlined in this book will contribute to the creation of healthy relationships for men and women of all ages and that you will find more joy and more pleasure in every aspect of your life. Check in with your body, observe your thoughts, feel your feelings, and examine what spirituality means to you; only then can any truth be witnessed as self-evident.

BIRTHING INTEGRATION

Reflection is another way of saying we must listen so we can hear.

—Jung

Conscious awareness of an integrated self can emerge when we take time to observe and reflect on our body's mind. A form of internal housecleaning, as easy as taking a shower or brushing our teeth, occurs once we learn to acknowledge our inner systems and the body's mind. When we become aware of the extrasensory sixth sense called intuition we expand ideas surrounding intimacy.

Human Beings are born helpless. We emerge from the womb after being cradled for nine months. Light and sound overwhelm us as we begin to sense our surroundings. As mother and baby separate, the pulsating beat of hearts continues the connection. We appear unable to do anything, but as we open our eyes, we attempt to focus on those around us. Many newborns mimic facial expressions. When we see a smile, we smile in return. If our caregivers feel uneasy or appear unhappy, we

reflect uneasiness and discomfort. We need to be comforted and pro-
tected. Protection comes through our connection with others. Intimacy
begins immediately; it is essential to be held and touched. If we are
neglected as infants, we fail to thrive. As we grow, our need for touch
and connection never ends. Under healthy circumstances, we receive
nourishment and then we rest, content and peaceful.

Babies explore the world through their senses. Everything within
reach goes directly into the mouth, where we have many nerve endings relating to touch. We delight in each new experience. Awareness
continually expands through touching, tasting, smelling, hearing, and
seeing—savoring it all. If one sense is weak, the others compensate by
becoming stronger. In addition to our five senses, we are born with a
sixth sense that allows us to experience a depth of feelings and emotional
reactions. Imagine this sixth sense as the *intuitive sense*. For some, this
sense is more finely attuned, similar to having an ear for music, an eye
for color, or an acute sense of smell. We use our intuition to perceive
both inner and outer worlds as we explore intimacy. Life becomes more
meaningful and expansive as intimacy develops. Intimacy is not simply
about erotic or sexual connections; it also refers to the bonding of parents and infants, as well as relationships between siblings, friends and
coworkers, even the partnership we must develop with any health care
provider. Learning new ways to explore intimacy is the major purpose
of this book.

*Have you ever felt a tingling up your spine or a tightening deep in
your gut? Do you sometimes know something is going to happen without
knowing how you know?*

INTO ME YOU SEE

The Human Awareness Institute (HAI) began in the 1960s to help
people explore greater intimacy. The originator, Stan Dale who died
in 2007, spoke of intimacy as *into-me-see*. He felt we achieve true
intimacy by looking within and taught that intimacy means becoming more visible to ourselves as well as to others. In HAI workshops,
facilitators consciously create a "room of love" where attitudes can
change through internal reflection. Thoughts and feelings of self-con-

sciousness are relieved, revealing renewed self-confidence. Through the HAI process, participants tap into a greater depth of intuitive knowing and intimacy increases. This leads to emotional intelligence, which includes

- self-awareness,
- motivation,
- empathy,
- mood management.

The intuitive sixth sense and these attributes are key ingredients as we learn how we learn. Fundamental factors for both learning and engaging in healthy relationships include ability to cooperate, capacity to communicate, confidence, curiosity, the intention to relate, and self-control.[1]

These skills increase as we mature, and lead to social intelligence. On the other hand, emotional sensitivity and the ability to form relationships can be diminished or enhanced when parents, caregivers, or teachers shun creativity and individuality. Most healthy children gradually learn to distinguish their own ideas from others and eventually determine that people have different points of view, and that we do not need to take their criticism personally. As we mature, we gain the capacity to make judgments about what we like and do not like, what we want and do not want. Intuition guides our decisions, whether we are aware of it or not. Some of us rely more on the intellect and others more on physical sensation as coping mechanisms for the emotional aspects.

PERSONALITY DYNAMICS

We are all physical, mental, and emotional beings, and these three universal principles combine in various ways to form distinct personality dynamics:

- The physical is pragmatic and practical; it is the creative, active, operating part.

- The mental principle is related to thinking, structure, focus, objectivity, values, and perspective.
- The emotional is concerned with relationships, feelings, communication, organization, and synthesis.

Each dynamic is distinctly different from the others in ways we learn, process information, communicate, problem solve, play on teams, and become stressed. Our preference for one over the other is characterized by different inner process and ways of functioning. The distinctions are so fundamental that they can be identified in babies and observed at every age level. They appear in every culture and characterize men and women in equal numbers. Each personality dynamic has characteristic traits and gifts as well as a specific requirement for optimal learning. Some of us are primarily mentally centered; others are a combination of mental and emotional. Additional categories combine emotional-physical, and physical-mental.[2] We need to understand the requirements for our own way of functioning in the world. Once we intuitively sense how these dynamics operate within us, we can enter into partnerships with an understanding of how they work together to make connections with others.

LOVING COMPASSION

For most healthy and emotionally mature people, connection leads to compassion. This sense of coming into passion is the embodiment of love for both self and others. Compassion is a foundation for sharing aliveness and building a more humane world.[3] Compassion connects us with all of creation, including animals, insects, rocks and minerals, mountains and trees, flowers and plants, creeks, rivers, and oceans. Eventually, this connection helps us to realize that nothing is missing; we need to bring in nothing and push nothing away. Some people describe this occurrence as complete joy or *compersion*. Compersion is the joy we feel when someone we love is also experiencing a sensual connection; it is the opposite of jealousy.[4] As we strengthen our intuitive sense, and learn more about human personalities, we begin to perceive the pervasive vital life force that permeates everything. In this expanded place, we cultivate the necessary skills for processing information and increasing opportunities to amplify loving compassion. It is through compassion that we achieve the highest peak and deepest reach in the search for self-fulfillment.[5] *Exploring Intimacy* will discuss ways to develop these skills from various points of view. We begin our journey by witnessing how Western thinking about relationships became separate from a more holistic Eastern way of accepting our intuitive wisdom.

BRIEF HISTORY OF THOUGHT

The English language has limited words to describe concepts and ideas regarding healthly relationships. Once we better understand how the body and mind work together, we can better grasp the idea of loving compassion.

The historical background of Western education can aid in our rediscovery of lost knowledge when we listen to the wisdom of scholars from diverse academic disciplines. As British and American universities developed separate schools of thought, a division grew between physical or *hard science* and social or *soft science*. Some students viewed the human condition through a microscopic lens while others looked through a large telescope. The vast field now known as social science included philosophy as the study of truth, beauty, justice, and validity; anthropology as the study of culture; and linguistics as the analytical use of language. History and political science often come under this umbrella, as well as the study of ethics. Later, courses included psychology, focusing on the individual, and sociology, studying people in groups. Most Western thought disregarded theories about loving compassion, intuitive connections, and the pervasive life force. However, *quantum mechanics* opened several interdisciplinary streams of thinking and the exploration of *quantum physics* has brought awareness of various interconnections. In today's world, we can simultaneously look through an assortment of lenses and combine various viewpoints to better understand intuitive knowing and emotional intelligence, which are not limited to any one academic discipline.

Emotional intelligence and intuitive understanding are not physical substances we can measure; rather they are *potentials*, or possibilities, that describe the vital life force that manifests in intimate, energetic connections. Various cultures and languages represent this potential for connection with different words.[6] Some traditions convey this phenomenon of an energetic connection as unspeakable, so sacred they do not give it a name. Some refer to it as a connection with God, Creator, First Cause, or Universal Source; others speak of Inner Wisdom. Some call it *conscious knowing*, others simply speak about *knowledge*. Central and South American cultures have honored *Quetzalcoatl*. !Kung people located in isolated areas of Africa call supernatural power *n/um*. In Japan vital life force is called *ki* and in China *chi*. The Kabbalah in the Jewish mystical tradition introduced the notion of *spark*.

Western literature originating in Egypt, Greece, and Rome addressed feelings of connection and mentioned light emanating from the body. Religious art often depicts light as if it is radiating out from or streaming into the body, especially around the head sometimes referred to as a halo or aura of glory. Pythagoreans referred to the idea of a luminous body and proposed the hypothesis of vital life force 500 years B.C.E. (Before the Common Era marked by the birth of Christ). Early Christians recognized light radiating from the body and spoke of it as the wisdom aspect of the trinity they named *Holy Spirit*. In prior centuries, scholars from both China and India created diagrams that revealed light radiating from specific areas of the body. These light areas are in the same locations as the organs of elimination and reproduction, the heart and lungs, and hormonal glands such as the adrenals, gonads, thymus, thyroid, pineal, and pituitary.

In the East, vital life force is represented by two symbol systems called the *aura* and *chakras*. *Aura* is a name given to the biofields surrounding the body, and *chakras* are said to provide an information-processing function within the nervous system. The earliest mention of the chakras, a Sanskrit term for wheel, is found within the Hindu *Vedas*, which originated in India about 700 to 600 B.C.E. About this same time, Egyptians developed the alphabet as a word system, and the Aramaic language replaced Hebrew characters. However, Chinese, Japanese, Sanskrit, Hindi, and other Eastern languages continued to use symbols that conceptualized wholeness and cooperation.

Over the next centuries, ideas began to formulate regarding the split between the mind and the body, the masculine and feminine. Alphabetic letters replaced symbolic pictures and the metaphors of the spoken word. As time passed, the alphabet dominated Western thinking and influenced our perception of the world. Eastern philosophy, which does not use an alphabetic word system, often made connections and associations in physiology and psychology that Westerners overlooked. The thought system that included auras and chakras was overshadowed by more linear and less symbolic communication.

BRIEF HISTORY OF MEDICINE

Drawings on cave walls and artifacts from archeological digs confirm that people have always searched for ways to heal wounds. Eastern traditions assumed the physical body could be healed by mental control. As an example, five thousand years ago the Yellow Emperor of China observed that frustration could make people physically ill. On the other hand, Western scholars believed that powerful forces far beyond human control were responsible for mental and physical health. Five hundred years ago, a Western physician and early alchemist named Paracelsus taught that illness was the result of outside agents attacking the body. The art of alchemy eventually evolved into chemistry and pharmacology. Paracelsus, who wrote the first manual of surgery in 1528 and a manual for anatomy in 1537, also theorized that the body was composed of an invisible force as well as visible matter. Many scholars ignored these ideas until the Age of Enlightenment, in the eighteenth century, when a few medical doctors noted that people gave off an energetic force that was capable of causing an interaction between individuals, even from a distance. They believed this force could have either a healthful, positive or harmful, negative effect on both self and others.

About this time, Western medical practices became strongly rooted in scientific methods, and analytical, linear thinking became the driving force. Eastern and Western systems tended to omit the insights of the other. Emerging professionals who practiced Western medicine discounted many ideas from Asia and focused on discoveries that could be tested and replicated. The dominant paradigm considered humans to be flawed by nature and measured health by the absence of disease.

As Western science became specialized, many scholars considered the study of human biofields and intuitive knowing as nonscientific.[7] People with physical symptoms consulted specialists who had little knowledge of physical, mental, and emotional integration. Conventional education

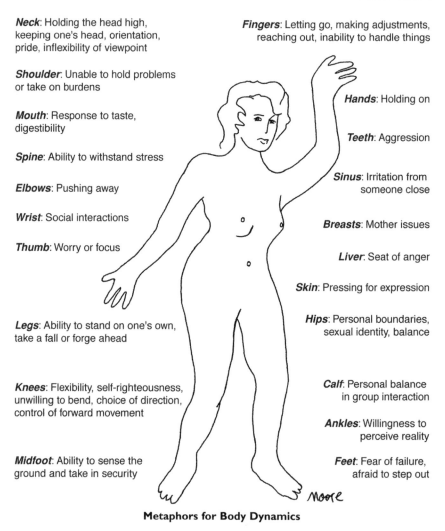

Neck: Holding the head high, keeping one's head, orientation, pride, inflexibility of viewpoint

Fingers: Letting go, making adjustments, reaching out, inability to handle things

Shoulder: Unable to hold problems or take on burdens

Hands: Holding on

Mouth: Response to taste, digestibility

Teeth: Aggression

Spine: Ability to withstand stress

Sinus: Irritation from someone close

Elbows: Pushing away

Wrist: Social interactions

Breasts: Mother issues

Thumb: Worry or focus

Liver: Seat of anger

Skin: Pressing for expression

Legs: Ability to stand on one's own, take a fall or forge ahead

Hips: Personal boundaries, sexual identity, balance

Knees: Flexibility, self-righteousness, unwilling to bend, choice of direction, control of forward movement

Calf: Personal balance in group interaction

Ankles: Willingness to perceive reality

Midfoot: Ability to sense the ground and take in security

Feet: Fear of failure, afraid to step out

Metaphors for Body Dynamics

completely overlooked the sixth sense of intuition and basically outlawed methods of healing such as massage and later chiropractic. Human touch was not valued, and healers who used herbal remedies could be persecuted as witches. Wisdom regarding an interconnected universe and compassionate intimacy became part of religious studies far outside the realm of the newly forming American Medical Association. *Holism*, which involves looking at the whole picture, was placed in a category with spiritualism, a response to a crisis of faith experienced by many Americans during the 1850s.

However, many traditional teachings from other cultures were also being practiced. Some included the idea that vibrations of light and sound could both produce discomfort and cure disease. Music and drumming always have been powerful forces in most cultures as a link between the physical-mental and emotional-spiritual realms. As the Industrial Revolution progressed, artificial light changed the way our bodies related to sunlight and darkness. At the same time, many fail to recognize how much human beings tune into the rhythms of the earth. Currently, Americans are most familiar with medical interventions that include radiation (x-rays), surgery, and pharmaceutical drugs that have received a patent after development in a controlled laboratory setting. Conventional medicine is now referred to as *allopathic*, which means treatment with remedies and substances that bear no relationship to the signs and symptoms of the disease. It is the opposite of homeopathy, which is based on the fact that "like follows like." Vaccinations are based on this principle. The practice of allopathic medicine removes the symptoms and produces an outcome different from the original disease. Allopathic doctors tend to use a mechanistic model asking: "How can I repair this machine called the body? What parts need to be replaced?"

Today we are moving toward a more integrative approach that often uses metaphors to understand symptoms that cause discomfort and disease. For example, when one gets a sore throat or a cough it might be useful to ask, "What is it we want to say that is not being said?" or "What feeling or thought has gotten caught in my throat and needs to be expressed?" "Is some desire not being met?" Most mainstream doctors have not listened to the symptoms of the digestive organs and wondered if a well-to-do patient feels insecure about life's basic needs, or asked if someone suffering a heart attack is satisfied in his or her love life. This is changing as many doctors discover that a significant healing occurs when, together with their patients, they consider the mechanics of the heart along with other metaphors regarding the organ systems. Numerous physician's assistants and nurse practitioners now ask pertinent questions inspired by Eastern models of thinking about the way the body and mind work together. This dynamic figure suggests other issues that might correlate to pain or discomfort in particular areas of the body.

This model on the opposite page can lead to an expansive awareness of illness, and this awareness is one explanation of the parallel between how we register what happens to us and how we hold the resulting consequences. Monitoring internal responses and moderating external motivations that result in visiable behaviors can change the outcome of our health and our relationships.

Aura and Chakra System

Western doctors are once again honoring the wisdom of the body and moving away from the notion that only medicine and surgery have the power to heal both physical and emotional wounds. *Integrative medicine* has become the key term used by those who acknowledge that drugs and surgery are necessary in many cases, but they also realize that, in some instances, prescriptions do not work and surgery might cause more complications. Modern medicine has made significant strides in the relief of pain and suffering from chronic illness when both allopathic medicine and holistic approaches are combined. Integrative practices include several modalities for solving specific problems in addition to using modern technology and medical interventions.

Holistic practitioners view individuals in the present moment while at the same time considering the future. Integrative medicine addresses questions about natural birthing and conscious dying, for instance setting up family birth centers and hospice care for the end of life. Doctors remember that they have not failed when someone dies, and they make distinctions between a cure and healing. The National Institutes of Health (NIH) has designated a group of healing modalities as nonallopathic. They refer to complementary and alternative medicine (CAM) and include diet and exercise, massage and vitamin therapy, chiropractic, herbs and other plant-based nutrients, homeopathy, Ayurvedic medicine, which originated in India, and Chinese medicine, which uses acupuncture, acupressure, and the external flow of vital life force. Some of these approaches have evolved over thousands of years, and they aim to prevent illness and promote wellness by balancing body, mind, emotions, and spiritual aspects, including consideration of how we relate to others. Neither CAM nor conventional practices provide standalone solutions to any problem. New fields of treatment referred to as vibrational medicine and energy psychology take into consideration the vital life force that moves within the body, as well as between and among people.[8]

COMBINING APPROACHES

Throughout the ages, the practices of yoga, meaning union; and tai chi, meaning movement of energy, have promoted the concept of connection through centering, focusing, and visualizing. Even without performing yogic postures or engaging in martial arts, it is possible to embrace life's challenges by learning to center or ground, to focus, and to visualize. These practices are different from meditation, which requires an empty mind.

As children, we learned to bathe and brush our teeth as ways of staying healthy; it is equally important to learn about personal reflection and how to observe inner thoughts and feelings. As we learn to use a more holistic approach to health and relationships, and we look at symptoms through a different diagnostic lens, then we can become skilled at mental exercises that are as quick and easy as brushing our teeth or taking a shower. Through the practice of simple exercises that will be outlined in this book, we can learn more about our internal processing systems and therefore improve our immune system and increase our capacity for healthy partnerships and maximum well-being. Most energetic processes for health and wellness apply the metaphors found in the aura and chakra systems. We can better understand how these integrative systems work once we understand the history. The concepts summarized throughout this book are not unique, but when we view them in a new light, each new day presents additional opportunities for their application in forming healthy relationships.

BEGINNING OF CONSCIOUSNESS STUDY

Charles Darwin observed behavior in the animal kingdom and later compared it to humans. He published *On Origin of Species by Natural Selection* in 1859, which spoke of the survival of the fittest. Questions about the widespread use of alcohol, psychopathology, and abnormalities dominated a new field of study called *scientific psychology*. Scientists in European and American laboratories began to research personality and genetic differences as they observed different outcomes when two people were exposed to the same stimulus. In their pursuit of scientific knowledge, they not only rejected information from East Asian cultures, they also often ignored earlier Western philosophical teachings that considered the consequences of cultural and societal influences on behaviors.

During this period, an Austrian medical doctor named Sigmund Freud borrowed Darwin's ideas and applied them to people in a more expanded fashion. Freud was the first to suggest that memories formed in early childhood caused the body distress. However, he followed Darwin's lead when he assumed that the same biological urges of sex, hunger, and aggression motivated human behavior. He proposed that to become a healthy adult repressed and denied issues needed to be resolved. He developed a process of therapy called *psychoanalysis* that included hypnosis and dream interpretation. Many regarded Freud's ideas as unscientific, just as they discounted Traditional Chinese Medicine (TCM) and Aryuvedic principles from India, which were becoming readily available as new travel opportunities and communication networks developed.

In 1907, Freud first met Karl Jung and they became friends as well as professor and student. The exploration of inner space became the focus of their work, and they began to discuss conscious and unconscious thoughts in the treatment of their patients who were seeking medical assistance for various physical and mental complaints. As a young man Jung had studied Eastern teachings, such as the I Ching, Taoism, and the Hindu Sutras. He looked to Zen masters for vocabulary to substantiate his theories. During his early college years, he visited tribal people in Africa, America, and India. Later, he questioned Freud's teaching that the immediate family was the main influence on individuals. Jung had observed the nuances of individual personalities within a larger context, and he realized that the myths and stories of various societies also provided input into a child's development. Internal, intuitive information can reach far beyond the responses that children are witness to within their immediate families.

Jung determined that each person had the ability to respond to various situations with specific preferences, which in turn led to different outcomes. He proposed that individuals, regardless of gender, have a wealth of intuitive knowing. Jung suggested that this information might be accessed through what he termed the *collective unconscious*. This understanding influenced his psychological theory of archetypes, two of which he named Anima and Animus. He saw them as "formless forces that only take on form when clothed by the symbol-making function of the unconscious psyche."[9]

Both Freud and Jung contributed to the field of *developmental psychology*, which will be explored in the following chapters. Jung's thinking broadened Freud's idea of bringing unconscious material to awareness and contributed to the expanded interpretation of dreams and free-associations. Those who were more interested in scientific proof regarding behavioral responses largely ignored Jung's acknowledgment of how the intuitive sixth sense and gender might influence the choices people make. As the Second World War ended in 1945, a few medical

Trace and color this mandala or create your own!

students became interested in how unconscious memories of past events might work in unison with physical awareness of current illnesses. Jung became a prolific author, instrumental in helping to open the Western mind to Eastern thinking. Eventually, *depth psychology* and the study of personality were based on the results of his insights. He believed the interpretation of symbols could aid the resolution of internal conflict and introduced mandalas into the therapeutic process.

A mandala is a symbolic illustration related to chakras. Mandala designs are also found in the round, stained-glass windows that enhance gothic cathedrals. The purpose of a mandala is to provide a soothing activity for a busy mind by drawing attention to the center. Mandalas work just by looking at them, coloring them, or creating one. Make time to create your own original circular symbol, or copy and color the one above as a first exercise in developing intuitive knowing and emotional intelligence. You might want to begin a journal using words or pictures to describe your experience and ideas regarding personality dynamics, or reflect on new ways of learning about the body, relationships, and intimacy. A lot of information has been presented and the next chapter will expand our ideas about the emotion we call love.

❦ 2 ❦

EVOLVING DEFINITIONS

Our sixth sense of intuitive knowing can provide a new basis for understanding our desires. Knowing the words for different forms of love will enable us to participate more fully in a variety of relationships. All of our partnerships benefit when we recognize the need for self-love. A renewed understanding of actualization helps to create loving compassion.

❦

Newborns require warmth and loving care. For generations, basic physical and emotional needs must have been satisfied in order for human beings to survive. Under the best circumstances, love is freely given to babies. Every experience contributes to the neuronal pathways forming within the nervous system, which determine behavioral responses. Small children require constant supervision as the muscles develop and they begin to move around. As we assert free will, the struggle between the child's demands and the caretaker's ability to satisfy needs and wants is set into motion. Unfortunately, some households and day care centers neglect to provide consistent attention and clear boundaries; others overindulge childhood desires. In either case, children learn to manipulate those around them.

From early childhood, we use the sixth sense of intuition to engage others, avoid others, or push others away; this is the *fight/flight/freeze* reaction of the reptilian brain. When we feel overwhelmed by demands, we move into defense mode, emotionally run away, or go blank. Various circumstances lead us to attack others or separate from them. These same responses occur when we desire something that appears out of reach. As our personalities develop, we cultivate individual ways of internalizing and processing information. Some people have an *external locus of control* and never cease looking outside to meet their needs. They constantly seek approval and often blame others for shortcomings. Others become more self-sufficient and less reliant and display an *internal locus of control*, which can lead to harsh self-judgment and, therefore, low self-esteem.

Too often people ignore and therefore diminish their sense of intuition as a way of protecting themselves, while others strengthen their sensitivity, also a means of protection from life's tensions. The key is to graciously handle the external stimulus while balancing our inner emotional response, taking responsibility when necessary and letting go in circumstances that are beyond our control. This requires intuitive sensitivity and emotional intelligence that allow us to realize what we can change, and to accept what we cannot change. This includes the ability to acknowledge a range of feelings as they occur, to gather emotional reactions and then to choose a response relevant to the current situation. When we do this, we recognize similar feelings in others as we tune into their verbal and nonverbal cues. In time, we willingly initiate negotiations to resolve conflicts that improve all of our partnerships.

EXPANDING IDEAS OF LOVE

Many people connect to intuitive knowing and increase emotional intelligence through what they call the aura and chakra systems and find that this connection provides harmony both internally and in their affiliations with others. Flexible, dynamic stability maintains balance in the vital life force. Balance is a key to loving compassion, conscious evolution, and self-actualization.

Is self-actualization the same as self-love? When we are taught to "love your neighbor as yourself," what or who is the entity we call Self? What does it mean to love self as we might love someone else? Must we initiate self-love before we can respond to others?

To explore these questions, it is important to examine emotional and spiritual as well as physical and mental aspects of love. Many cultures idealize erotic romantic love, and many people think about love and intimacy primarily as aspects of sexual relationships. Others view love as a component of spirituality or religion. For many, loving compassion is a necessary dimension of conscious evolution. Some have suggested that awareness of love means to be open to negative emotions as well as the positive events of life.[1] The experiences of grief, sorrow, and disappointment, as well as joy, pleasure, satisfaction, and fulfillment, are part of the spectrum of loving. Another model speaks of love as a positive emotion that contributes to happiness and optimism about the future. This model includes six *love styles*:

- Altruistic, selfless love (*agape*)
- Passionate, romantic love (*eros*)
- Friendship and family love (*storge* or *philia*)
- Game-playing love (*ludus*)
- Practical, logical love (*pragma*)
- Possessive, dependent love (*mania*)[2]

Ludas, pragma, and mania are easy to understand. Other Greek words further describe love's many functions:

Agape represents active, unconditional, self-sacrificing, thoughtful love, and it suggests a universal, as opposed to personal, love that is a conscious choice. Agape includes love of truth or love of all humanity, and it can encompass compassion in the way we think about and act toward others. It is most similar to generosity and charity and implies the wish to share our bounty with others. Some people say agape describes love from a higher power many call *God* or goddess.

Eros is passionate, personal love that usually involves sensual desire and longing. Although some think of eros only in terms of attraction to a particular person, with contemplation it can encompass an appreciation of the beauty within all people or even appreciation of beauty itself. Some translate it as "love of the body" and others use it in reference to feelings of the heart. Eros, the base of the word erotic, was the son of Greek gods Aphrodite and Zeus. The Roman version of Eros is *Cupido*, or Cupid. We will learn more about this influence in later chapters.

Philia love translates as friendship, implying a dispassionate lovethat includes loyalty to family, friends, and community. Philia can be very conditional often seeking equality and familiarity. Philia is the root of brotherly love and the love of knowledge. Philia involves the desire to enjoy activity with others, and it is the base for words such as philosophy, philology, homophilia, and pedophilia.

Storge (pronounced *stor-gay*) means natural affection, for instance the instinctual bond parents are supposed to have with their children and the expectation their children will feel the same. Storge can also be self-seeking, as there are rewards involved. An example is a child who quickly learns that "if I cooperate, I will be showered with more attention," often in the form of rewards. Storge involves friendship that is more automatic than Philia and nonsexual affection that can include attachment to material possessions. It can also imply bearing with or tolerating a person or situation, as in stoicism.

Xenia is a form of loving hospitality offered to a foreigner or stranger. In ancient Greece, xenia was a reciprocal obligation, passed down to descendants who were required to return hospitality in a ritualized way to former hosts or their descendants. It is the root of *xenophobia*, the fear and often hatred of people from other cultures, or the opposite xenophilia.

Most everyone agrees we cannot live without love. But, in these models there is not a word about self-love. Aristotle's mention of "love of self" appears to imply the selfless love of agape. Perhaps some Greeks feared that any emphasis on self-love leads to *narcissism*, which is an unhealthy absorption in self-admiration. In Greek mythology, a young man named Narcissus rejected the advances of the nymph Echo. In retaliation, she doomed him to fall in love with his own reflection in a pool of water. Of course, this became a one-sided, unreciprocated love. This myth hints at the idea that infatuation and obsession can lead to the pursuit of one's own gratification and an ambition for love that excludes the needs of others. Many people may still avoid self-love and self-pleasure.

Erich Fromm, an internationally known psychologist, psychoanalyst, and philosopher, commented on the widespread belief that while it is virtuous to love others, it is sinful to love oneself. When he wrote *The Art of Loving* in 1956, many people took his stance that if we love ourselves, we would not be able to love others. He traced this belief to the Protestant Reformation, which moved philosophical thinkers away from the biblical recommendation to love our neighbor as ourselves. Fromm also attests to Freud's assumption that love can only be turned toward others or turned toward self, making other-love and self-love mutually exclusive in the sense that the more there is of one, the less there is of the other. A balance between self-love and love for others is required to become aware of the internal or external locus of control mentioned earlier.

MOTIVATION FOR CHANGE

New ways of thinking about self-love and interdependence are necessary to cultivate healthy relationships. Between the First and Second World wars, when religion was no longer the dominant force for the explanation of morality and ethics, independence and individualism became the basis of democracy. New views regarding conscious and unconscious attitudes emphasized the concept of personal choice. After the Depression of the 1930s, American authors such as Napoleon Hill, Dale Carnegie, and Norman Vincent Peale began to promote new concepts regarding the possibility of everyone achieving success. These businessmen popularized capitalistic ideals such as the accrual of assets for individual gain through the power of positive thinking and self-determination.

Individualistic thinking led Americans to believe that control over our destiny meant control of the world economy, even at the expense of others. To achieve this meant ignoring emotional reactions that involve loving compassion. During this period, many male authors accentuated the idea that control of wealth resulted from attunement with a higher power that ruled rational, linear thinking. It implied that self-improvement alone was a signifier of success and that positive thinking would lead to perfect results. Well-being meant being well to do and accumulating material possessions far beyond what is necessary for survival.

Selfish wants and needs resulted in careless behaviors. Wealth became proof of goodness and godliness. This premise led to a hierarchy of control that negated emotional intelligence and ignored intuitive wisdom.

This emphasis on self-determination introduced the study of *motivation* into the growing field of psychology after the Second World War. Abraham Maslow proposed a theory for explaining motivation when he introduced the Hierarchy of Needs in 1954. His model starts with a foundation that requires the basic biological and physiological needs of fresh air and water, adequate food, shelter, and clothing. Next, he feels we need safety, security, and a stable, predictable environment. He pointed out that we are social creatures who need to love and be loved; therefore, he followed this base with the psychological need to belong, to have affiliations and affection. Maslow advocated that we could only attain the integration of love by satisfying the first three needs, which he labels *deficiency motives*, before moving toward the *being motives*, closer to the top.

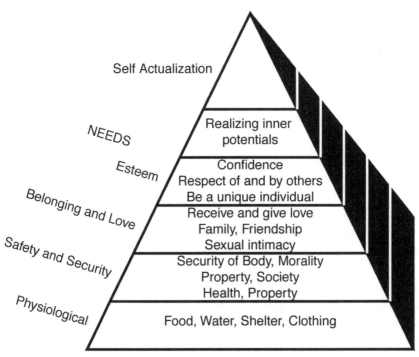

Maslow's original hierarchy of needs.

According to his theory, in the progression from the bottom to the top of the hierarchy, once we satisfy deficiencies we become concerned with the need for esteem. Self-esteem includes achievement, status, and responsibility as we gain competency in some aspect of life. In Maslow's model, this creates self-respect as well as respect for others and a cognitive desire "to know." Knowing includes the ability to be self-determined through a personal philosophy of life. Maslow taught it was essential to fulfill all of the lower biological and psychological needs before reaching the fullest potential, which he labeled *self-actualization*.

Before Maslow developed this hierarchy, personal success was not the pinnacle; instead marriage and creating a family were the most important aspects of becoming an adult. Most people moved from their parent's home directly into a marriage contract; this contract satisfied the need to belong. For centuries, some families have participated in prearranged marriages, usually as a business transaction where the bride accompanied a piece of land or a livestock inheritance. Even if the marriage was not prearranged, partners were chosen because they lived close by, and they also needed to be homogenous. This meant that if you were white, you only considered marrying another white. If you were tall, you looked for someone tall. If Catholic or Jewish, your mate needed to be the same. Once married, women became the property of men. Being a housewife implied being married to the house. Extended families, with several generations living under the same roof, were often the norm.

Now, there is no longer shame in remaining single and childfree. Many adults live alone and maintain separate households, we choose partners of any kind from anywhere. In many societies, having a variety of sexual partners outside of a marriage contract is acceptable. At the beginning of the twenty-first century, both women and men in many cultures accomplish their goals without being dependent. They do not see themselves as belonging to anyone. Students question Maslow's concepts, arguing that the achievement of self-esteem may be more important than the need for belonging. Perhaps it is time to reevaluate Maslow's hierarchy. Rethinking this hierarchy can be a call to conscious awareness, reminding us that the larger community is influenced by individual intentions. Both men and women are realizing that clarity of intention and being "on purpose" are not possible without inner reflection. Although we are familiar with the illusion that opposites attract, deep self-reflection often reveals that like attracts like in both positive and negative ways. We will address this later in regard to projections.

In the meantime, too much focus on personal success and autonomy can become a form of narcissism that works in opposition to the goals of the collective. Larger problems, such as ignorance of the fact we are polluting the environment and harming other species, can result from consumerism and overconsumption of natural resources. As capitalism flourished, so did self-indulgence and greed. When the Second World War ended, women's roles diminished as working-class men moved into middle-management positions and gained a greater measure of financial success. The more women strived for equal opportunities, the more they were held back. Nevertheless, the new ideas regarding self-determination provided the foundation for the second wave of the Women's Liberation movement. This brought about many changes in our ideals regarding love, marriage, and healthier lifestyles. Personal health and well-being came to mean feeling personally satisfied regarding desires as well as awareness of the impact our behaviors have on the planet. Fortunately, many more people are focusing on disciplines such as yoga and tai chi and they are taking actions that improve life for everyone, demonstrated by the "green movement." This movement toward becoming environmentally savvy has its roots in moving away from strict, linear thinking toward a softer, more intuitive loving compassion, and understanding the importance of using emotional and social intelligence to create health and healthy relation-ships and to save the planet.

THINGS KEEP CHANGING

Conscious evolution requires personal growth and new ways of talking about old ideas. The story and beliefs about the psyche have come a long way since Freud first posited his ideas about the basic biological urges of sex, hunger, and aggression. Medical technology now allows researchers to witness the nervous system in action, and doctors can perform brain surgery and track how the body repairs itself in ways that were previ-ously unimaginable. Through computerized axial tomography (CAT or CT Scan) and functional resonance imaging (fMRIs), we can observe synaptic connections between brain cells that form neuronal pathways.

The current theory is that these pathways actually influence the plasticity of the brain as we encode, store, and retrieve information.

In past generations, people had little access to information. They were influenced by the limited thinking of the dominant paradigm, which included information provided by the local culture and mainstream media controlled by advertisements. Now that we have exposure to the World Wide Web and opportunities to travel the globe, most of us have increased our ability to think outside the limited boxes previously created within families, neighborhoods, churches, and schools. However, many remain unaware of the power of the dominant culture until something new and different calls our attention.

Every family has a particular attitude regarding health. In some families, exercise and good nutrition play a central role. Others neglect these things. We now know that some attitudes are transmitted while we are still in the womb, and they often affect the choices we make later in life. Some families insist children follow rigid rules; other families are much more relaxed. In many cases, teenagers want to do things differently from parents. We rebel against the norm, while we develop our own philosophy about how we want to take care of our bodies.

One demonstration of how thinking changes over the years is found in regard to what used to be known as the *Four Food Groups*. In the past, we learned about nutrition through the dairy industry, which suggested we eat equal amounts of meat and dairy products, fruits and vegetables, bread, and grains. Eventually, the U.S. government replaced this grid with a healthier food pyramid that can be personalized for age, gender, and body size.[3] The Department of Nutrition at Harvard School of Public Health (HSPH) offers a healthier alternative to the government's pyramid.

In addition, Dr. Andrew Weil created a pyramid that includes whole soy foods; cooked Asian mushrooms; herbs and spices; white, green, and oolong tea; red wine, and healthy sweets, such as dark chocolate.

Having knowledge of food's influence on the body's mind, and eating with awareness, become a path to better health and a more holistic way of thinking. Hopefully, we will realize that we are capable of avoiding disease and disharmony when we make conscious choices about what we eat and drink. Being healthy also requires maintaining a sense of intimacy that allows us to broaden our connections and

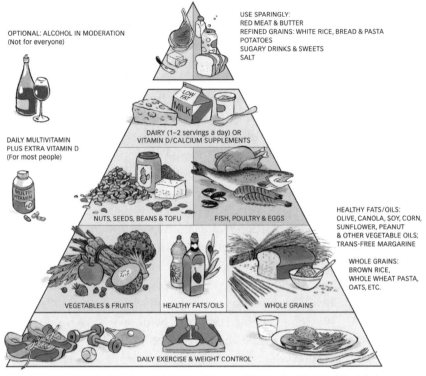

OPTIONAL: ALCOHOL IN MODERATION
(Not for everyone)

USE SPARINGLY:
RED MEAT & BUTTER
REFINED GRAINS: WHITE RICE, BREAD & PASTA
POTATOES
SUGARY DRINKS & SWEETS
SALT

DAILY MULTIVITAMIN
PLUS EXTRA VITAMIN D
(For most people)

DAIRY (1–2 servings a day) OR
VITAMIN D/CALCIUM SUPPLEMENTS

NUTS, SEEDS, BEANS & TOFU   FISH, POULTRY & EGGS

HEALTHY FATS/OILS:
OLIVE, CANOLA, SOY, CORN,
SUNFLOWER, PEANUT
& OTHER VEGETABLE OILS;
TRANS-FREE MARGARINE

WHOLE GRAINS:
BROWN RICE,
WHOLE WHEAT PASTA,
OATS, ETC.

VEGETABLES & FRUITS   HEALTHY FATS/OILS   WHOLE GRAINS

DAILY EXERCISE & WEIGHT CONTROL

Healthy Eating Pyramid from Harvard School of Public Health.[4]

keeps compassion flowing. As we develop a healthy, integrated self, we can both imagine more and know more about the kaleidoscope we call life.

As we pay attention to our intuitive feelings, we discover our own inner truth rather than accepting what others tell us is true. This discovery can provide a pleasurable sensation when we slow down and observe what is going on within the body's mind. When we take time to pause and look inside, we form new neuronal connections required for greater into-me-see. Love must include dignity, respect, understanding, and trust, as well as assurance, encouragement, praise, and physical affection. We must truly love our self before we can offer love to another. In the words from a popular song, "Learning to love yourself is the greatest gift of all."[5] When we choose to love Self first, we are open to the revolutionary process of becoming more authentic and transparent in our everyday interactions.

Self-love is best cultivated when we breathe deeply and become aware of the expansion and contraction of our lungs. Striving toward integration involves taking time for reflection. In the drive to succeed in relationships and in life, it is important to stop, observe, and apply the insights we gain. An easy way to experience mental activity is by noticing four different levels of awareness:

- First, observe what is going on outside the body.
- Second, feel the emotional sensations inside the body.
- Third, pay attention to daydreaming, fantasy, or imagination.
- Fourth, be still and witness what comes from the intuitive sense.

The fourth level is different from observation, sensation, or fantasy because intuition is the connector between thoughts and emotions. Our sixth sense of intuition fosters emotional intelligence, which has the capacity to generate ideas and it is capable of yielding more than one argument or position. This is the ability to *reframe*, which means to change our thoughts about a situation, and it is a most important aspect of free choice. Sometimes reframing happens spontaneously and other times we must make time for contemplation and reflection before we realize what is happening or how to feel differently. We must stop, think, and feel all four levels of awareness in the present moment. In doing so, we are able to move forward with less clinging and attachment.

Coming into conscious awareness means responding after thoughtful consideration. On a personal level, sometimes we overeat, drink too much, take drugs, or have sex without considering the result of our actions. On the global level, many people have failed to pay attention to how the Industrial Revolution and a consumer-based society have affected the next several generations. Responding to these problems involves initiating loving compassion rather than simply having an immediate reaction without thinking. In this way, we are capable of embracing both personal wants and needs as well as becoming engaged in actions that involve making the planet a better place for everyone. Loving compassion is a necessary component to improving connections with family members, friends, co-workers, spouses, partners and even those who provide our health care. At the same time, it is important to feel genuine affection for our self as well as for others.

THE BIGGER PICTURE

The more self-love we generate, the more we increase our capacity for creating loving partnerships. Our desire to love others brings us back to the need to love our self, even in such simple ways such as becoming more aware of how everything we ingest is significant to our well-being. Using the food pyramid can be a simple guide to making healthy choices. Knowing how and where food is grown also has a bearing on what we ingest. Even the way we transport products from one place to another is relevant to the whole picture because the amount of pollution produced affects the air we breathe. Another example is knowing more about the water we drink and how that has an influence on how healthy we feel.[6] When we make time to reflect and listen to how our body responds, we cultivate more love and intimacy. Paying attention is one manifestation of self-love.

As we enjoy the pleasurable feelings provided by working with our body's mind, it is important to remain aware of future consequences generated by our present actions. When we are truly in loving compassion, for both self and others, we experience each moment with less concern about our personal past or future, less influence from outside sources, while at the same time having more passion and freedom to become our highest and best, happy self.

3

UNDERSTANDING LIFE FORCE

Vital life force remains a curiosity as it flows throughout the body and generates creative expression as well as behavioral responses to external stimulus. When this force is not flowing freely, dis-ease and dis-harmony manifest on the physical plane. Life force or vitality can be cultivated through the breath. We must be in good health to have healthy relationships.

Loving compassion provides the opportunity to explore concepts of interconnectedness. For centuries, oral traditions, handed down from teacher to student, have related how to develop this compassion. Before words, symbols such as a coiled snake or serpent lying at the base of the spine illustrated the idea of flow moving up the spinal column. The first recording of this ancient knowledge is attributed to a yogi named Patanjali. His work illuminated the necessity of working with mental, physical, emotional, and spiritual levels simultaneously to optimize health.[1]

Since then many people study yoga, which refers to yoke or joining together in union, and tai chi as movement of energy. These people discover the vitality provided when energy flows easily throughout the system, and they harness this power by using meditation, focusing techniques, and creative visualizations. Through concentration, they are able to increase their intuitive abilities and to develop skills that heal themselves and others, or to see the future or understand the past. Some believe the rotation of the planet around the sun, as well as the cycle of the moon around earth, influences mental, emotional, and physical states. They all agree that learning to use the breath is essential to health.

Breath is the vital life force; if we are not breathing, we are not alive. *Prana* is a Sanskrit word meaning *first unit* that relates to breath as the basic constituent of life. Breathing deeply brings physical, mental, emotional, and spiritual aspects into balance. Vital life force is often depicted as two polar forces, called yin and yang that constantly flow back and forth as regular as day flows into night and night into morning, each one containing an essential element of the other. This balance is dynamic rather than static, because as one recedes, the other increases. We are constantly exchanging energy with others. The transmission and reception of positive or negative energy is contingent on tuning into the same frequency; for instance, we talk about being "turned on" or "turned off." In positive interactions, we might describe the experience as if our heart were on fire with love; in a negative experience, we might feel repulsed. Everything in the universe is energy that penetrates, receives, absorbs, conducts, and transmits; therefore, it plays a role in both particles (mat-

Yin Yang symbol.

ter) and waves (motion) as it turns matter into force or movement.[2] Our biofield extends outward from our dense physical body and comprises the necessary crucial life force. Looking into the biofield can explain many phenomena that are critical to health and well-being that cannot be explained in the conventional biological model.

A BRIEF HISTORY OF HOLISM

Holistic health combines Egyptian knowledge of the healing arts with the yogic system from India and China's understanding of chi. Healers who use the aura and chakra systems were previously referred to as *psychics*; today they are known as *medical intuitives*. The most striking attribute of these medical practices is the emphasis on diagnosing disturbances of *chi* or *qi* (pronounced *chee* or *key*) as an indication of wellness. These systems base the diagnosis of illness on observation, questioning, and listening, feeling for pulse quality throughout the body, palpation and reports of sensitivity in the organs. Conventional medicine also employed these methods until the recent availability of technological devices for diagnosis. Energy medicine includes these techniques along with the fact that *meridians* are electrical pathways within the body that connect to the limbic system. Meridians are major factors in traditional medical practices of several indigenous cultures. For instance, acupuncture points involve several meridians that run from the hands to the feet along each side of the body. The neck and face also contain several meridian points.

Anthropologists have found detailed maps and drawings of these systems from China and India that predate descriptions of the skeletal-muscular, respiratory, hormonal, reproductive, and nervous systems used in Western medicine. A component of the nervous system is the limbic system, which includes the neocortex and primitive brain. This system is indispensable because it is responsible for control of cardiac, pulmonary, and intestinal functions. Instinctive reactions and commands that allow for involuntary actions, as well as mechanisms of aggression and repetitive behavior, are located here. This includes most emotions and motivations including fear, anger, aggression, and the desire for intimacy. Feelings of joy and pleasure, derived from survival activities such as eating and sex, are also part of this system. For example, the level of oxytocin rises in a

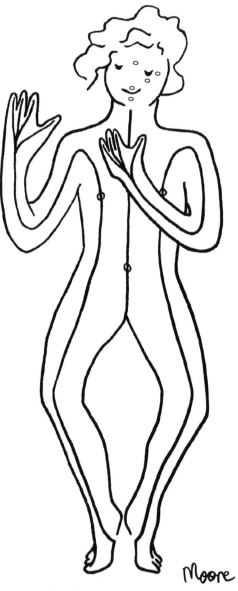

Simplified meridian system.

pregnant woman before and after birth to stimulate labor, then nursing, and eventual bonding. A rise in this hormone also occurs during any activity that involves a pleasing stimulation, such as gentle touch between people or even during face-to-face conversation without touch.

Twelfth-century scientists Émile Boirac and Ambroise-Auguste Liebeault reported that it was possible for people to have an interaction with each other from a distance. In the 1600s, mathematicians Franciscus Mercurius van Helmont and Gottfried Leïbnitz noted movement in matter that appeared fluidlike with a center of force. They too felt that this force that was around everything could influence both animate and inanimate objects. Much of this was not understood until the eighteenth century when Wilhelm Von Reichenbach began the study of electromagnetic emissions from the sun and their relationship to the forces of energy contained within the body. He found properties unique to the body and discovered that a person's energy, which he named *odic force*, could move through a piece of wire. The magnetic property of the odic force is not specifically magnetic but rather a polarity similar to that found in crystals, which can either amplify out or draw in energetic forces. In this same way tuning forks and older clocks with mechanical gears become synchronized with other similar devices. This theory of entrainment and law of attraction are based on the idea that we attract everything according to the vibrations of intentions.[3]

WHAT IS ENERGY?

Von Reichenbach observed that the polarity contained in odic force concentrations were within the red and blue-violet range of the solar spectrum. He stated that the opposite charges produced subjective feelings of warmth and cold in varying degrees of power. He used individuals who were sensitive to color and light to test his findings, and they demonstrated that properties contained within the biofield could actually be seen. The colors they saw were labeled as "hot, red, and unpleasant" or "blue, cold, and pleasant." Von Reichenbach determined that part of this odic current could be focused like light moving through a lens, while another part flows around the lens the same way a candle flame will flow around a nonburnable object. His experiments showed that what is now called the *auric field*

actually contains focused particles as well as fluidlike properties. Although some medical intuitives claim they can actually see these properties, most of us do not have this ability. These experiments were instrumental in moving ideas regarding the *essence of being* from the realm of philosophy and religion into settings that were more scientific. However, little funding was available to work with extrasensory perception, and further exploration was eliminated within most scientific circles.

Regardless, throughout the ages many people have spoken about their ability to perceive the biofield or the chakras and meridian systems, such as Mikao Usui, a Japanese spiritualist who helped popularize one type of vibrational healing, known as *Reiki* (pronounced Ray-Key). Another example is C. W. Leadbeater, an accomplished psychic who also claimed he could see the auric field. He worked with artists to depict the colors he perceived emanating from auras and chakras. He proposed that qualities such as habitual jealousy, pride, anger, irritation, sexual depravity, and depression were visible in the colors. Most of Leadbeater's works were published by the Blavatsky Center. In the late 1800s, Helena Petrovna Blavatsky helped to spread Theosophy derived from the term *theosophia*, literally meaning "knowledge of the divine." As author of *The Secret Doctrine* in 1888, she promoted the idea that Western science needed to acquaint itself with Eastern philosophy. Academic scholars were leaving an era of proclaimed cure-alls to pursue investigation that was more scientific. Many of her ideas were incomprehensible to the science of her time. Her contemporaries called her teachings "pretentious nonsense," although she was very good at exposing fallacies of materialistic science and attacking claims of spiritualism. She wrote in a powerful style that challenged the confusion and absurdities of the reigning medical and religious orthodoxy that regulated the practice of medicine at that time. Blavatsky's work can be summed up in one of her maxims: "Compassion is the law of laws." This implied that if all people simply displayed loving compassion, we would not need laws to govern health care policies.

WESTERN INTEGRATIVE PRACTICES

Compassion was the motivation for another medical practitioner who was writing during this time. While in medical school, D. D. Palmer reasoned that the body might have an ample supply of natural healing power, which he referred to as *innate intelligence*.[4] He wondered if per-

haps when single organs were not functioning, they might not be receiving the necessary supply of nutrients ordinarily transmitted throughout
the body. His thinking led to the premise of spinal misalignment or
subluxation, and he developed a procedure for adjusting the vertebrae.
Palmer performed his first adjustments on the spine in 1895, relieving
one man of deafness and another person of heart trouble. He founded
the Palmer School and Cure under the laws of Iowa in 1897, but it
took until 1961 for chiropractic to secure its current position among
the health sciences. Palmer helped to set the stage for a quantum leap
toward cultural acceptance of more holistic practices.

Another idea concerning medical diagnosis and healing included
radionics, a system that detects the biofield from a distance. Radionics
uses the word to describe how a healthy person has certain frequencies
that define health, while an unhealthy person exhibits different frequencies that define certain disorders. Radionic devices are purported to
diagnose and restore health by applying healing frequencies that will
balance out the discordant frequencies of sickness. This knowledge is
based on the concept that all life and matter contain vibrations and
harmonics.

Albert Einstein first published his article about the special theory of
relativity in 1905 and posited that reality did not obey Newton's laws of
gravity, which had been the main model for understanding the workings of the material world. This led to a new branch of physics called
quantum mechanics. According to Leonard Shlain these quantum ideas
turned science and common sense upside down by introducing the
mathematics of chance into the equation of understanding. In the early
1900s, William James, one of the fathers of psychology, was teaching at
Harvard Medical School when his work *Varieties of Religious Experience*
exposed medical students to a Buddhist influence. Concurrently, a new
health field called *naturopathy* included knowledge about herbal remedies and mental practices such as meditation, focusing, and visualization
borrowed from Eastern cultures. Naturopathy also promoted a mostly
vegetarian diet and the importance of physical exercise.

In 1911, William Kilner noted that he was able to sense a field around
humans using various colored screens and filters. He observed that the
appearance differed from subject to subject depending on age, gender,
mental ability, and health. He claimed that certain diseases show up as
patches or irregularities. This led Kilner to develop a system of diagnosis
on the basis of the color, texture, volume, and general appearance of the

energetic field that forms an envelope around the body. Shortly after, Neils Bohr showed that the movement of electrons produced light in a very precise quantity. Under Bohr's theory, an electron's emissions were viewed as concentric circles around the nucleus, similar to the field Kilner imagined around the body.

Bohr soon conceived the principle of *complementarity*, which meant objects could be separately analyzed as having contradictory properties. For example, light behaves as either a wave or a stream of particles depending on the experimental framework. In addition, Bohr witnessed ways in which the mental state of investigators influenced the outcome of experiments and suggested that bystanders predisposed or changed the reality they observed. This led others to assume that everything in the universe is mysteriously interconnected; no event happens anywhere that does not affect events everywhere else. At the time, Einstein preferred the determinism of classical physics. New quantum theories suggested that probability rather than possibility was the basis of physics. He and Bohr had good-natured arguments over the validity of these principles, and eventually Einstein published the unified field theory in 1914.

Questions regarding how to work with the energetic life force continued to be asked. In 1939, Semyon Kirlian, a female Russian inventor and electrician, discovered that when an object was placed on a photographic plate in the presence of a high-voltage, high-frequency, low-amperage electrical field, an additional image appears. This glowing, multicolored emanation is believed to be the physical manifestation of the life force surrounding all living things. The method, referred to as *Kirlian photography*, looks like a colored halo or the effect of a coronal discharge.[5] This image may be due to quite natural phenomena such as barometric pressure, electrical grounding, temperature, and humidity.[6] Changes in moisture reflect changes in voltage and barometric pressure, which in many people causes a change in emotions that may in turn produce different colors in the biofield at different times.

As the Second World War began, Wilhelm Reich, a psychiatrist and colleague of Freud, was also interested in this unified field theory as he studied the relationship between physical and psychological disturbances. Using a specially constructed high-power microscope, Reich observed pulsations of energy that he named *orgone* radiating not only from microorganisms but also around all animate and inanimate objects. He observed the same energy pulsating in the sky and built a device to capture this energy. In 1941, Einstein tested Reich's orgone accumulators and commented that if Reich's findings were true, they would violate laws of thermodynamics that were currently accepted. In 1954, the Food and Drug Administration (FDA) issued a complaint for an injunction against Reich, charging that he violated the Food, Drug, and Cosmetic Act by delivering misbranded and adulterated devices through interstate commerce, and making false, misleading claims. The FDA called the accumulators a sham and orgone energy nonexistent. Reich also believed sexual orgasms had healing potential. Sex was a taboo topic at this time and he was arrested because of his threat to the status quo.

Authorities feared that these concepts regarding *energetics* used for healing would interfere with the progress on the lucrative development of pharmaceutical drugs. Although some natural practices did in fact prevent and heal chronic illness, the medical mainstream ignored them because the results from energetic healings could sometimes be more thorough and long lasting. The discovery of penicillin sent naturopathic medicine into decline and advanced synthetic drugs including antibiotics, cortisone, and steroids. Only doctors who graduated from elite medical schools and passed a regimented set of board examinations could administer the new prescription drugs. These drugs were effective in protecting people from various bacterial infections that had begun to spread, but they did little to help with chronic pain and other psychosomatic ailments. In many cases, taking one prescription drug led to the need for another and this helped the pharmaceutical industry to flourish. On the other hand, many people began to use chiropractic, acupuncture, physical therapy, massage, and other means of alternative healing.

Reich was later released, in spite of the fact that many political lobbyists were working to pass laws in favor of the American Medical Association (AMA). Surgery and other medical procedures became popular, and concepts of holism and ideas about sexual orgasms were discounted. The FDA again deemed Reich's orgone accumulator devices harmful, although many people reported overcoming aches, pains, and emotional disturbances. They destroyed many of these devices and burned several tons of Reich's publications. He continued to teach and write and, by 1956, made outrageous claims. He was once again imprisoned where he died of heart failure a year later. Research on Reich's explorations continues, and some psychotherapists utilize his ideas and the remaining devices in their practice. Sexual activity has proven to benefit overall health. However, the AMA and pharmaceutical companies persisted in discouraging funding for investigation of biofields or meridian systems.

EAST MEETS WEST

In philosophical and theological, rather than psychological circles, the Eastern mode of thinking applies metaphors and symbols for explaining vital life force. As an example, instead of understanding the act of sex as a basic biological urge that either needs to be followed through for the purpose of procreation or kept under control, some Eastern practices hold the ideal that the use of sexual energy can be a path to gain greater understanding regarding how thoughts and feelings might be constructed. One of the most popular of these practices is Hatha Yoga, which include postures or poses known as *asanas*. Tantric yoga and some Taoist practices also involve sexual union that can demonstrate different, more holistic ways of experiencing libido through the energetic connection called *kundalini*. People who subscribe to these ideas propose that this powerful energy is always available as the creative life force within each of us. They suggest we take time to acknowledge and evoke its presence through self-reflection in order to access its power.

Translations of texts that presented the principles of transcendent Eastern philosophy were becoming acceptable in various circles during the intellectual revolution in the 1960s. As an example, *Autobiography of a Yogi*, written by Paramahansa Yogananda in 1946, became popular after the British musicians known as the Beatles went to India to study meditation. Pop psychology was born as the publishing industry continued to grow. Authors such as Alan Watts, who held both a master's degree in psychology and a doctorate of divinity, were able to bridge the divergent worlds of psychology and theology because they presented methods for experiencing, and therefore understanding, conscious and unconscious ways of knowing. Books, magazines, expanded radio programming, and the new media of television spread a wealth of information. In the early 1970s, the use of psychotropic drugs and computers also gained wide acceptance along with Eastern mysticism. Many young teachers popularized interconnectedness and nonduality after studying sacred texts such as the Hindu Vedas, the Upanishads, and Bhagavad-Gita.

Popular authors including Michael Talbot, who died at the age of thirty-nine, in 1992, were scientific intellectuals who dropped out of the academic world in order to pursue their own direct experience of mental practices such as meditation and the observation of the body's responses. Throughout his life, Talbot experienced psychic, paranormal events. In *Beyond the Quantum*, he hypothesized how interior experience manifests in the outside world. In *Mysticism and the New Physics* and *The Holographic Universe*, Talbot gave a highly developed exposition of the notions of the holographic model and of morphogenetic fields.[7]

Many other academics, for instance, Timothy Leary and Ram Dass (Richard Alpert), used psychedelic drugs. As a result, Americans and Europeans began to embrace ideals around a more humanistic mode of thinking rather than the mechanical and behavioral models based on the laboratory testing of animals. Many authors incorporated information about mental and physical processes from Eastern thinking. Those who still work on these topics, such as Fritjof Capra and Rupert Sheldrake, have published several books translated into many different languages that are readily available in paperback editions. They comment on how the ego influences the vital life force and therefore contributes to the wellness of an integrated self. Those who remain in the academic field of scientific psychology persist in testing their hypotheses regarding abnormal behavior by observing measurable outcomes rather than allowing for any direct experience of ego, which incorporates the body's mind as well as the emotional and spiritual aspects.

EXPLANATIONS OF EGO

A currently popular philosopher, Ken Wilber, explains *ego* as an emotional concept that causes us to feel separate from others. Wilber contends that there are two primal emotions of the ego: fear followed by resentment. In other words, whenever we experience opposition to another person, which Wilber contends happens every time we do not immediately receive instant gratification, then the ego fears that others might harm or cause conflict with the idealized separate ego-self. If we insist on identifying with this separation rather than the idea of interconnection, the ego becomes bruised, insulted, and injured. Wilber writes, "The ego is kept in existence by a collection of emotional insults; it carries its personal bruises as the fabric of its very existence. It actively collects hurts and insults, even while resenting them, because without the bruises it would be, literally, nothing."[8] In both Freud's and Wilber's way of thinking, by the time we reach puberty we all have individual egos, which have the potential to be insulted and injured. Most of us bring this separate, bruised ego into all of our relationships, especially those that involve an erotic connection.

Another contemporary philosopher, Eckhart Tolle, refers to the ego as our *pain-body*. We are beginning to understand that in order to love fully we must give up the notion that we are separate beings. Feeling separate makes us small and vulnerable, as if we were riding a bike with one flat tire on a crowded highway. People are meant to work and play and love together. A Buddhist perspective views attachment as the cause of both physical and emotional pain. The trick is that we must learn to share our lives with others without clinging to them. This process of acknowledging that we are different from one another is as important as it is to grasp the concepts of differentiation and interconnectedness. In the same way that the body's physical and mental processes must be in balance, we must learn how working and playing and loving others can occur in healthy and balanced ways. Traffic systems would never work unless we all agree to drive about the same speed, to stop when the lights are red, and go only when the light turns green. Cars constantly move on and off ramps in an orderly fashion because drivers agree to a set of rules we all trust.

In relationships rather than a set of rules, we need both trust and clear communications to form healthy, balanced partnerships. We are able to gain a sense of trust through mindfulness even if we were neglected or traumatized as children. Mindfulness is the practice of intentional awareness and a prerequisite for developing the sixth sense of intuitive knowledge. John C. Lilly, made an important contribution to the process of gaining mindfulness following his work with dolphins. Lilly, who died in 2001 at the age of eighty-six, designed tanks where people would lie in warm water, in total darkness and silence, to still the busy mind often referred to in Eastern mysticism as the *monkey mind*. He advocated that a busy mind must become quiet in order to observe both emotions and mental processes. His experiments with these sensory deprivation tanks revealed that people could bypass the language center of the cerebral cortex and therefore concentrate on greater control of relaxing the central nervous system. Lilly found that when people fully experience thoughts and emotions through the processing system of the body's mind, they learn to trust these feelings, which in turn contributes to the possibility of a richer understanding of the interconnectedness of all life that goes beyond a separate ego.

Anodea Judith is an author and teacher who explains this interconnectedness as she illuminates ideas from both developmental and depth psychology. In her work called *Eastern Body, Western Mind,* she suggests that while still in the uterus, and certainly at birth, the chakra system expands and contracts in response to stimulation in every situation. She teaches that a newborn's sixth sense of intuition has the capacity to provide information beyond what we are able to perceive with our five senses of hearing, seeing, smelling, tasting, and touching. New babies need attention, touch, and close connection for survival. When these needs appear unattainable, even for a moment, the internal organ systems of the body spontaneously respond by either expanding or contracting. Judith theorizes that this intuitive defensive response results in an unbalanced flood of current throughout the body. This response encodes the body's mind in protective and sometimes destructive ways. An imbalance impinges on the vital life force, and this can result not only in immediate discomfort but also later in disease.

CHANGES IN THINKING

In 1990, the National Institutes of Health (NIH) began to study the field of complementary and alternative medicine (CAM). During this time, the insurance industry and pharmaceutical companies dictated the level of care physicians could provide, and they also determined who could be a provider, often without a true sense of compassion in regard to what is the optimal best for the patient. Once a national health care policy is established, perhaps previous ways of dealing with sickness and health will come around full circle and Americans will have a plan that actually cares for health rather than supporting disease.

Recently, scientists in both the Eastern and Western hemispheres have made many strides in the measurement and recording of the evolving brain. Neuroscientists have identified receptor cells throughout the nervous system that respond to thoughts. This study of *psychoneuroimmunology*, which explains how thoughts influence the immune system, recognizes how the interplay between attitude and observable behavior can result in either health or illness. This awareness leads to rehonoring the intuitive process as the power of the inner healer. We have the capacity for better relationships with others when we are physically, mentally, and emotionally healthy.

If we are in pain it is almost impossible to fully enjoy intimacy with anyone. Pain can alert us to the importance of developing into-me-see that allows us to find ways to eliminate or at least minimize distress. In 1971, medical doctor and researcher Norm Shealy developed an effective treatment for chronic pain. Shealy, who adheres to idea that "the secret of the care of the patient is in caring for the patient,"[9] developed the Transcutaneous Electrical Nerve Stimulation (TENS) unit, which uses small electrical currents to adjust the electromagnetic fields along the spinal column. Later, he discovered that almost all patients suffering chronic pain and depression had low levels of dehydroepieandrosterone (DHEA), a naturally occurring steroid hormone produced in the adrenal glands. His further research developed a procedure he calls *biogenics* that effectively raises DHEA levels without the use of medications.

Because of the need to address memories that result in pain and distress, such as in the case of post-traumatic stress disorder (PTSD), many people have worked toward finding ways to overcome past traumas that block the full flow of vital life force. Stanley Keleman, a pioneer in somatic or body-centered therapy, began the Center for Energetic Studies in 1975. This new branch of *formative psychology* focused on intuitive knowledge, personal relationships, emotional stability, and self-actualization instead of pathology. Keleman builds on Reich's previous work with bioenergetics to describe *character structures*. Character structures are patterns of behavior and ways of holding the body in a particular posture as a result of traumatic or insulting injuries. Keleman teaches specific exercises to move the life force through the body and remove *body armoring*. Body armoring forms when the body defends itself from family and cultural conditioning. This armor can keep us from feeling healthy and peaceful. When we are able to pay attention to the messages the body provides in the moment, then we tap into the healing process called *somatic experiencing*, further developed by Peter Levine, as a gentle way to relieve and discharge unresolved stress and trauma. These methods often use a process of stimulating and tapping the body along meridian lines to increase the flow of energy.

While most sports, as well as yoga, tai chi, martial arts, dance, and movement of any kind including walking in nature, require us to be aware of the body and mind simultaneously, there are other methods for reducing stress levels. Slowing down breathing to quiet the mind provides the opportunity for the physical, mental, and emotional systems to connect with the spirit of enthusiasm. Sometimes this includes the practice of a shamanic journey, using guided imagery or creative visualization with the intention to focus and enter an altered state of mind.

Embracing the stillness of mind, whether we are at rest or moving, allows the release of memories that may be stored in the body's mind. Meridian-based and chakra therapy are two methods of working with vital life force energy as the interface between the body's mind and the spirit of enthusiastic participation in life. We reinstate the natural flow of aliveness when blocked energy is moved through exercises such as tapping, qigong, yoga, and visualization. Unless we address the issues stored in the tissues of our body, we cannot change our unconscious responses. Habitual responses become inextricably linked as holding patterns in the body. This means they are entwined and entangled in an intricate fashion that is difficult, but not impossible, to undo.

The younger we are when we become conscious of opportunities to undo past hurts, the easier it is to avoid forming the neuronal pathways that become addictive patterns. When we can observe our behavior and thoughts, without judgment, we are in the present moment and therefore we can harvest the power available from being fully alive.

FREE FLOW OF ENERGY

Contemporary writers highlight the interaction of brain chemistry and hormonal components. Although some psychologists still ignore the precept that these things are related, Western scientists are beginning to have sufficient language, metaphors, and symbols to explain how this interconnectedness might occur. This remains a difficult concept because we can only grasp the connection through direct experience. Often this experience involves a relationship that helps us to understand shortcomings in a new way. Deep connections often cause altered mental state when successful relaxation is achieved. In the past, some people who reached this realm of feeling connected to everything were viewed as mentally ill. Stanislov Grof was the first to recognize that these people could be having what he calls a *spiritual emergence* rather than a psychotic break. His work with the breath has allowed many people to become consciously aware of the difference between the "difficulty of mental illness and the gift of mental stillness."

Relationships are healthier when we feel good about our self. The ability to be in the present moment has the capacity to reduce stress and soothe tension. The energy from burning calories is more available when we are relaxed. When this energy is flowing freely, the life force enlivens the body's mind and we feel enthusiastic motivation. When internal energy flows smoothly, the vibrational field around us gently touches the boundaries of interpersonal relationships, and we connect more easily. Being in the present moment is similar to having a rapid Internet connection and mobile phones that allow us to contact people around the world in an instant by having push-keys at the tips of our fingers and thumbs. When our internal systems work in harmony with each other, we are embodied in a way that is present, active, and aware of the connections between the mental, physical, emotional, and spiritual aspects. The practice of deep breathing and reflection moves us toward greater awareness, harmony, and eventual intimacy.

Electrical charge is a form of energy found in the body. Just as the hardware and software of the computer need electricity to operate, so does the body. If there is no energy or vital life force, we are dead. If the current is not flowing smoothly, if the voltage is too high or too low, the programs will not run correctly and the hardware itself may even become damaged, resulting in sickness or injury. Our psychological process links to the body and the resulting physical experience is looped back to the psyche. This synergistic linking forms a unified flow of energy that runs through the cells, muscles, and meridians and is then converted into action and observable behavior. When unconscious childhood experiences are not processed into conscious awareness through an integration of several modalities, we cannot make the necessary changes in behavior that will improve relationships.

Healing modalities, such as massage and hypnosis, subscribe to the idea that everything that has ever happened to us is recorded and stored on the cellular level. Talk therapy can be helpful in getting to the source of issues, but it is often unable to address chronic tension held in the muscles. In addition, unless talk therapy is long term, it often does not have a permanent influence on health problems. However, newer modalities that include the tapping of Emotional Freedom Techniques (EFT) and Eye Movement Desensitization and Reprocessing (EMDR) are rapidly becoming comprehensive, integrative approaches. Others include psychodynamic, cognitive, behavioral, interpersonal, experiential, and body-centered therapies that attend to past experiences that may have caused the present difficulty. Practitioners also consider the current situations that may trigger dysfunctional emotions, beliefs, and body sensations. Bodywork, such as massage and physical therapy, helps to release muscular tension but does little to address any trauma held in the neuronal pathways of the brain.

The body consists of nerve endings that act as sensory receptors for the brain. Simple aches and pains are warnings that something needs attention. Stress and the resulting tension also call us to *at-tension*. When we ignore these early signals, physical and mental discomfort can follow. Many body-mind techniques involve using the breath as a tool for healing, and most note the difference between healing and a cure. When we are able to bring stress and tension messages to awareness, the memory can be released from the body through various meridian therapies. When we focus on the breath, the tension is free to dissolve as the vital life force finds a new pathway through the tubes of the body. Our nerves, veins, arteries, bones, and the hollow of the organs are a complex series of pulsating, structured spaces. The tissue and muscle that shape around the bones contribute to our sense of identity.

Judith refers to the tubular structure as *tissue undergoing a being experience* or the *tough underbelly of existence*. Rigidity and calcification form within the tubes when we stick to one viewpoint or remain in negative, harmful relationships. If we fail to integrate new behaviors and incorporate new ways of thinking, we often experience health problems such as indigestion, acid reflux, gall bladder attacks, high cholesterol, hardening of the arteries or other heart problems, as well as depression or any other mental discomfort.

When we become aware of how our internal systems perform, we are more fully alive. Learning how Eastern and Western traditions complement each other allows us to grasp important facets of well-being and personal development. As we appreciate how the ego might influence us, we can keep Freud's basic biological urges of hunger, sex, and aggression within our control by satisfying natural impulses, motivations, and desires.

All parts of an automobile are important so the car can move: the gas tank is as necessary as the spark plugs, all four tires must be fully functional, AND there must also be a driver and a key. Some people appear to be driving with a few flat tires, a nearly empty gas tank, and corroded spark plugs. How does this happen?

For some, soothing behaviors include negative addictions to alcohol, nicotine, drugs, gambling, or mindless sexual activity. As we become more conscious of our behaviors, we become less defensive and stop acting out of habit or avoidance. This moves us toward becoming more integrated. For example, we begin to realize that the drive for sexual release is not more important than observing the flow of energy throughout the body. Activating energy does not eliminate the desire for sex; both bring aspects of joy and satisfaction. However, learning to move energy provides an alternative means of tension release and self-pleasure. Other methods include a long bath or shower, the enjoyment of a great meal or favorite food, exercising or deep breathing, as well as masturbation. The goal becomes the connection with the water, the food, or the breath rather than satisfying the need to release hunger, sex, or aggression through unconscious overeating, drinking too much, smoking, having unprotected or unwanted sex, or becoming aggressive, violent, or depressed. As we evolve, the body's mind motivates us toward various creative desires, and we learn to run energy that may or may not be sexual in nature.

Intimacy that includes into-me-see embraces the ability to use the sixth sense to examine the concepts of ego and individualization. The more we know about how our body's mind functions, the better our relationships will be. Once we have insight into what is going on within us, we can allow others to see us more clearly. As we explore various teachings from other cultures, we can learn more about how we appear in relationship to others. This leads to transparency, an important aspect of being open and expressive. By expanding our understanding beyond our traditional cultural viewpoints, we can embrace universal facets of the body's mind essential to the exploration of our sixth sense. This expansion provides the intuitive knowing that leads to greater intimacy. Conscious awareness of our intuitive sixth sense through self-reflection and visualization has an effect on the way others react toward us. Healthy energy flow between inner experiences and outer expectation optimizes connections.

↬4↫

DISCERNING SYSTEMS

Models from other cultures regarding the body's capacity to heal itself provide a base for holistic health programs. An understanding of our internal processing systems contributes to an explanation of how the tangible physical organs work together with subtle energy fields. Together they foster greater vitality and the overall sense of well-being that leads to healthy, meaningful relationships.

↬∞↫

The study of how the body's mind might work to process information has come a long way since the 1600s, when René Descartes first made the distinction between the mind, understood to be the seat of intelligence, and the body. He argued that the nature of the mind is a thinking, non-extended thing, completely different from that of the body, an extended, non-thinking thing. He clearly identified the body as mechanical and the mind as self-aware, which led to a *dichotomy*. This eventually became known as the *mind-body problem* as if somehow one could exist without the other.[1] A dichotomy is any splitting of a whole into exactly two non-overlapping parts that are both:

- mutually exclusive, nothing can belong simultaneously to both parts, and
- jointly exhaustive, everything must belong to one part or the other.

In spite of this flaw in reasoning these ideas became part of the scientific model and led many scholars to undervalue the body. Mind is not a separate entity from the physical body. Feelings are essential to what it means to be an embodied human being.

The study of how the body's mind might work to process information has come a long way. An introduction to the internal systems that includes other cultural contexts can reveal the link between the psychological realm of thinking and the physiological realm of feeling and emotion. Various tests performed on students, prisoners, and mental patients provide a basic understanding regarding the five senses. Scientists study how we perceive information and the effect it has on behavior. Medical students dissect human cadavers to validate the body's internal systems. The interactions of the entire biochemical and nervous system, the secretion of hormones and their flow within the endocrine system have all been well documented. In spite of this, we do not know why we behave the way we do under various circumstances.

Scientists cannot exactly measure the entire progression of human thoughts and feelings, but each of us has the capacity to become aware of our internal psyche and emotional processing systems just as we are able to be aware of our physical body. When we combine emotional intelligence and intuitive knowing with psychological theories, we attain a greater appreciation about conscious and unconscious processes. When we are receptive to knowing our personal thought patterns, we gain control over automatic reactions and responses that often get in the way of developing intimacy with self and others.

CHANGE IN THINKING

Ken Dychtwald wrote a pioneering book called *Bodymind* in 1977 at a time when more women than ever before obtained higher education. Some studied the essence of being human, along with the history of holistic medical practices. Others explored theories of quantum physics. Ten years later Marilyn Ferguson wrote *Aquarian Conspiracy* and began the publication of the *Brain-Mind Bulletin*, a popular newsletter that brought together different viewpoints on science and mysticism and furthered the work of the previously mentioned consciousness studies. Ferguson stated that the "energetic life force is organized by a holistic model that marries biology to physics in an open system."[2] Barbara Ann Brennan, a former NASA physicist, remains one of today's principal teachers of the marriage between biology and physics. Her well-illustrated *Hands of Light* was influenced by her friend Rosalyn Bruyere's *Wheels of Light: A Study of the Chakras*, published in 1987, the same year as *Wheels of Life: A User's Guide to the Chakra System*, written by Anodea Judith. Joan Borysenko also picked up this theme in *Minding the Body, Minding the Mind*. During these pivotal years, Richard Gerber brought these concepts into medical terms through his book *Vibrational Medicine*. The almost simultaneous publication of these works demonstrates a *zeitgest*, which occurs when particular ideas and thoughts originate from different sources at the same time.

Gerber explains the chakra system, not in esoteric philosophical or spiritual terms, but as a step-down transformer that condenses the body's energy into deeper levels of consciousness. His work recounts how higher frequency energies can become useful in the process of healing the body once we become aware of the auric field that surrounds us and the chakra system within us. Most of today's authors on this topic agree that the chakra system influences hormonal levels. Medical intuitives actually see energy patterns in the aura and chakra systems that affect behavior. Some scientists maintain that using medical concepts to describe how the body's mind works is alien to empirical science. Others interested in integrative medical practices insist that it is essential to bring these ideas together in order to gain greater understanding and, therefore, more control of both our health and healthy relationships.

What if our intuitive processing system has a direct effect on all intimate connections? If we learn more about emotional intelligence, would it make a difference in how we feel about ourselves and toward others?

Current teachers illustrate the seven primary chakras and several layers of auric field as characterized by location, color, brightness, form, density, fluidity, and functionality. They describe chakras as discs or vortexes of energy that correspond to the seven main nerve ganglia emanating from the spinal column. Some believe chakras to be a part of the memory system that gathers, stores, and retrieves information. Anodea Judith teaches that the job of the chakra system is to receive, assimilate, and transmit information throughout the body. Some teachers hypothesize that an electrical current is emitted within the body that directly affects the endocrine system, which in turn influences our reactions and therefore our behavior. This change in hormones triggers a response in behavior. We often react to information that originates externally at the same time as we become internally aware of thoughts, feelings, and emotions.

IMPORTANCE OF BALANCE

According to these teachings, our life is in balance when our energy is flowing gently throughout the system. One possible way to envision a single chakra is similar to the iris of a camera based on the working of the eye. An iris has a range. It is capable of being wide open to let light in or tightly closed to keep it out. Another way to picture the working of a chakra is to use your own hands and experience the feeling of what it means if this vortex of energy is too open or too closed. If you spread your fingers wide apart, so much so that it hurts, this would be an example of a chakra being too open and causing the energy moving through to flow out quickly; this is referred to as a *leak*. If you close the same fingers into a fist, again so tight that it hurts, you have an example of blocked energy. Just as it would be uncomfortable to walk around all day with fingers spread wide open or pressed tightly into a fist, the chakras also need to relax into a more flexible, centered, and balanced position. We are out of balance when the energy is either leaking or blocked. We are in our fullest state of aliveness when this energy flow is neither excessive nor deficient.

Practitioners who integrate this information believe these leaks and blockages are a cause of both chronic illness and fatal disease. They teach that if any chakra is either too open or too closed it is difficult to experience well-being. They imply that once we learn to pay attention to this internal information-processing system, we may become able to discern leaks or blockages, and this awareness will allow us to respond differently. Illustrations of chakras show them closely linked in prox-

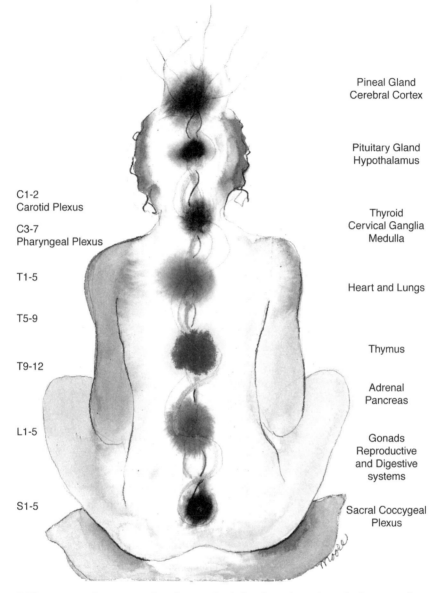

Pineal Gland
Cerebral Cortex

Pituitary Gland
Hypothalamus

C1-2
Carotid Plexus

Thyroid
Cervical Ganglia
Medulla

C3-7
Pharyngeal Plexus

T1-5

Heart and Lungs

T5-9

Thymus

T9-12

Adrenal
Pancreas

L1-5

Gonads
Reproductive
and Digestive
systems

S1-5

Sacral Coccygeal
Plexus

Different vertebrae are related to each chakra based on the spinal nerves that innervate the ganglia and the corresponding organs and glands.

imity and function to the feedback mechanism within the spinal cord; therefore, it is believed they have a direct effect on both behavior and physical condition. When energy moves too quickly or slowly along the body's central axis, a deficiency or excess may result in the function of the corresponding organ.

In the past, Western science ignored the possibility of this correspondence and little academic research was done in this area; therefore only a few serious studies exist on how this reactive, intuitive system might work. On the other hand, numerous books, tapes, websites, videos, and DVDs have been published outside of academia on this worldview. They offer exercises and solutions to problems that may result from this imbalance in the flow of the vital life force.

Many of these ideas were originally part of oral traditions and various authors interpret the correlations to the organs differently. Judith's view is that the legs, knees, ankles, and feet relate to the *first chakra*, in addition to the area at the base of the spinal column in the sacral-coccygeal plexus in the perineum area. Brennan's interpretation connects this root chakra to the adrenal glands and kidneys, and Gerber's model connects it to the gonads and reproductive system. Judith relates disorders of the anus, colon, and large intestine to this chakra as well as all solid parts of the body such as bones and teeth.

In Brennan's model the *second chakra*, called the sacral or sexual, consists of the reproductive organs in the lower abdomen. Gerber associates it with the genitourinary tract, which includes the organs of elimination, and the interstitial cell-stimulating hormones of the endocrine system. Judith includes both and adds low back pain, sexual pleasure and dysfunction, as well as deadened senses.

The *third chakra*, which these teachers all describe as beginning at the navel and ending at the breastbone, is called the solar plexus. This area includes the stomach and contains a large network of sympathetic nerves and ganglia, which have branching tracts that supply the abdominal viscera. This chakra may include the adrenal glands and digestive system according to Gerber, and the pancreas, stomach, liver, gall bladder, and nervous system according to Brennan. Judith relates that eating and digestive disorders as well as muscular dysfunction can impact this region.

The *fourth chakra* contains the complex circulatory system of the heart and lungs, and many authors include the thymus gland here as well as the vagus or cranial nerve, which connects several organ systems to the brain. Judith suggests the breasts and arms are included here, as well as immune system deficiency and even tension between the shoulder blades. She and other practitioners believe we receive information into the heart chakra through the fingers and hands via everything we touch.

In these models, the *fifth chakra* is associated with the thyroid gland located in the neck area. According to Gerber it connects to the nerve plexus known as the cervical ganglia medulla. The throat chakra is said to include our ability to express thoughts through the respiratory and bronchial apparatus that encompass the vocal cords and the alimentary canal. Most models also include the sense of hearing as well as the taste buds.

The *sixth chakra*, often referred to as the seat of intuition and the third eye due to its location between the eyes, is said to contain the sense of smell as well as sight. Both Brennan and Gerber associate the hypothalamus with this nerve plexus and the pituitary gland, which helps to control the autonomic nervous system.

The top of the head is the crown and the last of the seven major chakras. The crown is believed to be the connecting point to the pineal gland, which governs the central nervous system including the cerebral cortex. Gerber notes, "Currents of energy are taken into the body through a stream." Various teachers agree that each chakra is associated with a different vibrational frequency similar to a ray of light, which enters a prism and then splits into the seven visible colors of the rainbow. In other words, each chakra acts as a prism for the incoming stimulus perceived as a thought or feeling. "Inherent in the white light are all seven colors," Gerber continues. "Cosmic energies enter the crown and the vibrational currents are refracted from the single higher stream containing all the colors . . . and distributed to the appropriate chakra attuned to that specific color frequency."[3]

Those commenting on these topics often compare the physical body to computer hardware. The constant incoming flow of information entering through the five basic senses acts as the electrical or battery-charged energy source. We can understand this as similar to the USB hub that can route data to the correct device. Our intuitive sixth sense may contain the genetic encoding and cultural conditioning similar to a software program. An integrated self acts as the computer operator who ultimately has control of the system. Obviously, the more knowledge we have about our hardware and software systems, the more efficient operators we become.

Another way to grasp the notion of this available cosmic energy is to relate it to the breath taken in through the nose and mouth, which then flows from the lungs throughout the body in the form of oxygen. Some nonmedical explanations contend that vital life force can also enter the body at the cellular level through the soles of the feet and the palms of the hands.

Valerie Hunt, a pioneer who holds advanced degrees in psychology and physiological science, has provided evidence of the human biofields. Her techniques for protection of the aura and chakra systems have contributed to the understanding of how subtle energy healing works; however her research projects are often viewed as unscientific. Hunt developed an AuraMeter that correlates the auric layers with frequency wave patterns in the reverse order of a rainbow color sequence. Hunt and others, including Jack Schwarz, a medical intuitive and naturopath who died in 2000, have observed the healing power of colors, both as light and in the use of the imagination. The larger medical community has ignored many of their discoveries. Schwarz is quoted as saying that "it is time to come out of ignorance where we perceive only from our physical environment." His teachings state that when we disregard a relationship with the larger cosmos, we shun everything else that would provide greater awareness. Thus, Schwarz felt we interfere with the capacity of the laws of the universe, which he saw not as psychological or physiological but as "metapsychophysiological." He taught that we expand our ability to see more and feel when we are not in defiance of physical laws but rather in an expansion of these laws.[4]

Gerber, noted earlier, emphasizes the concept of the transformer. Although he uses medical terms, his explanation is similar to the descriptions translated from the ancient texts of China and India:

> Subtle energies are converted to endocrine signals in a manner akin to a step-down transformer . . . and transmitted as information of a more physiologic nature. Subtle energy is converted into hormonal signals from each of the major endocrine glands linked with the chakra. Through the release of small amounts of powerful hormones into the blood stream, the entire physical body is affected. In addition, each chakra distributes vital energy to a number of different organs that are in the same body location that tend to resonate at a similar frequency.[5]

One interpretation of this is that when any stimulus enters into our perception through the five senses, the sixth sense sends a signal to the corresponding organ. At the same time, thoughts and feelings are also triggered and we respond with an observable behavior. According to this explanation, it would mean that when the vibrational energy from other people enters our personal space, their energetic force connects to our own. This interchange relates to behavioral action and emotional response. In other words, their energy affects our behavior and creates an internal reaction to whatever is happening. When one energetic force bumps up against another, it creates a reverberation in the flow of energy. As this happens, our internal organs resonate in either harmony or cacophony. We might feel a rush or tingle, which we could describe as joy or pleasure or as anger and frustration. When we do not resonate at the same frequency with the people or place around us, we often become distraught, distressed, and argumentative. We may want to move away to end the discomfort, or we may automatically shut down our feelings, thereby blocking the vital life force that must flow freely in order to retain control.

Our biofield seeks the flexible stability of homeostasis, and it adjusts and responds the same as when we are feeling too hot or too cold. When our body temperature fluctuates, a message is sent throughout the nervous system so that we consciously desire to change the thermostat in the room, open or close the window, or take off or put on clothes. In this way, we return to a more balanced body temperature. Some believe the chakra system begins to expand or contract from the time we are infants. Because of stress, a chakra might remain too opened or leaking, causing us to overreact, or too closed, therefore blocking out any good feelings that are coming in as well as the bad sensations we want to avoid.

To feel this energy, simply rub your hands together for a few seconds, and then move them an inch or two apart with palms facing each other. Do you feel a pulsing sensation or heat radiating from your hands?

Another descriptive way to illustrate this also uses the hands, which connect to the heart. If we are thirsty and there is no means to get the water except with our hands, but our fingers are wide open, we will not be able to bring water to our mouth. If we try to carry the water with our fingers closed into a fist, we will not be able to drink that way either. However, instinctively, or perhaps by trial and error, we know or learn how to cup the hands in order to hold water and therefore quench our thirst. Our internal systems also need to be in a relaxed state for us to feel balanced and centered and experience joy and pleasure.

Again use your hands to represent bodily energy. If you greet another person with arms outstretched at shoulder height, hands up with palms facing outward and fingers pointing to the sky in a "keep away" position, it is most likely the person will get the message. If our energetic stance is with closed fists in a protective, defensive "I'm ready to fight" posture, we are likely to trigger fight, flight, or freeze response. When we greet another person energetically, in a way that invites a hug, most will understand that invitation. As we become aware of the subtle energy we emit, based on our internal action and reaction to outside stimuli, we will better understand why people respond to us the way they do.

Once we grasp the importance of inner reflection, we can create more possibilities for noticing and responding to the subtle energy and behaviors of another person. We then have additional choices in the way we react in various situations. These choices continuously help determine our destiny. The more choices of response we have, the more opportunities we have for connections through intimacy, loving friendships, and personal growth. When we are fully in control, it is easier to manifest wants, needs, and desires into reality. Visions and wishes are only one step toward achieving intuitive knowing and emotional intelligence for the highest good for all concerned. Learning the developmental stages of childhood can bring greater compassion for our self and others. As we mature, we begin to notice how the earliest emotional experiences have a continuous, life-long effect on the way we process information. We have the opportunity to change past conditioning through insight and intuitive awareness.

～5～

SENSING PERCEPTION

A combination of nature and nurture forms the personality. As we perceive the outer world with our five senses, we record these perceptions in our mind. How do we define mind? How do we differentiate emotions from thoughts and memories? None of these can be seen or heard, they do not smell and cannot be tasted or touched, yet we continuously make distinctions about the role they play in all of our relationships. New theories regarding how we think can provide ways to access our powerful sixth sense of intuition and to gain greater intimacy.

～⬥～

From infancy, most of us have a consistent style of behavior, which includes activity level, emotional reactions to outside stimuli, and preferences for social interactions that are aspects of temperament. Ancient Greek philosophers believed inborn predispositions led one person to be *melancholic*—doubtful and uncertain—and another person *sanguine*—full of confidence and certainty. Today, we use the words *pessimist* or *optimist* as characteristic components of temperament, which is different from personality. Some people look at a glass that contains liquid up to a halfway point and see it as half empty, and others will see it as half full.

We inherit both temperamental and biological aspects from our ancestors. Our biology includes race, aptitude, and physical characteristics; genes determine skin tone and eye color, biological genital structure, and whether we are tall or short, large or small. Once we reach adulthood, under normal circumstances, these things do not change. On the other hand, age can alter the color and/or texture of our hair, as can environmental causes such as sunlight or humidity, the foods we eat, or conscious decisions we make to apply chemical products as change agents. It is also easy to modify our personality as we learn more about emotional and social intelligence. It is more difficult to change temperamental traits.

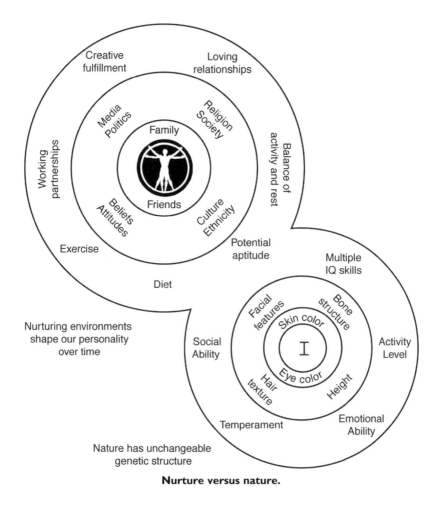

Nurture versus nature.

Over the past several decades, Jerome Kagan led research that followed a group of infants through adolescence and into adulthood. At the beginning of this long-term project, Kagan theorized that a young baby's early responses might determine later patterns. His team recorded breathing rates, facial expressions, eye contact, and movement patterns of the arms and legs during the first year of an infant's life. As they observed the same children over time, they discovered a consistency in body movements and physiological functions. The team tested these same children as they reached puberty. Based on the fact that those babies who displayed vigorous arm and leg movements became active children, and those who made more constant eye contact were outgoing and sociable teens, Kagan then defined temperamental differences based on measures of activity and social responses. He found people unwavering in their emotional response from birth, consistent throughout childhood into adolescence and adulthood.

In contrast, personality is malleable, sometimes strong and sometimes submissive. Because personality is impressionable, we are capable of changing behavior, developing self-awareness, managing our moods, motivating ourselves, feeling empathy, and therefore capable of greater intimacy in respect to these aspects of emotional intelligence. As we become consciously aware of our internal reactions, we can acquire the ability to alter thoughts about situations and make different choices about how to respond. It is possible to change our thoughts, which will change our life; for instance, we may begin to think about the glass as half full, even through our first response may have been that it was half empty.

Scientists have since discovered that we can actually modify our biological chemistry when new neuronal pathways modify the actual folds within the gray matter of the brain. Psychotropic drugs also alter the chemistry of the body's mind. In the same way, we can alter hormonal secretions and physicality of the gray matter by adjusting our attitude and monitoring our responses to the circumstances around us. This way of controlling stressful situations can be achieved by focusing, practicing tai chi, holding yoga postures, learning how to meditate and to visualize. Other methods include acts of forgiveness and compassionate kindness, learning about meridian-based therapies, and nonviolent communications (NVC). Each of these approaches to greater self-loving requires discipline. Practicing these skills will actually cause the synapses to fire throughout the nervous system in unique ways. When used consistently they transform the neuronal pathways that in turn determine future behavioral responses.

The work of Kagan's team highlighted that physical activity and emotional and social responses are constant, and more difficult to change because he felt they were part of our genetic nature rather than stemming from the nurturing we receive from childhood. In psychological circles, the words *nature* and *nurture* are used in an unusual way. Nature in the "nature versus nurture" context is our genetic, chromosomal coding. Psychologists refer to nurture as the input of sensory stimuli received from our first caregivers, regardless of whether these influences are positive or negative. The idea of nurturing goes beyond the influences of family, friends, and teachers; we are also exposed to input from the *environment* or neighborhood where we are raised. Other nurturing influences include ethnic background, religion, school, politics, and all varieties of media. In many homes radio and TV become a constant background noise, full of advertisements and commercials as well as information and entertainment. Although the general public may still debate the nurture or nature question as to how each one influences a child's development, most psychologists consider that the outcome of our lives is shaped equally by both genetics (nature) and the environment (nurture). There is no doubt we are a combination of many different influences.

MULTIPLE INTELLIGENCE

Howard Gardner proposed that we are born with innate potential and an aptitude toward certain abilities. He introduced the concept of multiple intelligences to understand how different people learn and process information. The intelligences that he identified include:

- *Bodily-kinesthetic intelligence:* the potential of using one's whole body or parts of the body to solve problems. The ability to use both mental abilities and physical activity to coordinate bodily movements.
- *Intrapersonal intelligence:* the ability to understand oneself, to appreciate one's own feelings, fears, and motivations. This involves an effective working model of integration and the ability to apply this information to regulate our lives.

- *Interpersonal intelligence:* the capacity to understand the intentions, motivations, fears, feelings, and desires of other people. Combined with intrapersonal this composes the emotional and social IQ that allows people to work effectively on teams or in groups.
- *Linguistic intelligence:* sensitivity to spoken and written language, the ability to learn languages easily, and the capacity to use symbols or sign language to accomplish certain goals.
- *Logical-mathematical intelligence:* the competence to analyze problems logically, carry out mathematical operations, and investigate issues scientifically.
- *Musical intelligence:* skill in the performance, composition, and appreciation of musical patterns. An aptitude for recognizing and composing musical pitches, tones, and rhythms.
- *Spatial intelligence:* the propensity to recognize and use the patterns of wide space and more confined areas.[1]

Although we may have a natural inclination for one of these intelligences, we have the capacity to learn from each of them. Recent research suggests we have more control than previously believed.

I AM NOT YOU

From the first moments after birth, the processes of *differentiation* and *individualization* begin. We soon realize we are separate and different from other individuals. Freud described this individual self as the *id*, and he understood *ego* as the mechanism that helps integrate the individual into society by cooperating with the norms of the culture. Norms are constantly in both a progressive and reactive flux from generation to generation. Every culture has its own variation, and they also differ from family to family within a given society.

For the current generation, electronic media are rapidly expanding normal boundaries and our capacity for multiple intelligences. Historically, learning was handed down through traditions and myths, songs and storytelling. The information age provides the opportunity to expand cultural norms far beyond what was available to previous generations. Now music, books, radio, movies, television, and the vast array of information available from the Internet are all part of what is called the *nurturing environment,* although some of it does not appear nurturing in a positive sense. Exposure to ideas beyond the environment we grow up in allows us to change our thought processes and become more inclusive of others' points of view. Many healthy children now have access to information far beyond the prevailing, conventional mindset of any particular culture. Because of the World Wide Web, most affluent families can easily access information our ancestors never had available in any form. Although in some cases the availability of computers segregates the wealthy from the poor, the hope for the future is that all economic levels and people in every society will have access to technology.

As a rule, different cultures have distinct ideas about raising children, and individual families use a variety of words and phrases to express ideas and enforce values. Strict parental constraints often fail to encourage the traits necessary for emotional and social intelligence, such as confidence, curiosity, cooperation, and communication. In most American schools, students learn only English. In other societies, children are encouraged to learn English as well as their native tongue. Young children who learn more than one language often find it easier to differentiate from parental and cultural conditioning as they mature. In poorer countries, people may be exposed to a variety of verbal communications, but without books, television, or the Internet, they have little experience with English. Although they appear to have fewer opportunities for growth and development, they may be less stressed and more peaceful and content. The visual stimulation and new technological information currently available to affluent children may be causing stress and depression. In addition, many fail to develop imagination, therefore losing touch with intuitive knowing.

We are able to see things from different perspectives only when we are encouraged to form and express our own ideas. Exposure to different ways of knowing expands our thought processes to be more inclusive of others. Currently, family and societal restraints are weakening in many cultures, and we have no idea what future outcomes may be. Knowing about multiple intelligences is one way to increase the potential of human dynamics.

Through the developing field of quantum physics we are learning how we are all interconnected. This connection is encouraging many to view the world through various lenses simultaneously rather than sequentially. When we connect the dots between our self and others, we recognize that we are inseparable from a greater whole. The intuitive sixth sense constantly provides information from within, and the combination of nature and nurture provides input from thoughts and feelings,

INTERLOCKING CIRCLES ILLUSTRATE AN INTEGRATED SELF

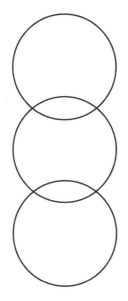

in addition to the sounds, sights, smells, tastes, and textures that surround us. Our ability to act and react in all situations is informed by our various intelligences, and they determine the outcome of our behavior.

The integrated self has the ability to explore the world through the senses. The body is where we perceive *tangible reality* through our skin, hands and feet, eyes, ears, nose, and mouth. Our sensory systems constantly convey information to every muscle and organ as we interact with the external world. Our body responds as we take oxygen into our lungs; our heart beats, blood flows, and limbs move. These systems work automatically. We usually do not stop and think about the internal working of the body unless something goes wrong and draws our attention toward the problem.

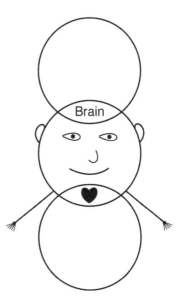

We often view the heart as the place where we feel love. We also damage the heart by fueling the body with a poor diet, alcohol, or other toxic substances. Because heart problems are the number one cause of death, it is important to become aware of these organs and the effect they have on our entire system. We can easily become aware of our breath or heartbeat when we pause and observe them. Reflecting on the breath and heart rate is as easy as observing the way we move, or noticing our behavior and emotional reaction to various external stimuli. Taking time for quiet, inner observation of our heart and lungs allows us to have more control over all of our actions and reactions. Focusing specifically on the heart, bringing in and sending out compassion and loving kindness is a practice well worth pursuing. HeartMath techniques for reducing stress are another great avenue for changing the way we approach the world.

LEARNING HOW TO LEARN

The brain is the information-processing center that works along with the mind. In this model, the mind is the recorder and responder of both mental and emotional activity found in every cell throughout the body, including the heart. Both brain and mind are essential to the Integrated Self, as is intuitive knowing, which is suggested by the aura and chakra systems. All are engaged in exploring and developing sensitivity. Information processed through all six senses forms the *cognitive* aspect. Cognition is perceived within the central nervous system (CNS) as both tangible and intangible reality. Internal energetic interactions become the learned knowledge called experience.

An explanation of this is found in the work of Jean Piaget, who outlined a theory of mental development in the mid-1950s that is now readily accepted. His model explains how young children move into higher levels of learning or cognition in predetermined steps beginning with what he called *sensory-motor* and moving to *preoperational* thought. According to Piaget, the *concrete operational* and *formal operational* stages follow. During this progression of internal mental growth, most of us have less awareness of our biological, physical body as we concentrate on the accomplishment of various tasks. This is what Freud called the latency period. Just as young children must follow the directions of others at first, the body follows an internal lead by retrieving previous learning and experience and making independent decisions about when to eat, sleep, play, exercise, or what clothes to wear. As we mature, Piaget found we make decisions without consciously thinking too much about them. These decisions become routine until we are tired or hungry, emotionally or physically hurt, and then our senses automatically focus more on the physical body.

As an example, when we are not hungry, we do not usually think about eating, but as time passes and the stomach empties, our attention is called back to the need to find food. When we experience hunger or thirst, we must get something to eat or drink, similar to the desire for sexual release, it becomes difficult to think about anything else. When we are preoccupied with our body, we can be overwhelmed with both physical and mental input, and soon we are unable to function in other areas. Just as when we first learn to drive a car or we are driving in an unknown area, we must fully concentrate on other cars and the flow of traffic, but as our experience on the road increases, our ability to operate the vehicle becomes more automatic. This is also comparable to the performance of a car; mechanically things can be in order, but if we do not have a key for the ignition, then the car does not function. In order for a car to be most useful it also needs gas, oil, and other fluids to keep it moving, in addition to a driver.

Knowledge about the sixth sense is similar to the driver of the car. Not only do drivers determine where the car might go, they also can regulate the temperature inside the car, decide how fast to go, and when to stop. In the beginning of learning about the car's engine, the driver simply glances at the gauge to see if the gas is low. As we increase our understanding about the body's response through our intuitive awareness, then it is as if we put the car on a diagnostic computer to see what might be out of order and potentially cause a disturbance in the future. In a similar way, the body's mind is regulated as we gain knowledge and experience through our intuitive sense.

Our body's mind responds to both internal and external stimuli through *innervation*. Innervation occurs by sending signals through the nerve ganglia that stimulate *inhibitory* and *excitatory* responses in the nervous system. If we move our finger too close to a hot candle, we will automatically pull back unless we have made an intentional decision to touch the flame and experience pain. In the same way, if a mother is carrying a hot pan full of food toward the table and suddenly realizes the pan is too hot, she is not likely to drop it because the thought of feeding her family will over ride the autonomic system and inhibit the fact that her hands are feeling an uncomfortable amount of heat. One way to think about this phenomenon is that a higher power or inner wisdom takes over. Eastern teachings use the aura and chakra systems to explain how such information becomes part of our experiential learning. In turn, this learning becomes part of the response mechanism that regulates the integration, storage, and retrieval of memory.

LEARNING HOW TO LOVE

The Integrated Self includes spirit or soul. Think of spirit in terms of motivation or enthusiasm. Some discuss spirit as the seat of morality, where right and wrong are established. In this model, spirit encompasses the sixth sense. Sometimes, we call intuitive knowing *common sense*. Common sense usually refers to logical, rational, coherent thinking. But it can also be something we "just know" without questioning. In this same way the sixth sense, or paranormal thinking, provides information in addition to common sense and sometimes even in opposition to it. Without all six senses, we would be rather "senseless." Scientific instruments cannot yet measure this "spiritual" characteristic, and hard science contends that if we cannot see it, hear it, smell it, taste it, or touch it—IT does not exist. Although this component is impossible to observe, some philosophers refer to it as the *Observer*. The simplified model presented here explains it as part of the processing system that discerns, evaluates, and judges information perceived through all six senses. As incoming information is processed, outward behavioral responses are determined, as in the example of not dropping the hot pan of food. When we are paying attention, the information provided by the internal processing system warns us about what is important to our well-being and the best path to take for the highest good of all concerned.

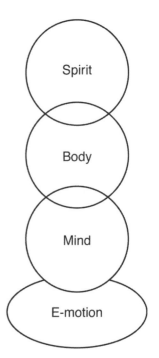

In addition to the body that perceives, the mind that does the cognitive recording, and the spirit of discernment and determination, the base of this model is *e-motion* or energy in motion.

E-motions are influenced by the biochemicals called hormones in the endocrine system, which determine how we appear as masculine or feminine, as well as how we respond in various situations. Various biochemicals regulate the response to what the brain-body perceives, the heart-mind records, the soul-spirit evaluates. As we become adults, we are capable of being consciously aware on several levels and in several directions at the same time. To elaborate on how these internal systems might work together, let us agree that we are always aware of our body even when not directly thinking about it. For example, if I suddenly ask about your feet, your attention automatically moves in that direction and you become aware of your feet. All six senses are constantly providing information, although we cannot process every bit of incoming data. Therefore, some of the input must be filtered out, and we usually do not pay much attention to our feet unless they are too hot, too cold, or in pain. Some believe the filtered out information is recorded on the cellular level and that we are constantly susceptible to underlying memories and vulnerable to belief systems of which we may be unaware. We take in and process information through the internal systems influenced by temperament, as well as family background including ethnic, cultural, and religious beliefs handed down for generations.

CONSCIOUS EVOLUTION

It was previously thought that babies entered the world as a tabula rasa, or blank slate, with no other instinct but to search for the nipple to suck and stay alive.[2] Now some believe memory begins soon after the sperm meets the egg and that this zygote is a separate, viable being. Others believe the storing of memories and recording of information begins in the fetal stage twelve to fourteen weeks after gestation. Many current theorists hold that information is recorded throughout the pregnancy and that the process of labor and delivery also has an effect on future personality. Still others teach that memory can occur only after we pass through the birth canal, once the umbilical cord is cut and we are actually separate, breathing and functioning without the aid of the mother's body. To simplify the debate for the sake of this explanation, let us agree for now that all perceived information from the time of labor and delivery is encoded and stored at the subconscious level and is available for later retrieval. Generally, most theories acknowledge that the neonate perceives, records, and makes decisions during the first hours after birth. This means that thoughts from the very beginning of life form attitudes and personality traits that, in turn, influence us for the rest of our lives.

Freud believed that we denied and therefore repressed certain thoughts in what he termed *unconscious mind*. In his theory, both memories and desires caused anxiety, which leads to hysteria. In this newly proposed model, we will define *unconscious* to mean when we are not aware of what is happening around us or inside of us. We will label the recorded and stored memory of all we experience *subconscious* information. As with any model, we must understand that words are simply symbol systems to clarify and label complex concepts. These operational definitions make arbitrary divisions for simplification of the complexities of our internal systems rather than denote separate areas of the body. The words placed within these circle drawings are designed to lessen confusion as we blend different models and theories.

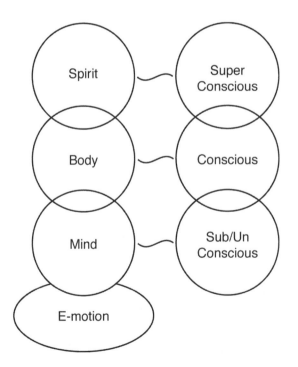

The top circle, across from the soul-spirit level, is labeled *super-conscious*, which we can also understand as an aspect of *conscience*. It includes the internalized rules from family and society that are called *mores* (pronounced "mor-aes"). These mechanisms of the nurturing environment enable us to make decisions about what actions to take, which then manifests as our behavior. As part of this model superconscious is the linear, analytical thinking sometimes called the *left brain* and often referred to as the *rational mind*. This aspect makes evaluations and judgments regarding what we understand as hot and cold, as well as "good and bad." A healthy conscience is similar to what Freud called *superego* as it is derived from our childhood and is continuously modified by other life experiences. The intuitive sixth sense forms evaluations and judgments that become our code of morals or ethics. The society we live in, our cultural background, and our family are all influences that we use to determine what is right or wrong in any given moment, and together these influences generate the resulting behavior. Freud named *defense mechanisms* and Jung highlighted *projections* that come into play and influence our relationships. We will come back to both in the next chapters.

This responsible, critical, moral aspect of thinking can be condemning and prejudiced, and in turn it can cause us to act in irrational or immoral ways. Therefore, what appears to be rational under one set of circumstances can also be illogical and can damage our connections with others, for instance, when we close our minds to hearing another person's point of view. It is important to remember that most of us have the intuitive experience of knowing something without knowing how we know. Some refer to this phenomenon as *the one who observes* because this part of our Integrated Self seems to have an awareness of the past, present, and future. Some people call this *Universal Mind* or *Inner Wisdom*, and others refer to *Supraconsciousness*. Jung named the *collective unconscious* to explain the fact that we have visions or dreams about the myths and stories from past civilizations that may or may not be known to us.

As we become more consciously aware, we can quickly change our reaction from the way we previously learned to respond. By observing our internal reactions, we can make a different choice about our behavior in any given moment. Within the blink of an eye the conscious mind can perceive the present, while the subconscious mind provides past memories regarding the many decisions previously made under similar circumstances. Simultaneously, the superconscious mind decides what action to take, based on what we know from the past combined with our desire for future outcomes. In this model, the superconscious encompasses our instinct for survival and the component that quickly provides a change in our behavior.

At the same time all of this is happening, the biofields are bombarded with information that is recorded within the bodily systems. Simultaneously, the chakras make connections with all previous information stored throughout the intuitive systems. In the present moment, healthy physical bodies take action and move forward. As we become more sensitive to our thoughts and feelings, we experience all of these steps taking place in every moment before every reaction. This is not an easy task.

Neurobiologists continue to ask if thoughts precede our physical emotional response. Or do we first have a feeling followed by a thought that prompts us to act? Perhaps the response is different for different people in different situations? Each individual can only answer these questions after internal observation. Is it possible to experience any feeling without first having a thought, or do our feelings create our thoughts? Science does not yet have answers to this puzzle. Although many people find it relatively easier to change thoughts, others still believe that circumstances beyond our control generate the feelings inside the body. If we believe outside forces determine the way we feel, it follows that we would look outside for solutions. If this were so, we could just eat or take a pill, get a drink, watch TV, or have sex, then we would feel better, and no one would ever get sick.

What if our thoughts were the main determinate of how healthy we feel? What if we were able to continually monitor our breath and heart rate? What if we were consciously aware every time we put something into our mouth? What if we always stopped to think before we speak? How would our worlds be different?

Information from family, friends, teachers, and various media constantly bombards us. We are waking up to the fact that our thoughts may create what we experience. This is changing the therapeutic process and how practitioners deliver health care. People are discovering information for themselves and asking more questions when they go to a doctor or therapist. Advertisements for medications are helping us to become more aware of possible side effects and therefore are becoming more selective about what we ingest.

When we perceive information through the senses, a synapse fires in the nervous system that creates a neuronal pathway that becomes the memory of the event. Our thoughts are the documentation of what happens around us, and this documentation is recorded within the plasticity of the brain's gray matter. Current theory about memory suggests that our internal interpretation of outer events is our reflection on the situation rather than the actuality of what just happened. It is similar to looking into a mirror and imaging that we are fatter or thinner than factual reality. As another example, we have constant choice about how we react to what we see, hear, smell, taste, and touch. If we are close to traffic noise that we find annoying, we can pause, take a deep breath, and reframe what we are hearing. We might mentally change the label from *noise* to *soothing ocean sounds* and therefore think only about ocean sounds. In this way, the body's mind can better tolerate an uncomfortable situation. This does not mean that we are unaware of the traffic or that we believe the traffic is the ocean, only that we are relabeling or reframing our experience of the noise and therefore integrating the stimulus in a novel way.

In this undemanding and seemingly effortless way of becoming more mindful, we can influence our overall well-being. Every word we hear and speak, every touch we give and receive, each choice and decision we make influences our individual development throughout our life span. All of our previous experiences, and the memory of those experiences, have an effect on the connections we have with each other. These connections are important aspects of health and happiness. Several studies have found that people with strong emotional support systems are more likely to be healthy and happy than those who isolate themselves and become lonely and depressed.

Our body reflects the thoughts in our mind. How else can we explain why some people get the flu or are infected by a cold virus, while others in the same situation do not get sick? Why do people respond to the same bacteria differently? How do we account for the fact that some bodies become cancerous when others do not? Some people can easily control their thoughts and emotions while others must overcome chemical imbalances, but the more we work with our internal systems the more control we are able to gain. If we feel sick with a fever or toothache, it is often a warning that something in the body's mind is out of balance. After we learn to walk, humans do not usually fall down when the body is out of balance unless something is drastically wrong. Under the best circumstances when we feel out of balance, we must determine the necessary actions to restore the body to a healthy state. But too often we fail to pause and pay attention to the body's warnings. Pains that we experience may exist so that we will correct the situation. Many people simply ignore pain, hoping it will go away. Denial of early warning signals often leads to further complications. The pain increases until it gets our attention.

Proponents of complementary and alternative medicine (CAM) agree that thoughts and emotions play an important role in determining the outcome of health. In addition to specific behaviors, such as getting enough sleep, exercising, and eating well, we need to comprehend the workings of the internal systems to become an Integrated Self. CAM practitioners are now referred to as integrative, rather than *alternative*, because they propose that concepts of holism and traditional practices from other cultures must become integrated with conventional medicine. Contemporary insurance must cover other modalities to improve the system of delivery for the highest good of everyone concerned. Manipulation of the system from pharmaceutical companies must end. We must become a nation that provides true health care rather than disease control. To do this each one of us must become aware of the root causes of health and pay attention and eliminate any discomforts, instead of simply controlling the symptoms.

Most of us are capable of examining thoughts and feelings that underlie physical discomfort and emotional conflicts when we reflect on the issue or tension. To do this, it is necessary to slow down enough to attain a state of mental as well as physical awareness. Most people can become consciously aware when they know about the varieties of learning and possible intelligences thereby improving the integration of the perceptual body with the cognitive mind. When we pause to observe how thoughts and feelings provided through the intuitive sixth sense come into play with behaviors, we can overcome inner tensions and prevent the anxieties that can cause sickness. Using our sixth sense and multiple intelligences to make conscious decisions about physical, mental, emotional, and spiritual health on a regular basis will enhance relationships with everyone around us.

❧6❧

CONNECTING TENSIONS

We sometimes confuse our need for connection with a desire for sex. When we understand the concept of libido as the vital life force, we improve our capacity to make connections, and we become receptive to intimacy that does not necessarily lead to sexual encounters. When we are able to let go of angry, aggressive, or fearful responses, we move past defense mechanisms and fixations that no longer serve us.

❧❧❧

From birth most of us enjoy being touched, stroked, and hugged. In healthy situations, children receive affectionate touch spontaneously. In most families, the amount of physical contact diminishes as puberty approaches. Talking becomes more important than touching. As we get older, touch is often reserved only for sexual encounters. Some families encourage open, honest communication regarding sexuality, and others cannot even mention it. Some consenting adults approve of sexual loving encounters outside of marriage.[1] For others, all sexual interactions can occur only within a marriage contract; any affairs are hidden and kept secret.

When we desire to know someone better, we often want to touch. We do this by reaching out with our hand or asking for a hug. Using our senses of seeing and hearing supplies limited information about another person's energetic field. To be truly intimate requires that we are in physical proximity without a phone line or computer between us. This is true for family, friends, co-workers, and health care providers as well as potential romantic partners. When we are together our sense of smell is activated. We share meals, a drink, or treats that allow us to enjoy the sense of taste together. We offer a hug or ask for a kiss. But for some people any touch, except a handshake as a formal greeting, is viewed as inappropriate outside of erotic situations. Physical closeness often brings up strong emotions, and these feelings may block the impulse to touch. A lack of physical contact can cause some people to become inwardly focused and connected to books, computers, iPods, television, video games, and other media rather than to each other. Self-soothing behaviors such as overeating, smoking and drinking, masturbating, even exercise or shopping can become distractions to avoid intimacy with others, as well as a way of ignoring our own internal responses and desires.

Sometimes in social situations, we experience an internal response similar to a surge of energy or charge moving throughout the body, and simultaneously we have a stimulating thought and emotional reaction that is a judgment, for instance, "I like that" or "I can't stand it when that happens." These e-motions are the actual energy charge in motion, as a basic part of the sixth sense and intuitive intelligence that formulates ideas about other people and our reactions to them. Perceptions formed through our sense of intuition relate to our ability to "read" another person's energy fields, which is different from the perception of how the body is positioned in space. We detect location, orientation, and movements of the body through the nervous system, especially visually and within the semicircular canals of the inner ear. Reaction to others occurs within the internal systems of the body's mind. Different streams of information combine to send signals to the brain. These signals allow us to make a judgment and choose a response. The more aware we become, the broader our range of responses. The body's mind also experiences emotional tensions that bypass awareness. For some people, too much visual input, loud sounds, and strong smells overly stimulate what Jung called *innate sensitiveness*. People with this trait are now known as highly sensitive persons (HSPs). They cannot differentiate between what is happening outside their body and what they are experiencing on the inside. They shut down and move away from the stimulation. Others seem able to ignore everything around them. They are in their own world and appear insensitive to whatever else is going on. Both of these are ways to avoid intimacy. We need to make connections, both within our internal systems and with others, to overcome the deep sense of separation, which is the normal result of having a human ego. These connections can occur with or without touch. Becoming aware of the choices of response that we have in different situations can provide a greater depth of intimacy.

The study of psychology or developing a yogic or Taoist practice strengthens the body's mind through both physical and mental applications. Mindfulness, focusing, creative visualization, and/or meditation are most useful. Creative visualization involves filling the mind with pictures and imaginations. Focusing is about noticing what goes on inside the body, and mindfulness is paying careful attention to what is going on outside of the body. Meditation, similar to prayer, is an act of emptying the mind. When we experience a surge of energy, we use our intuition to determine if it makes sense to reach out at this particular time. This is difficult when blocks or leaks are present in the energy flow. Because there are different ways of moving the body through space and different methods of presenting and receiving information, what works for one person does not always work for another. And, what is applicable at one time may not be at another. Practicing observation and awareness, without judgment, can help us determine what is best in the present moment and therefore allows us to be less self-conscious and more self-confident.

FREUD'S PHASES

In the early 1900s, Freud focused his attention on childhood experience and forced his colleagues to consider that children might have sexual feelings and desires. Furthermore, he explained how individuals might internalize the values and norms of their society. Freud labeled his understanding of mental processing as *id, ego, and superego*. He believed that thoughts and feelings from childhood might influence adult behavior through *intrapsychic conflict*. Intrapsychic conflict occurs because of the strain created between a child's pleasure seeking id and the mediating response of caregivers, who often have anxiety from their own childhood trauma. He explained *id* as the irrational aspect of self that simply operates on a *pleasure principle* to maximize satisfaction and reduce tension and the *ego* as the rational feature that operates on the *reality principle*. The *superego* is the mediator between the two, which develops as we mature.

During Freud's lifetime, most psychologists were not interested in how we received and processed information; their studies reflected a mechanistic view of human nature, and many regarded thoughts, feelings, and emotions as uncontrollable and therefore not able to be studied. Freud filled his theories with a concoction of teachings from this era. As his medical practice began to focus more on psychoanalysis and the interpretation of dreams, he continued to theorize about the biological urges of hunger, sex, and aggression. He drew conclusions that still permeate Western culture in a multitude of ways. His teachings became so ingrained that many people understand them to be facts. In spite of his insubstantial base regarding energy in motion, his theories provide a solid groundwork that articulate individual as well as cultural development.

Strict sexual constraints dominated Europe and America at this time. Most people were exposed to only a small circle of family and like-minded friends and little sex education of any kind was available. Sexual issues were a taboo topic. In proper society, erotic encounters outside marriage were restricted, available only to men who had money for prostitution. In the lower class, neither men nor women were to enjoy sexual activity outside marriage. And even within marriage, sex was more a necessity than a pleasure. Some upper-class people sought medical treatment because of the physical discomfort caused by these puritanical, Victorian constraints. Others rejected them, and some learned to use vibrators. Traditional Jewish and Catholic religions remained sexually repressive. American protestant religions developed more tolerance, but this is not true for most Baptists. Mormons and Muslims condemn any sexual expression outside of sanctioned marriage. Fundamentalists from most religious backgrounds do not endorse lesbian, gay, bisexual, or polygamous relationships. Nor do they encourage self-examination and reflection outside of their own doctrinal writings.

Pleasure in general, including masturbation for both women and men, is often strictly forbidden. On the other hand, Hindus, Pagans, and people who identify as Wiccan are more open about heterosexual behavior. We are beginning to understand that it is natural to explore our bodies and to befriend a variety of people over the course of our lifetime. To become a truly Integrated Self, it is important to explore deep friendships with caring people of different ages and both genders. In many cases, these relationships are not explicitly sexual, but discussions regarding sexual behavior are allowed and encouraged.

To further explore issues of sexuality, we will use a model of *psychosexual* behavior. Freud suggested that children pass through five developmental phases, which he named *oral, anal, phallic, latent, and genital*. In each phase, he imagined that pleasure and gratification were focused on a particular biological function. He wrote about infantile desires, demands, and needs that remained hidden from awareness because he felt they would disturb the individual's mental state within the restrictions of society. Freud noted that a newborn's pleasure focused on oral stimulation because it was obvious that sucking satisfied hunger. Next, he theorized that an infant's attention shifts to the anus when she or he becomes aware of producing the by-product of eating, and then to the genitals, especially the phallus, when the male child discovers the pleasurable feelings that come from touching the penis. It is important to note that only the male pronoun was used during this period of writing, therefore any female experience was not specifically mentioned.

In these first three phases, the self-absorbed id represents primitive drives as the raw, unorganized, innate part of personality. The pleasure principle is in control until the ego automatically, under healthy conditions, provides a warning that it is dangerous to be too self-centered. At this point, the reality principle becomes a protective force. Freud taught that unless the basic urges related to hunger, sex, and aggression were restrained the child would not become a mature, well-adjusted adult. Freud wrote about the function of the ego as helping to integrate the child into society by learning to cooperate with cultural expectations. According to Freud, the ego is the more reasonable aspect of personality, and it mechanically becomes the buffer between the desires of the inner child and the expectations and demands of other people.

Freud labeled the fourth developmental phase a period of latency, during which attention is directed toward learning experiences. At this stage, tasks performed in the outside world become more important than our inner world. Following this latency period, he noted the fifth phase as the genital stage, when young teens become aware of a physical arousal in the area of the genitals. He felt this was caused by an attraction to and thoughts about the genitals of others. Arousal occurs in the area of the body that an Eastern model would call the *lower chakras*. Freud proposed that this arousal leads to the development of the superego, which is an impulse similar to the function of conscience. For many, the concept of *conscience* has a religious connotation that incorporates distinctions between right and wrong, good and bad, and includes morals and ethics learned from one's parents, teachers, and other significant authority figures, especially those involved with religion. The id is controlled by the superego.

FIXATIONS AND DEFENSE MECHANISMS

After World War II, desire became a topic for everyday discussion. Pop psychology spread Freud's ideas into conversations throughout all levels of society. People learned about sexuality and consciousness through an influx of books and magazines, radio, movies, and TV programs that exposed them to a wide range of views. Freud's definitions of *fixations* and *defense mechanisms* became useful as ways to increase or avoid into-me-see. Fixations are behaviors that a person exhibits later in life resulting from unresolved conflicts during a particular developmental period. When children are not sufficiently able to gratify the need for pleasure and satisfaction during a particular stage, or if a child is overindulged and provided with too much gratification, a fixation can occur. All of us experience fixations along with anxiety left over from childhood. The outcome of childhood tension depends on the conflict or cooperation negotiated between the needs of the caretaker and the needs of the child.

Fixations become a problem only when they interfere with normal activity and manifest in a behavior that is socially unacceptable or difficult to overcome. For instance, if a newborn is over- or underfed during the oral phase, this might cause the future adult to be focused or fixated on activities of the mouth, such as overeating, nail biting, smoking, or talking too much or too little. As the ego develops, someone fixated at the anal phase tends to focus on cleanliness, neatness, order, or the opposite. People who are self-centered or self-conscious and shy demonstrate fixation at the phallic phase. They may be unable to socialize because of too much or too little inward focus during this stage of self-discovery. Someone who pays more attention to the production of goods and services rather than to relationships often reflects a fixation in the latency phase. This could also be a homemaker intent on maintaining orderliness or someone so involved in her or his career they fail to balance work with relationships. Those overly focused on the genital phase might show more concern with sexual encounters and relationships than any other activities. These people can appear overly dependent and needy. They may never have a satisfying sexual relationship, or they may have an inability to reach climax or have an orgasm even within relationship. On the other hand, they may display a sexual addiction, constantly seeking and often engaging in sexual activities that are harmful to themselves or others. In any case, Freud taught that in order to resolve these conflicts the individual needed to examine early childhood influences through psychoanalysis.

Freud's analytical process included hypnosis, free-association, and dream inquiry as a way to understand the root of both fixations and defense mechanisms. He found that defense mechanisms altered and distorted the original impulse until it became tolerable. His definitions can become self-help tools that can eliminate therapeutic analysis as the only solution for correcting imbalances in the flow of energy. Often defense mechanisms are used to display resentment toward a particular issue, such as:

- Compartmentalization—a process of behaving with two separate sets of values. For example, an honest person cheating on an income tax return.
- Compensation—counterbalancing perceived weaknesses by emphasizing strengths. "I'm not a fighter, I'm a lover" is one example.
- Denial—the refusal to accept reality and to act as if a painful or pleasurable event, thought, or feeling does not exist.
- Displacement—the redirecting of thoughts, feelings, and impulses from an object that gives rise to anxiety to a safer, more acceptable one. Being angry with the boss and kicking the dog is an example.
- Fantasy—the channeling of seemingly unacceptable or unattainable desires into the imagination. This can protect one's self-esteem. For instance, when educational, vocational, social, or erotic expectations are not met and one imagines success in these areas to ward off self-condemnation.
- Intellectualization—using a cognitive or mental approach without the attendant emotions. An example is someone with a life-threatening disease focusing exclusively on the statistical percentages of recovery because s/he is unable to cope with fear and sadness.

- Projection—attribution of undesired impulses onto another person. Thus, an angry spouse accuses their partner of being hostile.
- Rationalization—the reframing of perceptions to protect the ego in the face of changing realities. For example, when an expected promotion is not attained, we could rationalize that it was a dead-end job.
- Reaction Formation—converting wishes or impulses that are dangerous into the opposite. For instance, a parent who is furious with a child then becomes overly concerned and protective of the child's health.
- Regression—reverting to an earlier stage of development in the face of unacceptable impulses. An adolescent who is overwhelmed with fear, anger, and growing sexual impulses becomes clingy and begins thumb sucking or bed wetting is one example.
- Repression—blocking of unacceptable impulses from consciousness.
- Sublimation—channeling of unacceptable impulses into acceptable outlets.
- Undoing—attempting to reverse behavior or thoughts. An example is excessively praising someone after insulting or thinking badly about them.

We use defense mechanisms in an attempt to protect us from unpleasant emotions. However, both fixations and defense mechanisms are deterrents to a healthy, Integrated Self, and they can also cause problems with into-me-see.

JUNG'S SHADOW

Fixations and defense mechanisms are part of what Jung later termed the *shadow*. The shadow side of personality derives from our prehuman, animal past, when concerns were limited to survival and reproduction. In many ways the primitive, limbic brain still has control over our physical responses. In other ways, we evolve as we become aware of the connection between thoughts and feelings. Jung thought the basic instincts of hunger, sex, and aggression represented *archetypical* behaviors. As an example C. George Boeree, a current professor of psychology, writes:

> In Jung's teaching, [the shadow] is the dark side of the ego, neither good nor bad, just like animals. An animal is capable of tender care for its young and vicious killing for food, but it doesn't choose to do either. It just does what it does. It is innocent. But from our human perspective, the animal world looks rather brutal, inhuman, so the shadow becomes something of a garbage can for the parts of ourselves that we can't quite admit to. Symbols of the shadow include the snake, the dragon, monsters, and demons.[2]

Part of evolving awareness is recognizing how these symbols appear in the form of defense mechanisms and fixations that influence the intuitive body. Freud had developed rather rigid interpretations regarding physical and mental dysfunction, while Jung allowed for more freewheeling, mythological explanations. The disparity in the discourse between Freud and Jung was the beginning of opportunities for future students to form their own ideas and to agree or disagree with their professors. As time passed, many analysts and psychotherapists have worked with the shadow and helped clients take control of their emotional energy.

ADULT STAGES

The evolution of Freud and Jung's teachings can be understood through the eyes of one of their students. Erik Erikson emigrated from his native Germany in the 1930s to become a developmental psychologist. He researched childhood memories and their influence on adult behavior and motivation. For Freud, basic urges of hunger, sex, and aggression were biological, mechanical responses to family influences. Freud thought that an individual's ability to obtain food and sex sometimes resulted in aggressive behavior and produced defense tactics to protect the ego-self. Jung took Freud's thinking a step farther and taught it was not just the family but also the larger society and culture that influenced the individual. These external influences both challenge and shape the superego or higher consciousness of everyone.

Erikson's teachings bridged these concepts. He described psycho-social growth that ignored the sexual aspect. His stages represent the tension between internal drives and cultural demands. He began to articulate the cause and effect of conflicts within social interactions, and labeled the forces that determine both behavior and personality traits. His work clarifies how early conflict can affect partnerships, including sexual connections, as well as the decisions we make to satisfy desire. To better appreciate Erikson's theory of development, which will be presented in the next chapter, we must first recall Freud's early hypothesis that every child is born with an internal sex drive or psychological energy he labeled libido, from the Latin desire.[3]

Freud characterized sexual drive as a gradual buildup to a peak of intensity, followed by a sudden release and then decrease of excitement. He wrote about libidinous activity as the emotional or psychic energy derived from the basic instinct for survival. Freud and Jung disagreed about the meaning of libido and desire. This discussion between students and teachers spawns new beliefs and opinions. When we move beyond the limited thinking of our predecessors, we can open to the ideas of others and find new solutions to old problems.

DESIRING CONNECTION

The historical context continues to be necessary to understand the events during the time when Freud began teaching. Although automobiles were becoming available, horses were still the main mode of local transportation. The power of electricity had recently been discovered. Darwin's hypothesis regarding survival of the fittest was accepted as truth, and most people regarded aggression as a self-defense necessary for survival. Freud, trained as a medical doctor, may have modeled his scientific philosophy on the basic discoveries of the new physics and chemistry when he wrote about the instinctual drive to create life balanced by a desire for death. Freud himself was at the mercy of these two instincts, as noted in several biographies. He believed a strong death instinct called *thanatos* was the source of our destructive urges. In mythology, Thanatos is the force of death that destroys and divides, and Eros is the force of life that allures and unites.[4] Freud wrote that these were constructive, goal-directed activities that could not be avoided. He felt libido, specifically in the form of sexual attraction, often came into conflict with the conventions of society. Freud taught that if a form of erotic drive did not remain present and active within our lives, we were moving toward death. His socioeconomic standing and the religious thinking of his time demanded that sexual encounters occur only within the confines of life-long monogamy as previously mentioned.

When Freud's writings referred to sexual energy as the vital life force, he spoke about the defense mechanisms of sublimation and denial as ways of moving beyond the biological urge for sex. Based on the hydraulic model developed during this period and the principles from physics regarding conservation of energy, he taught that when sexual urges were blocked they would seek release. He implied that libido might be a finite amount of energy that powered our internal battles. In contrast, Jung argued that we must maintain balance between denial and satisfaction of needs. He taught that libido was the creative or psychic energy that moves us toward personal development. In spite of Jung's interpretation, the connotation of libido continues to be cast mainly as a drive for sexual contact.

The difference between sex drive and the need to resolve tension by moving this energy requires clarity. If we understand *drive* as the need for release, then masturbating with the goal of climax or ejaculation would be an outcome of sex drive, whereas self-pleasuring with no particular outcome is one method that can be used to move vital life force. Once we comprehend this distinction between sex drive and the movement of energy, we can grasp the similarities and differences between loving our self and loving others. In order to love our neighbor as our self and to practice the golden rule of "do unto others as we want them to do unto us," it is necessary to be aware of how desire works with emotional and social intelligence. Although we often feel the charge of energy that we identify as arousal in the genitals, the need for connection is more about fading the boundaries of the ego-self that keep us separate. It is also important to dissolve the defense mechanisms, which are different from *coping mechanisms*. Coping mechanisms can be a more positive method of self-soothing and finding our way through complex relationships.[5] When we broaden our thoughts regarding the drive for sex to include the desire for connection, then we can better understand libido as the vital force.

Libido can be understood as the flow of creative energy directed into the liberation and manifestation of all wants, needs, and desires. The vital life force moves and flows throughout the entire body most of the time, although the experience of orgasmic response will vary across the lifespan. Variations in libido and loss of vitality might occur when we are depressed, have low self-esteem, or are under the influence of legal or illegal substances, such as alcohol, caffeine, tobacco, or pharmaceutical drugs, as well as when we grow older. But most people experience creative impulses and the desire for physical affection, which may or may not lead to erotic interaction, throughout life regardless of chronological age or the ability to achieve erection or ejaculation. When we bring feelings of arousal up into our heart center, hormones such as oxytocin and dopamine are released to help us feel bonded rather than depleted.[6]

It does not matter if we are alone or with others; when a true connection occurs there is a feeling of expansion and union. Suddenly, we know we are in the flow when we experience overall balance and harmony. This aroused, connected state is sometimes described as *bliss consciousness*, which includes a marvelous feeling of delight. Some call it a connection with God or they might say the *divine*; others refer to *divine order*, meaning all things are perfectly aligned. Jung understood *synchronicity* to be the coincidental occurrence of events that seem related but not explained by conventional causes. *Serendipity* is another term used when several events line up to be just perfect.[7] Some use the word *brilliant*, which can mean highly intelligent, bright as a shining star, or perfectly clean and shiny, as well as a great idea. Therefore, this idea of a divine or brilliant connection involves our internal sensations and our reflective experience, as well as to behavior that includes contact with others.

We all need to love and be loved. The requirement to touch and be touched never ends. Making love and practicing safer sex with or without the exchange of bodily fluids needs to be a consensual choice in every situation. In addition, celibacy is also to be honored. Although some people might think of celibacy as a punishment or sacrifice, for others it is a way to celebrate one's self. For some it means avoiding sexual feelings for self or anyone else, and for others masturbation is allowed. Each new level of awareness moves us beyond translating sexual thoughts, feelings, and encounters as simply a way to satisfy the basic

biological urge for sex. As we mature, we can proceed in all of our partnerships with less clinging and attachment, less concern about the past
or future, and less influence from outside sources. In this context, eros
is a living force that unites us in love, rather than a desire for release or
the instinct to procreate. To become fully integrated, we need time to
reflect on what is truly important to us.

Self-discovery can only occur when we slow down enough to observe
energy flow. This discovery has the potential either to become joy filled
and provide pleasurable sensations or to provoke anxiety. Once we understand that the need for connection is an instinctive biological urge
and that the creative impulse of libido continues across the lifespan,
then we can expand beyond the drive for sexual interaction limited by
intercourse. If we disregard the moral issues surrounding erotic encounters between adults of the same or opposite sex, who may or may
not be married, then we can embrace intimacy in an expanded sense.
In spite of differing morals, many sex education classes continue to
teach abstinence. This means that the sex drive must only be activated
in the context of a marriage and for the sake of bearing children. For
many people, young and old, this requires unnecessary denial and self-
restraint. Tantra and Taoist practices explain how libido can include the
desire for connection across a spectrum, not just in the limited context
of coitus or other sexual behaviors.

We require positive feedback and meaningful interactions with family and friends who are important to us, as well as with lovers. A desire
for intimacy often means we want to be understood for who we are. We
want our thoughts listened to and actually heard. We *individualize* as a
necessary outcome of personal growth and development when we move
away from restrictive parental and cultural influences. As we progress
with compassion and loving kindness, we gain greater emotional and
social intelligence as well as the freedom to become our highest and
best Integrated Self.

~7~

DEVELOPING STAGES

How can we use our past to understand our future? In order to become an Integrated Self and have true intimacy, it is important to discover the tensions and possible demons that may have developed in the early stages of childhood that might keep us from reaching our full potential. This awareness is essential to deepening our intuition in order to experience intimacy in a diverse range of relationships.

⌐∞⌐

Decisions we make about past circumstances, and the defense mechanisms cultivated as a result, can be viewed as the cornerstone of adult development. When we take time to reflect on how the past affects the present, we have the capacity to behave differently in the future. Freud and Erikson both taught that we emerge from each stage of childhood in a fixed pattern that was similar for everyone across race and gender. Although the age-related correlation in each of their models is not consistent, both attest to the fact that the developmental process continues to unfold whether or not the crisis or tension from the previous stage is adequately addressed.

Erikson's work titled *Eight Stages of Man* was unique in 1956 as he was the first to comment on adult development throughout the entire lifespan. Erikson's study of Native American traditions as a young adult helped him to broaden Freud's ideas regarding the stages of psycho-social growth. His theories encompass Jung's understanding that the individual is always responding in reaction to others as well as a part of a particular society with certain cultural conditioning. As Erikson describes each stage, he finds that stress and tension are created by a crisis or conflict that must be resolved. Through his work we can appreciate the interaction between internal drives and cultural demands. His labels provide insight into the tensions people face throughout life under a variety of circumstances:

- Trust and Mis-trust
- Autonomy versus Doubt and Shame
- Initiative versus Guilt
- Accomplishment versus Inferiority
- Identity versus Role Confusion
- Intimacy versus Isolation
- Generativity versus Stagnation
- Ego Integrity versus Despair

These tensions are never completely resolved during childhood, therefore we confront the same issues later in life, hopefully before they create an actual crisis. These theories could be illustrated in a linear mode as steps, but in reality life progresses more as a series of overlapping circles that loop and spiral around each other. The spiral is a symbol often used to illustrate holism and a holistic point of view, which takes into account that personal growth happens in repeating, cyclical patterns, that includes several twists and turns, as well as giant nosedives that often throw us off course.

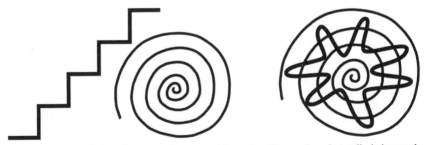

We used to think development happened in a step-like order. Actually it is much more complicated.

Does holistic theory insinuate that each generation develops at a quicker pace? Does this quickening suggest a process of conscious evolution? Does awareness create the generation gap? How does it affect other relationships?

NEW PARADIGMS

The historical background of psychological thinking once again provides clues to these questions. German medical literature from 1922 introduced the mind-body connection to illustrate psychosomatic interrelationships. The term *psychosomatic* came into English usage in 1935 when Helen Flanders Dunbar wrote: "Medicine can come to its fullest flowering only when the medical profession takes into account the integrated nature of the human being, and learns to treat psyche [mind] and soma [body] as the inseparable phenomena they are."

Most clinical psychologists agree that a range of angry and defensive responses result from early, unresolved stress and tension. Some actually believe that perception begins before birth. Tension adds to the synaptic pathways that make up the folds in the brain. Neuroscience can now demonstrate how synapses fire throughout the nervous system and form millions of neuronal pathways, especially during the first several months of life. When imbalances occur in the internal systems, as leaks or blocks, failure to address these concerns show up later as inappropriate behaviors. Some believe that stress contributes to the bone and muscle structure that determine posture and character structure. Somatic or body-centered practitioners agree this is one possible explanation for the root cause of disease. Several healing modalities come under the somatic umbrella, for instance, the work of Arthur Janov on primal scream and Leonard Orr founder of rebirthing. In addition, Wilhelm Reich's work evolved into *core energetics* and *bioenergetics*.[1] Most practicioners believe we begin to contract soon after the trauma of entering the world through the narrow birth canal. The operation called *cesarean section* does not eliminate this disturbance because the drugs used for surgery often cause different problems for the newborn. Entering the world is a difficult step.

We know for certain that emotions and thoughts activate the perceptive body and cognitive mind as gateways to intuitive knowing. In order to recognize how these tensions begin, we need to consider the temperament and personality of both the child and caregivers, as well as the potential moodiness of both. The emotions that surround the family are equally important, as well as what is happening in society at any given moment. Therefore resolution of tension from each stage depends on ever-increasing skills. These skills later become crucial in partnerships with others. Becoming aware of the mental and physical crisis from each stage of development is one way to use the powerful sixth sense of intuitive knowing, which in turn strengthens our capacity for intimacy in all relationships. Peaceful, positive feelings and hurtful, negative circumstances both contribute to the development of emotional and social intelligence that in turn influences conscious awareness. Learning to use the metaphor of the aura and chakra system is one way to increase awareness.

DEFICIENCY OR EXCESS?

Eastern philosophy and western psychology both explain how the infant expands toward pleasurable feelings and contracts away from pain. The chakras and intuition come into play as an explanation for emotional responses. The root of *emote* means "to move." Energy in motion is the energetic life force that creates health and well-being. This vital life force constantly moves us toward pleasure and away from pain. Throughout life we long for a full belly and sound sleep. Anodea Judith suggests that working with these issues through the internal chakra system might bring a greater sense of control and help to alleviate feelings of imbalance and disintegration as we learn more about the excess and deficient aspects.

Judith introduces the notion of *demons* or imbalances that oppose the natural activity of our inner systems. She is not referring to demons as an evil force but rather as a counterforce that takes us away from feelings of love, joy, and pleasure. When any one of the chakra centers is out of balance, that imbalance or demon interferes with the healthy working of all the internal systems. The earlier we identify the counterforce, the less we are thrown off balance. Judith suggests that becoming aware of the possibility of demons and consciously working with the information will strengthen the functioning of the entire system. Judith finds practicing various yoga postures can activate energy that would otherwise keep us from moving forward. She recommends that if we challenge the demons and explore the lessons their imbalance brings, we can gain a deeper understanding of our motivations. For example, if at any age we admit that we are afraid, this admission enables us to face the fear and become more confident.

This acknowledgement is necessary for each of the demons:

- *Fear* arises when something threatens our survival mode. Fear prevents us from feeling secure, focused, and calm. It creates hypervigilance, yet it also protects us from harm.
- *Guilt* undermines the natural flow of emotional and sexual energy throughout the body and inhibits us from reaching out. This can diminish both emotional and social connections with others.
- *Shame* has the ability to undermine esteem, spontaneous activity, and joy. Instead of radiating power outward in the form of anger or determination, personal power is turned inward, sometimes showing up as depression.
- *Grief* contracts the potential expansiveness of the heart and causes it to feel heavy and closed.
- *Dishonesty* and lies twist our relationship to the outside world through distorted information, which then blocks intimacy and successful partnerships with parents, peers, family, co-workers, lovers, and everyone we come in contact with.
- *Illusion* causes an under- or overinflated sense of accomplishment.
- *Attachment* may lead to co-dependency, away from healthy interdependence and the strong independence of an Integrated Self.

From an Eastern perspective, the *kanji* symbol for crisis translates as an opportunity to learn. A review of the unresolved crisis from each developmental stage is one step to eliminate wounds that may cause mental or physical pain. Noticing where we feel tension in the body aids our ability to resolve any lingering damage. It is important to notice the feelings and focus on bodily sensations on a regular basis. Understanding how this all works together can help reframe or even eliminate the demons that may be causing a blockage or leak in the flow of the internal energy.

Judith's hypothesis regarding demons, along with Freud and Erikson's theories of childhood development, provide a basis to comprehend the human potential for healing. Their combined ideas provide language for what they saw happening during each developmental stage. When applied in real-life situations, their theories suggest solutions for problems that may be lying dormant. Looking back at our childhood can often result in dropping defense mechanisms and noticing projections. After working with thousands of clients, Judith and other practitioners who directly access bodily sensations have proven that we can become more highly functional when the consequence of early stress is addressed and eliminated. This can create greater harmony in relationships.

GROWING THROUGH STAGES

Shortly after conception, the lungs of the embryo begin to form. The heart beats as blood is pumped through tiny arteries to the developing organs and throughout the nervous system. The eyes, ears, nose, mouth, and hands begin to sense the surroundings when the fetus is still inside the womb. Immediately after passing through the birth canal, the tangible reality of the *neonate* begins. Our mouth instinctively grasps for the nipple of mother's breast or bottle and our tiny hand automatically enfolds a held-out finger. We sleep more than we are awake because the plasticity of the brain needs time to encode all the new information received through the five senses. Eventually the eyes focus and follow. Smells cause a reaction. A healthy newborn mimics facial expressions and sounds during the first hours after birth; we are immediately in relationship with those around us and cannot survive for long without their attention. The entire organism must have connection with others. Watch any young child within weeks after birth and you can easily observe emotional changes.

Erikson characterized his first stage, from the womb to twenty-four months, as the time when we embody trust or mistrust depending on the quality of care. All babies require a comfortable position to sleep and food when their tiny bellies are empty. Freud called it the oral stage because the sucking process is most active as we take in nourishment for survival, and we experience pleasure from the active motion of the lips and tongue. Judith describes this as a period of physical and emotional identity. The first root chakra, which is activated at this time, represents survival and the demon is fear. If security needs are not met, the newborn fears it may not survive and therefore develops a sense of mistrust. Fear and mistrust later affect our ability to give and receive love. We learn to trust and not be afraid when our needs for food and touch are met. Touching is essential as we perceive the physical presence of others. Karen Horney was the first to discover that well-fed babies fail to thrive when they are not touched or held. Lack of touch may cause abnormal mental and physical development related to depression. Inability to control impulses and violence has resulted from mother-infant separation.[2] One study observed that baby monkeys spent more time with a soft, towel-wrapped, wire surrogate mother than with a similar bare-wire "mom" that simply provided milk.[3] Attachment theory research led to understanding the need for a secure base to go out from so that the child can return to a safe haven. More recently, research at the University of Miami School of Medicine clearly demonstrates that premature babies who receive massage gain weight more quickly than those not touched in a particular way.[4]

During the first six months after birth, babies struggle to roll over and eventually sit up. As we become toddlers, in the sensory-motor period we gain awareness of movements that were previously automatic physiological responses. Most healthy babies move forward by first crawling on their bellies, eventually shifting to a kneeling position, and finally walking. Erikson describes this as a time of *autonomy versus doubt and shame*. The connotation of the word *autonomy* means "standing on your own two feet."

Most babies are also introduced to the cultural norms of hygiene regarding elimination between eighteen months and three years. Typically caregivers enforce the norms of their prevailing society when teaching cleanliness. If we are shamed during toilet training, or made fearful regarding early attempts at walking, we may doubt our innate ability to accomplish these simple tasks. When our attempts are affirmed, we overcome the tension or crisis of this stage and achieve a healthy sense of the ego-self. Freud referred to this anal phase when muscular control becomes the focus. We also discover our genitals and learn more about our own touch as well as integrating the touch of others. Caregivers and teachers either affirm or deny all activities with a preestablished system of reward or punishment. If we are rewarded, an atmosphere of stability is created. When we are punished, we learn to manipulate our environment in order to meet our needs. As we learn to walk and control our bodily functions, we also learn to want, and sometimes demand, more than what we are offered.

During the locomotor stage, between two and six years of age, we continue to become more assertive and social. We learn to run and climb and move about without constant supervision. Both large and small muscles are involved as we learn to hold a spoon and fork, pencil and crayon, and eventually scissors and other materials for creating crafts. We begin to master such projects as building with blocks or putting together puzzles. In addition, at this age most healthy children attempt independent reading. This takes coordination between the eyes and mouth in order to produce sounds independently without simply repeating what we have previously heard. A different level of cognitive thinking and brain processing becomes necessary in order to grasp the concepts and retell the story. Ideas regarding freedom and will power are learned, and emotions of regret and sorrow begin to develop as the child struggles for greater self-control. If a child is too forceful or opposes the will of the caregiver, feelings of doubt may develop when either reprimanded or ignored. Thus, creativity is the main element of the sacral chakra, and shame is the demon. Under healthy circumstances, we achieve fluidity of movement and opportunities to create pleasure. At this age, many problems occur when temperament and other personality traits are mismatched between the child and caregivers; when the match is adequate then social intelligence flourishes.

Erikson's next stage of *initiative versus guilt* corresponds with Freud's phallic phase, approximately between three and seven years. The tension now is the struggle for more independence and a need to have more social contact with other children. We gain willpower and a sense of purpose, as well as self-esteem and physical strength. As children learn to initiate activities, they also begin to feel remorse if their actions are met with disapproval. Unconscious thoughts and feelings are no longer dependent only on the immediate response of the caregiver. Now internalized memory of actual or imagined experience comes into play. The positive aspect of the solar plexus represents a well-developed sense of personal power, and the demon is guilt. At this age, we act more spontaneously and when reprimanded healthy children learn to regret what happened, and soon learn that behavior results in consequences that we can control.

Next, we move into Freud's latency phase, which Erikson labels *industry or accomplishment versus inferiority*. Normally, children have little interest in sexuality from age four to twelve when we are gaining additional physical dexterity and skills of information processing and competition. We begin to compare our self to others. If we are not allowed to achieve our own level of industriousness, and if we are constantly being corrected and held to a standard set by others rather than experiencing an internal sense of accomplishment, future development can be overcome with feelings of inferiority, failure, and incompetence.

Compassion, self-acceptance, and good relationships are the key elements of the fourth chakra. As the heart is opening to love, we may also encounter the demon of grief. If the heart has already been contracted and this fourth chakra is blocked or deficient, sadness can easily interfere with emotional development. In a healthy, nurturing environment, we embody the social skills of loving and being loved, as well as the ability to grieve something that has been lost or never found. We continue to learn the art of manipulation and co-operation as we become aware of choices and consequences.

The demon of the throat chakra is *dishonesty*. We need to speak our opinions and be heard. When we tell children that their feelings do not matter or that something they have actually witnessed did not really happen, a cycle of denial and learning to lie begins. When this fifth chakra of communication is activated, we are able to express our truth. If the throat chakra is excessive, bullying and gossiping may occur. If it is deficient, our voice may be blocked.

During adolescence from ages ten to eighteen, peer relationships with both genders become more important, and caregivers at home, school, or church have less influence than before. Freud named this period of puberty the *genital phase*, when physical changes reawaken repressed sexual awareness, and the child begins to seek gratification and release. Erikson labeled the tension of this stage as *identity versus role confusion*. Our sense of identity in relation to others is both internally and externally driven. During this phase we struggle to find a sense of identity that will determine choices we make about becoming an adult. Erikson pointed out two substages: one a social identity that focuses on group belonging and includes a personal philosophy and taking a stand on issues; and second, a personal identity, focusing on abilities, goals, and potential for future gender development. We begin to question what our roles will be in the world of work and whether or not we will chose to become parents. Erikson, along with Piaget, described conceptual thinking and the formal operational skills that are necessary to develop individual potential. As we reach puberty, we must make decisions regarding romance and intimacy. Throughout adolescence we see, hear, smell, taste, and touch in ways that a child cannot imagine. As adulthood approaches, healthy teenagers acquire a personal philosophy in order to understand their place in the

larger society. Collective- cooperative and independent-competitive activities are important to our emotional and social interactions.

The sixth chakra, known as the third eye, opens as we develop our
imagination and begin to cultivate strong likes and dislikes. Our intuition becomes more astute as we continue to perceive the world through
all six senses. We distinguish everything around us with greater focus
and begin to make judgments. The demon of illusion is present during
this period. If our vision is blocked or deficient, we have difficulty planning for the future. When it is excessive, we might be convinced that we
are in control of changing the world.

Judith views the central issue of adulthood as *awareness* and the demon as *attachment*. The main idea is becoming aware of conditioning
received in childhood and letting go of any attachments to old hurts or
injuries through the process of forgiveness. Doing so will help overcome
the natural impulse to blame parents for our shortcomings. It is important to remember that healthy parents do the best they can based on
the circumstances of their own lives and the conditioning they received
from their upbringing. As we move out of late adolescence into early
adulthood, we gain greater intelligence on every level and tap into our
intuitive awareness. Doing so can aid the process of understanding our
parents' points of view, and acknowledging how we want to raise our
own children. Now it is possible to know more about cultivating healthy
love and beneficial partnerships.

TIMES KEEP CHANGING

Many societal norms have changed in the half-century since Erikson first
labeled these stages at the height of his career in the 1950s. At that time,
most women and men did not remain single past the age of twenty-one.
Educated families followed a path of attending college, finding a spouse
and landing a career. The career was actually only for males, because
housewife was the job title for most middle- and upper-class woman.
The couple would likely purchase or inherit property. People expected
to stay with one job until retirement and with their spouse until death.
It was not much different for those in the working class. Although some
did not complete high school, they married young, and both men and
women worked at one or perhaps many different jobs until death or re-

tirement. Many could not afford to own a home. Whether educated or not, everyone was expected to produce children, who would eventually produce children, and the whole cycle would begin again following the social norm of the time. Choices at that time were limited; most people had few options, which is partially what led to the social revolution that culminated in the 1960s.

This revolution actually began after the First World War when women questioned the authority of their fathers and husbands and fought for the right to vote and own property. During the Second World War, many more women entered the workforce and earned income for the first time. They experienced more freedom and autonomy than ever before in history. Housewives began to desire more from life than being married to their house. Their ability to support themselves and their children meant they were less afraid of leaving their marriage. They demanded more emotional support from men. These changes escalated throughout the 1950s and 1960s when the advent of birth control furthered women's liberation.

Lifestyle options increased, and both women and men could choose to marry or not. Sexual freedom flourished with or without the "benefits of marriage." The concept of choice spilled over, not only regarding how many children to have and when but also whether to have children or not. Divorce or remaining single became acceptable norms. Today, some people stay in long-term monogamous relationships, others experiment with a variety of sexual expressions. We have more choices about changing jobs and careers, moving from place to place and owning or renting various types of housing. All of these choices contribute to the fact that adolescence lasts longer for some, and maturity comes sooner for others. As the sexual revolution and women's liberation progress, elements of the issues Erikson identified appear in some cases at a younger age and, under other circumstances, it is as if adulthood has been delayed.

According to Erikson, young adults face the tension of *intimacy versus isolation*. For some people, commitment issues arise again and again, often getting in the way of success in both work and relationships. In his time, this crisis presented the option of making a marriage contract or being independent. Because so few people remained single at that point in history, Erikson felt that someone without erotic intimate relationships meant that person was isolated. In today's social culture, the personal crisis of each decade would depend on a variety of choices.

Some people marry and/or become parents in their teens or early twenties, others wait until they are in their thirties, while a few do not begin a serious relationship or family until they are over forty, if at all.

As people mature, questions regarding *generativity versus stagnation* follow. Erikson theorized that if we did not generate something for the future, then our life would be stagnant. Here he was referring to the pro-creation of the next generation, but there are other accomplishments we can generate during adulthood other than, and in addition to, producing children. For instance creating a work of art, cooking a great meal, owning real estate, or building a bridge, among thousands of other choices.

The final crisis for older adults in Erikson's theory was to explore issues regarding *ego integrity and despair*. This meant finally attaining a sense that we are separate from our parents and free of social constraints. A healthy ego-self acknowledges accomplishments made over a lifetime, rather than despairing about things one can no longer do and regretting attempts that may appear to be failures. Again remember that times are changing.

LOOKING THROUGH A DIFFERENT LENS

To grasp the impact these theories have in today's world, consider the concepts of trust and mistrust. Most of us find that in every new relationship, and at the beginning of each activity where love or money is exchanged, this issue is revisited. Each and every time we meet someone, we must determine whether they can be trusted or not, and simultaneously they must decide the same about us. When we begin a new job, the manager or supervisor must evaluate whether we can be trusted to carry out the responsibilities, and we must determine if the information they are relating about the company is true or not. Will we receive the promised wage after we have accepted the position and worked a week or two?

These issues of trust are followed by questions of autonomy. When we meet someone for the first time, we often want to know their stories and hear about family and friends. We might find ourselves adjusting to their timetables and blending into their lives. In a way, we lose a bit of our own autonomy or independence in exchange for interdependence in most relationships. The same thing happens when we take a job. We are no longer separate, autonomous individuals; we are now part of a team with a task to accomplish. Either we are secure in our choice, or we may be filled with a sense of shame, and begin to doubt that the relationship or position is right for us at this time. In every case, we must face whatever fear or other demon may arise when doing something new for the first time.

If we decide we are doing the right thing, and resolve trust and autonomy issues, then Erikson's questions of initiative and guilt come into play. In the relationship example, we must have an interest in continuing contact and sharing information. If feelings of attraction do not flow in both directions, no friendship develops. We need to know if the other person is interested in taking the initiative in getting to know us. Without reciprocity, partnerships do not work. It is the same with the new job: either we take the initiative to show up when we are scheduled and do what is expected of us, or we wonder why we chose that particular occupation. This is often followed by feelings of guilt that we are not living up to our own expectations; plus if we do not produce the required results, there may not be a paycheck.

After we resolve tensions in personal or work-related partnerships around trust, autonomy, and taking initiative and we overcome fear, guilt, shame, and grief over the failed goal or relationship, the next crisis occurs between industry and inferiority. In the new relationship, we begin to spend time together, and either both enjoy the same kind of activities or we do not. We are either at the same level of industry toward achieving similar goals, or we are not. In either case one or the other might feel inferior. Again, it is the same at work: either we are engaged in what we agreed to do and do it industriously with a feeling of accomplishment, or we feel inferior for the job or that the job is not challenging us enough. In either case, the tension must be resolved if the partnership is going to continue. If it cannot be resolved, we start over again with a new friend or career. In every case, it is important not to deny what is happening.

If we continue with the same friendship or job, the next tension to be addressed is identity and role confusion. In relationships, we often use a title such as "best" girlfriend or boyfriend and eventually spouse or partner. Or we begin to feel confused about our roles in each other's lives. This can result in becoming merely acquaintances rather than friends or even breaking up and losing contact. The same applies in the world of work: we either identify as a member of that particular team, or we wonder why we are there and our performance falters. Again we may choose to move on, away from this particular situation and back to the initial trust questions, or we move into the next stage where intimacy and isolation are the focus. In the realm of relationships, it is easy to see how this plays out—we become more intimate or we feel isolated. The same is true with both the team members at work and the actual requirements of the job. We continue to become intimate with co-workers and understand our responsibilities, hopefully enjoying what we are doing, or we feel isolated from the people around us, lose interest, and eventually fail to do what is required. In both cases, it is important not to get caught up with the demon of illusion that all is well and it will all work out. Illusion diverts attention from seeing things accurately. On the other hand, if the intimacy continues, the tension Erikson called *generativity* follows. Intimacy helps to generate healthy relationships and good partnerships at work, which means we do not stagnate and there is no need to look for a new partner, friend, or different job. As we mature into greater intimacy, we attain ego integrity rather than feeling despair.

At each of these stages, we evolve past the tension and resolve the imbalance, or we begin to search for new challenges. The imbalanced demon of attachment comes into play when we narrow our attention so that it blocks our ability to manifest goals. Attachment often takes the form of manipulation and we might even take relationships for granted. Or it means we slip into co-dependence rather than the interdependence required for building healthy, beneficial partnerships. It has been said that men and women have different ways of approaching jobs and relationships. Do you think this is because of our genetic nature or the nurturing within the environment where we grew up? We will look deeper into these questions and the union of psyche and eros, as we discover more about the meaning of love and the movement of internal energy.

❦ 8 ❧

MAINTAINING BALANCE

Many forces bombard us throughout our lifetime, and we easily lose our sense of balance if we are not mindful of the information provided by our internal systems. Different "levels of being" contribute to understanding the concept of transcendence as conscious evolution. Discovering the ebb and flow of the psychology of mind brings self-understanding.

❦

Learning techniques of self-observation can help us confront the demons that develop throughout the stages of our lives. Reflection and mindfulness are two keys to health and healthy relationships. In the beginning of the life cycle, we are the center of the universe and we learn to trust or mistrust. We slowly gain independence and autonomy as we overcome issues of doubt and shame. Fascinated with everything as toddlers, we take the initiative to instigate tasks, still imagining we are the center of our universe. As young children, we glow when we can accomplish something without anyone criticizing us or making us feel guilty about not doing it right. As we mature, we become more industrious and begin to compare one thing to another, including ourselves. We gain high self-esteem when we recognize that we are not inferior to anyone else. Teenagers focus on questions of identity, and outside influences pull in different directions. We strive to eliminate confusion, develop a personal philosophy, and find our role in society. Healthy teens look for connections and begin the process of self-reflection. Ideally, our ability for into-me-see grows, and we avoid isolation. In the best-case scenario, we radiate more of our Integrated Self into the world and generate something of value. As we age, it is important to not stagnate but rather attain a sense of integrity and overcome separation and despair.

Throughout this developmental process not everyone achieves high self-esteem. If we are overly focused on the outside world and feel pulled in too many different directions at once, we tend to ignore feedback from our internal systems. Simultaneously, we feel stressed, depressed, or simply overwhelmed. Many of us reach for a pill, sex, food, drink, or smoke to feel better. On the other hand, if we can slow down and become mindful of our internal processes, we are better able to create a sense of peace.

MINDFULNESS

When we take time to become mindful of sensory input, we rediscover direct experience. Contemporary interpretations of integrative health include the belief that having knowledge can help us to attain a calm state of mind, thereby reducing stress. When our system is in balance, we develop an attitude of compassion and participate in the world at a more consciously evolved level. We are motivated to achieve goals, and we realize inner peace, intuitive knowledge, and the emotional intelligence that contributes to better relationships.

Many who teach that the aura and chakra systems are the basis of motivation and attachment have found that when these systems are leaking or blocked, we are out of balance. Blocks and leakages in the chakras can cause excesses and deficiencies, which produce stress and tension, and prevent us from moving forward. Too much attachment to the past or attention on the future closes us to new ideas in the present moment. If we are overly motivated and concentrate only on external issues, our life force is flowing outward. We quickly deplete our vital energy when we fail to take time to replenish it. Mental or physical health problems develop when the body's intuitive system is out of balance, because that means the immune system is out of sync. If we fail to honor emotional or spiritual upsets, they can show up as pain in the mental or physical body. One way to renew the system is through an internal process of self-reflection, for example, using prayer or meditation, guided imagery or creative visualization as described on page 77. On the other hand, if we maintain too much of an internal focus and do not participate in outer activities, then we block our fullest potential. Again, the key is balance.

BODY AS BIOCOMPUTER

Integrative medicine recognizes the possibility of working with intimacy, insight, and intuition as a potential path to provide adequate health care. Those who study the aura, chakras, and meridians take advantage of thousands of years of teaching that present the opportunity to understand the inner workings of the body's mind. Various theories overlay these systems of thinking and provide insight into temperament and personality, as well as to group development and the evolutionary process of civilization. Over the past decades, Anodea Judith and others have created many books, workshops, videotapes, CDs, and other products that demonstrate how to radiate positive energy. Judith has personally helped thousands of people improve their sense of intuition and well-being. Her most recent work, *Waking the Global Heart: Humanity's Rite of Passage from the Love of Power to the Power of Love*, provides suggestions and motivation for performing positive actions that will benefit the larger world.

Using the analogy of a computer, Judith points out that the chakra system supplies us with a set of instructions that we might use to reprogram our lives. She notes that it is quite common to have a perfectly good operating system but not know how to activate a particular program. Activation of the healing program requires us to consciously direct a charge of energy throughout the tubular system to bring about balance. Her theory is that once we learn how to create and direct this energy on an individual basis, then perhaps we can also apply the same methods to cultural and environmental concerns. The more we learn about self-love, the more we develop our capacity to create peace in the world.

For Judith, each chakra is an information-processing and memory-recording center for the interactions that occur between our inner and outer worlds. She views each chakra as a *vortex* of energy that empowers us to release hurts and negative tensions from the past. A vortex is a powerful circular current that is usually the result of conflicting ideas, similar to the conflicting messages we receive as children. She feels we must heal these conflicts in order for evolutionary connections to occur. Judith teaches that becoming mindful of balancing the chakra system and releasing negative energy will help overcome unconscious feelings of hostility, rage, anger, or aggression. This includes wanting to attack or take something away from another or the feeling that we must assume a defensive posture. She believes that when we remain attached to thoughts and emotions that no longer serve our highest good, we create harmful blocks or leakages that drain our reserves of vitality.

PARADIGM SHIFT

In order to have healthy relationships, we must be healthy. Attainment of this goal includes a simple model:

1. mindfulness of emotions and reflection on our thoughts
2. daily exercise that includes activation of the glandular and meridian systems
3. harmonious patterns of eating and drinking.

It is important to take this basic formula a step further. We must also consider the impact of energetic forces in the environment. Up until recently, most research has not employed principles of holism. A current psychology professor, William L. Mikulas, illustrates a comprehensive prototype for the convergence of Eastern and Western therapeutic processes, which he calls *conjunctive psychology*. He reminds us that at the time when Freud, Jung, and other Westerners began the study of consciousness, they chose to emulate the mechanics of physics rather than a more organic, holistic model in their quest to be acceptable to the scientific community. Mikulas points out that this bias caused most medical doctors to focus on controlling symptoms rather than finding the root cause and understanding the potential benefits of more inclusive models.

His book, *Integrative Helper* suggests a paradigm shift that incorporates indigenous healing modalities and concepts of traditional medicine for cross-cultural counselors and therapists. Many contemporary practitioners in both the medical and the mental fields are recognizing the importance of listening to the person and considering lifestyle as well as environmental factors when making a diagnosis and deciding treatment. Doing this includes a motivational interview, an assessment of everything one eats and drinks, and asking about exposure to toxins. Additionally, they consider the entire support system, including family, friends, personal intimate relationships, and working partnerships.

Whether or not we are at the point of seeking help from a counselor or therapist, Mikulas warns that we need to comprehend how the vibrational forces that surround us affect physical, mental, emotional, and spiritual levels of well-being. A moving electrical charge creates both an electric field and a magnetic field. An increase or decrease in an electric field creates a corresponding magnetic field, and an increase or decrease in a magnetic field creates a corresponding electric field. This mutual interaction creates the electromagnetic field. Electromagnetic force (EMF) is one of the four basic forces in nature; the others are gravity and strong and weak nuclear forces. Electromagnetic radiation (EMR) includes the circulation of various electric and magnetic fields through space. Increasing wavelength or decreasing frequency creates cosmic rays, gamma rays, x-rays, ultraviolet light, visible light, infrared rays, microwaves, radar, and radio waves.

Human brainwaves also generate and absorb EMR. In fact, every atom and molecule generates EMR. These vibrations persistently surround us, causing a relentless interaction and effect on the regulation of our biological, and therefore emotional cycles. The earth has a 10-hertz frequency, and now, at the turn of the twenty-first century, the level of EMR is so high that the natural background level has been masked by all of the other radiation present today. EMR influences our vital life force by having an effect at the molecular level on the magnetic crystals found in the human brain. It is not likely we will ever return to the natural level; therefore the questions become: *Is this harmful?* and *How will we adapt?*

In this age of microwave ovens, cell phones, and other WiFi technology, we each need to evaluate the amount of exposure we can safely tolerate and make a conscious decision of what we want to do about the unavoidable exposure. We have emotional responses to most stimuli that can be helpful or harmful to our personal growth. We are bodies of energy, and the "vibes" we give off effects others. Many products have become available for protection. There is currently not enough research to know if they are simply "snake oil." Perhaps in the evolutionary process we will safely adapt without a problem?

Have you ever noticed that you resonate with some people differently than others?

One example is when we notice the vibration of a person or place and comment on how it gives us a good or bad feeling. Another example is that menstrual cycles often synchronize when women live and work together. An additional illustration occurs when a group harmonizes and vocal sounds combine with drums or musical instruments. This brainwave synchronization or feeling "in sync" is called *entrainment*. When our head and heart, thoughts and feelings harmoniously work together, we have more clarity and inner balance. Input perceived by all six senses makes up our basic biological temperament, which continues to influence us throughout life.

Mikulas points out that over and above the vibes from the human energetic field, we are showered with EMR from mobile or cell phones, personal computers, iPods, radio and television signals, microwave ovens, electric blankets, digital alarm clocks, radar, electric subways, light-rail tracks, and the power lines themselves. Furthermore, visible light as well as sound vibrations, which include harmonious melody lines as well as syncopated drumbeats, have a range of biological and psychological effects on our well-being. Similarly, smells and tastes influence us in both positive and negative ways. Becoming more aware of the vibrational effects of various inputs, both tangible and intangible, helps to increase our sensitivity. Many holistic teachings suggest that we can become more aware of the intuitive sixth sense and substantially increase our capacity for healthy development and intimacy, when we take in vibrations from light and color, as well as sound, by using our eyes, ears, and throat to accentuate these vibrations.

We now know that even during the prenatal and infancy periods, sensory and motor stimulation can facilitate or hinder the learning process and alter the production of muscle and bone tissue. Auditory and visual stimulation are factors in our performance during every stage of growth. Various activities that involve motion induce the sense of touch. Our skin can be highly sensitive; most people feel the phenomenon of air as they move through space. Exercise that includes a full range of motion creates a further method of stimulation.

We all have varying degrees of sensation on the continuum of pain and pleasure. Tastes and smells can bring us either joy or disgust. Eating junk food can be pleasurable, however, healthy, organic food along the guidelines of the food pyramid mentioned earlier will build a strong immune system as well as powerful muscle and bone structures. All of these factors influence our sense of awareness. Moreover, the way we think about various stimulants determines the consequences of how they are "stored" in our body's mind. For instance, if one person smokes and truly believes it to be a perfectly harmless behavior, they are less likely to develop a problem than someone who constantly wants to quit, knowing smoking is detrimental to their health. In many cases, this placebo effect is not entirely true for the physiological addictive substances contained in many tobacco, alcohol, and drug products.

LEVELS OF BEING

These concepts regarding external stimulation complement four inter-related levels of being: biological, behavioral, personal, and transpersonal. Mikulas contends that we continuously move within these four levels throughout our lifetime. His system helps to clarify the ways in which we respond under different circumstances. To explain his model, imagine yourself in any kind of exercise class. The *biological* level refers to the genetic makeup of the person sitting still and silent on a mat. The *behavioral* level encompasses overt, outward, observable behavior as we speak, sit still, or move into a different position. The *personal* level is comprised of listening and processing the emotional responses and experiential, conscious concepts that include judgments, free will, and personal reality as we move in and out of particular postures. The *transpersonal* level denotes our connection to others in the room and includes the fact that each individual also has a story embedded in family, community, and a cultural and ethnic background. This transpersonal level relates back to Jung's concept of the collective unconscious.

EVOLVING SELF-ACTUALIZATION

The levels of being provide a comprehensive model for understanding human development. In the first biological level, an infant realizes, "This body is different from other things I perceive. I have control over my body, and things that happen produce various sensations. My skin separates me from not me." Eventually, the baby recognizes other tangible things and adds a behavioral level to the biological level. The maturing child begins to demonstrate familial, social, and eventually vocational roles as part of the self-concept. As we move toward the personal level, teenagers recognize that we are more than just our bodies, our possessions, and our roles in the world. As we mature, we come to understand that our personal, physical body is only one aspect of the complex vehicle that we inhabit. There is a constant and ideally consistent inner awareness in the midst of outside changes. We realize "something inside me is greater than the sum of my parts." This leads to the transpersonal level, which includes recognition of a higher or greater Self. Mikulas suggests transpersonal forces operate throughout the body's mind to select, construct, and provide awareness of the essence of the personal, behavioral, and biological levels. In other words, we find we do not know much about the core of a person even if the body is dissected for an autopsy.

Mikulas, along with Wilber, Tolle, and many other current writers, points out that self-centeredness is a key distinction between the personal and transpersonal levels. When we focus too much on our internal thoughts and emotions, we cannot move forward. On the other hand, too much external focus or too many ego attachments, either to past events or to material possessions, are also major obstacles to becoming a fully functioning, actualized adult. As a way of expanding Maslow's Hierarchy of Needs, Mikulas interprets actualization as a personal level goal rather than the highest level of accomplishment. He highlights that in 1964 Maslow added an aesthetic need that appreciates beauty, balance, and form as part of actualization. Transcendence became the height, a stage that corresponds to the superconscious or transpersonal level of being.

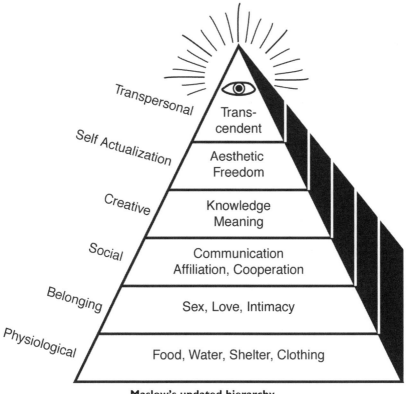

Maslow's updated hierarchy.

RETHINKING FREUD

As we fulfill the basic needs outlined in Maslow's hierarchy, we become an Integrated Self. Balancing the progression of what happened in the past with what is happening now and what we want to happen in the future is a major accomplishment. This progression enables us to acquire powerful tools for staying healthy and building better partnerships. We can facilitate this when we slow down and pay attention to the thought patterns that produce our inner dialog. The ability to become aware of what is going on in our mind was first mentioned by Freud, who is quoted as saying, "What is in your mind is not identical with what you are conscious of; whether something is going on in your mind and whether you hear of it are two different things."[1]

Freud compared the mind to an iceberg where only a small portion appears on the surface. He suggested that we must become more conscious of our thoughts through the process of analysis, dream interpretation, and free association. Another way to understand how past events activate current behavior is to become aware of the various defense mechanisms we utilize in different situations. The patients Freud observed in his medical practice ordinarily identified with only one level of consciousness. His descriptions of their problems parallel Mikulas's behavioral and personal levels. Layers of evolutionary potentiality incorporating Darwin's survival of the fittest theory have allowed us to become ever more complex in our ways of thinking. Yet, it remains a revolutionary idea that individuals are capable of becoming aware enough of what is going on within the body's mind in order to understand what triggers outward behavior. The movie *What About Bob?* provides a good example of how self-help techniques and taking small steps can aid recovery: Bob's psychiatrist (Richard Dreyfus) becomes very irritated with Bob (Bill Murray) and threatens to blow him up with explosives, literally tying dynamite around his neck. In his distress, Bob realizes he must untangle his own "inner knots" in order to stay alive.[2] The application of self-help tools such as contemplation, creative visualizations, focusing, mindfulness, meditation, and stimulating the meridians are steps toward untying those knots. Tapping or touching the meridian lines of the body have proven useful to eliminating past triggers and letting go of repressed and denied pain.

THE POTENTIAL OF QUIET MEDITATION

A Google search shows 5,000 completed studies on the effectiveness of meditation and mindfulness since the late 1960s and early 1970s when an intellectual revolution acknowledged information from other cultures. Some scholars experimented with various drugs and psychedelic herbs to achieve a state of balance, others began to practice yoga and learn practices such as TM or *Transcendental Meditation*. Eastern philosophy and the benefits of meditation and mindfulness became readily available through the media and word of mouth. For instance, after the Beatles traveled to India to study with Maharishi Mahesh Yogi, an assortment of colleges, institutions, and centers were created, both in this country and around the world, to study various forms of meditation. Jiddu Krishnamurti, another popular writer from India, made a valuable contribution during this time. His presentations at many American campuses focused on the purpose of meditation, human relationships, and how to enact positive change in a global society. Shortly before his death at age ninety, he was awarded the 1984 UN Peace Medal after he addressed the United Nations on the subject of peace and self-awareness. This evolution toward embracing Eastern culture began to illuminate a more unified, inclusive way of thinking as Mikulas, a Buddhist, has aptly illustrated. He follows in the footsteps of other integrative thinkers such as Alan Watts, Carlos Castaneda, and Joseph Campbell.

PSYCHOLOGY OF MIND

As the field of psychology continued to grow, Piaget and Erikson provided labels for the mental development they observed in their own children. Their students began to break down these mental processes even further. Many noted that the intuitive process provided by the sixth sense could proceed in different ways. For instance, Sydney Banks proposed a *psychology of mind* (POM) in 1974, which described two modes of thinking:

- processing or analytical model
- free-flowing or diffuse model

The *processing model* takes in information and stores it in the memory where data is sorted, compared, and organized into beliefs, concepts, and ideas. It is the mode of thought used to learn a new habit or skill. This model is useful for planning our lives because it creates a simulation of the future based on past memories and other aspects of our imagination. We compute and calculate the data in a way that is useful for organizing our lives and responding to various situations. A processing mode functions to remember information previously learned. This model is essential for living life effectively so we do not have to relearn everything every day. Our habits, values, skills, beliefs, attitudes, prejudices, expectations, preferences, likes, and dislikes all come through this mode. The primary advantage of this mode of thinking is that when we can know all of the variables, it is extremely fast and efficient. The downside is that when we are not aware of all variables, we too often obsess about the problem without results. This can be draining, frustrating, and stress filled. Most Western either/or, dualistic educational systems have used this method for the past several centuries. Although it is not the only learning tool, most school situations rely heavily on this analytical form.

The *diffuse model* is more like a river that is always flowing and brings new thoughts in the moment. They seem to come from some memory or recognition of the creative source, similar to Jung's idea of the collective unconscious. These thoughts seem original to us in the moment and sometimes we refer to this reflective mode, or effortless thinking, as creative intelligence. The primary purpose of a free-flowing way of thinking is to enjoy life. We operate at peak performance levels and we can solve problems easily when one or more variables are unknown. This kind of thinking is an aspect of the sixth sense often called intuition, insight, realization, wisdom, out-of-the-blue thoughts, or divine inspiration. This free-flowing form has the advantage of being stress free and nonfatiguing, and it provides the opportunity to deal with the unknown when creative, evolutionary thinking is necessary. The function of this more receptive and reflective mode may use memory, but in a new and creative way that is relevant to the moment and responsive to whatever is happening or needed at the time. It is an effortless state of mind where appropriate thoughts continue to bubble to the surface. It is better known as an Eastern nondualistic, both/and thinking. Most refer to this method as the pathway of acknowledging that we are one part of the whole web of life.

When we are in the flow mode, thoughts seem to float in from nowhere. Depending on how much confidence and trust we have, the thinking takes no effort; in fact, effort puts us back into the analytical mode. Children at play are frequently in flow mode, but we need a process model to carry out our responsibilities. We can do almost anything when we integrate the two ways of thinking, if we have the ability to move easily between the two. Although it is natural to be in either mode, we often focus too much on the processing model and forget how to get back into the flow. Our best ideas often come when we are relaxed, because we are able to slow down thinking enough to let creative ideas come through. Nonetheless, we must immediately switch back into process mode to remember these ideas and carry them through to complete a project. We cannot remain in flow mode without integrating analytical thinking as well. One mode is not better than the other, and neither one is good alone. The two ways of thinking work together within the body's mind in the same way that all of a car's parts are necessary, in combination with a driver, so that we can arrive at a particular destination. In this same manner, all of our senses work toward a common goal that combines a perceptual understanding with tangible reality. The ability to capture the flow and hold onto the process mode is often an "aha!" experience.

This natural function of thinking allows us to participate at peak performance while simultaneously being in a state of calm enjoyment. We can observe the ability to combine the process and flow modes when we watch Olympic performers or any great sporting event. Moving between the two ways of thinking is what happens when one paints, writes, creates, or fixes something without effort. We are in the flow mode when thinking is effortless and fresh; harmonious thoughts allow us to achieve our best. But in a moment, a memory might trigger us into the processing mode, and the self-talk that ensues can create feelings of insecurity that can ruin the performance or spoil the moment. This flip can often happen during sexual encounters, especially if there is a history of incest or abuse. As we become familiar with these two modes, the interplay between them becomes easier and more natural.

One way to understand the difference is to notice that when we are actively thinking, we are in processing mode. When we are more passively thinking, almost daydreaming, we are in free-flowing mode. Balance between the two modes is the key that opens the door of creative, emotional intelligence.

REGAINING BALANCE

To be open to learning, we have to admit what we do not know. Often this takes a level of humility. The ego prefers to review what we already believe and think we understand rather than to trust in a more subtle, unknown process; the ego does not like to be out of control. When we pause the busy mind, learning is easier, and we can sense the connections that allow us to receive answers, which are often brilliant, divine, unexpected, and just right for the situation. Simultaneously tuning into both modes of thinking is actually more natural than being encouraged to use only the process mode. As we tune into a balanced way of being in the moment while planning for the future, we are able to analyze, rehearse, and often retrieve information from several sources as it becomes part of our awareness. As adults, we can correct the errors we absorbed as children and teenagers. To do this, we need to become aware of how childhood conditioning shapes our thinking. We must embrace our demons and resolve the tension from each developmental stage to tap the strength that balanced thinking can produce.

As we observe different modes of thinking and learn more about our internal systems, we broaden our ability to respond in various circumstances. We can then direct our hopes and intentions toward extending the scope of our personal power. When we reach out into the larger world with ever-widening intimacy, we become aware of the motivations that can lead us to our greatest happiness. When we refocus from either/or to both/and thinking, we become more open and better able to act and react differently. This refocusing can change our future personality and alter undesirable character traits. In order to access various layers of our psyche, we are required to reflect and to listen so we can hear. This reflection increases our capability of radiating positive, healing energy as we slow down and gain control.

We can triumph over obstacles and surmount errors as we mature. We can appreciate life as a journey rather than a series of problems to be solved and lessons that we must learn. As we become more mindful and embrace natural, balanced modes of thinking, we can enjoy life rather than dwelling in fear, worry, and depression. Exploring intimacy means uncovering the emotional and social intelligence that includes self-awareness, motivation, and empathy. When we are able to manage our moods we conquer the shadow and rediscover joy and pleasure—therefore achieving greater levels of intimacy and compassion.

🍂 *9* 🍂

ACTIVATING ENERGY

Many people understand desire and being "turned on" as feelings associated with the sexual act. It is important to understand the difference between the drive for sex and the movement of energy. As we become aware of the internal flow of energy and the accompanying emotions, we can make conscious choices about our behaviors. In addition, flowing energy is a way to improve our health.

🍂

We give names such as joy and sorrow, pleasure and pain, to the energy in motion that arises from both internal processes and external circumstances. Anodea Judith refers to the body's mind as a rainbow bridge that carries intentions both upward in the "path of liberation" and downward in a "path of manifestation." These currents of energy can free us from constricting patterns and lead to the awakened awareness of an Integrated Self. Once we recognize how our various systems work together and we begin the practice of running energy, we can experience the sense of liberation and manifestation that can be as simple as brushing our teeth or taking a shower. Then, in diverse situations regarding both our health and our partnerships, our thoughts and desires are open to more choices.

This is especially true when it comes to concerns about sexuality and the essential need to touch and be touched.

In the mid-1950s, Alfred Kinsey began the first comprehensive study of human sexuality. People were quite interested when he reported on men's behavior, but he shocked people when his report covered women's behavior. Many were reluctant to hear about the variety of sexual experiences that both men and women practiced outside the confines of marriage and totally unrelated to procreation. In the late 1960s and early 1970s, during and after the Vietnam War, the sexual revolution continued as riots of protest erupted on college campuses. Some experienced "free love" as a way to break out of authoritarian constraints, and others experimented with mind-altering drugs such as marijuana and LSD.

In order to make sense of a society that appeared out of control, many other Americans studied Eastern practices, looking to understand the philosophy behind an alternative way of relating to reality. We have matured as a culture, and through interactions with a diversity of alternative thinking, we have learned additional ways of looking at the body's mind. We now understand that all sensory input, including that from the extrasensory, intuitive emotions, works to provide a broad spectrum of aliveness. We perceive the outside world through our five senses, and we process this information through the sixth sense that provides the emotional response that we translate as our perception of the event.

Through our sixth sense of intuition, we are able both to monitor our thought processes and to experience our bodily sensations whenever we take time to pause, feel, and observe. For instance, we are not usually aware of our liver or kidneys unless something goes wrong, then an internal physical pain may call our attention to these organs. We can cultivate awareness of our inner systems, which might include working with the biofield, chakras, and meridians, by making time to learn about their functions. As we become more sensitive, most people can actually feel the vital, creative life-force energy moving throughout the body. Some practitioners of yoga, tai chi, and qigong or kigung may actually experience the activation of vital life force as erotic energy. These practices move us toward greater awareness and harmony. In turn, as our internal relationship improves and natural impulses, motivations, and desires are fulfilled, partnerships with others are more gratifying. We truly become a healthy Integrated Self.

HEALING THROUGH THE ENERGY BODY

Health, both physical and mental, includes much more than the absence of disease. When we are stressed, depressed, or overwhelmed, most of our energy is directed toward survival. When this happens, we become disintegrated and we are not able to work toward either self-actualization or refinement of relationships. Fullness of well-being, even

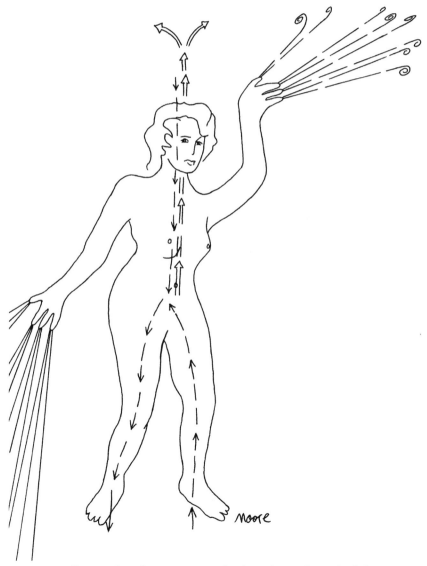

Can you imagine energy running in and out of your body?

when we have physical or mental difficulty, can be enhanced once we become consciously aware of our sixth sense of intuitive knowing. When teenagers learn how the endocrine system drives behavior, they have more choices about their actions. When women have a sensitivity and understanding of the hormonal changes at menopause, there are fewer symptoms. When we pay attention and become conscious of what we are thinking, we know more than what is perceived by our five senses through the perceptual body. Several studies currently show that when cancer and AIDS survivors tap into this intuitive healing power, they manifest fewer symptoms, need less medication, and live longer than others with the same diagnosis, even though they do not totally cure themselves of disease.

As mentioned earlier, Freud labeled the biological urges as aggression, sex, and hunger. The drive to satisfy sexual urges for the continuation of the species is as essential as the drive to satisfy hunger. Both are valuable aspects of a pleasurable life and both are necessary for the continuation of life. Although at one point aggression may have been crucial for the survival of the fittest, hopefully we are evolving as both individuals and separate societies to know that aggression is no longer a way to satisfy wants or needs. When we appreciate how id, ego, and superego influence us, we keep the basic biological urges of hunger, sex, and aggression under control. When we become aware of both the function and performance of our internal systems, we are more fully alive.

Most of us have observed that the drive to meet sexual needs varies from situation to situation and over time. Sometimes we can hardly think about anything else. Other times sexuality seems unimportant, although the underlying urge has not disappeared. Our need for connection remains in spite of not being interested in sex at any particular point in time. Learning how Eastern and Western traditions complement each other can provide an important facet of well-being and opportunity for personal growth. One way to achieve the kind of connection many of us long for is through moving energy or vital life force throughout our body's mind. We can accomplish this in a variety of ways.

First, it is important to note two things. Running energy does not eliminate the desire for sex, and sex drive is not more important than moving energy. However, when we run energy alone or with others, this movement of the vital life force supplies a method of self-pleasure. We move energy when we walk, dance, exercise, or play sports. Routine pleasuring could be a great meal or favorite food, a long bath or shower, or deep breathing, as well as masturbating. In these examples, the goal is the connection with the food, the water, or the breath. On the other hand, some people attempt to satisfy the need for connection through sexual contact that they do not really want or unprotected sex with many partners, which can have negative outcomes. For some, choices of pleasurable or soothing behaviors include the use of alcohol, caffeine, nicotine, prescription or nonprescrition drugs, shopping or gambling. Others might overeat and binge, or undereat and become anorexic. These forms of unconscious behaviors can cause us to become aggressive or depressed. Most addictions are fixations or defense mechanisms. As we work toward birthing an Integrated Self, we can become more aware of our behaviors and avoid acting out of habit or avoidance.

Activating energy can be healing. As we open our body's mind to various teachings from other traditions, for instance learning about Taoism or tantric practices, we can satisfy desires in new and different ways. These are ways of living rather than belief systems and both incorporate union with the eternal, vital life force. The Tao (pronounced *dow*) is basically indefinable but translates as the path or way.[1] Tantra means *to weave*, and this is similar to what happens as we process new data into the nervous system and synaptic pathways form that change the neuroplasticity of the brain. Usually we are not aware of these pathways forming, nor do we question how they form. As we change our internal sense of perception, it changes our external behavior. This has an effect on the way others react and respond to us. The eternal life force constantly flows throughout the body's mind and our emotional spirit. We increase the sixth sense of intuitive knowing when we practice reflection, focusing, and visualization that are incorporated into the Tao and tantra. As we increase in awareness, it is important to remember that we are constantly seeking action and reaction; however, we also need movement such as walking, dancing, or playing sports, as well as rest. Stillness is as important as moving. The idea of running energy moves the life force up and down the spine, and in and out of the body.

Many Taoist, tantra, and shamanic practitioners report that when they become aware of the aura and chakra systems, they not only have the freedom to feel their own aliveness but they also can sense the energy field of others. They accomplish this by gaining control of their thoughts and feelings regarding the energetic streams that move up and down, in, out, and around the body or other objects. Some experience this movement or energy in motion as a motivation to tune in with a higher power or a sense of spiritual presence; others focus on love. Many of these practitioners utilize movement of energy as a tool for healing. They witness the chakras as forces that both create and animate the entire universe, and suggest using the energy of chakras provides the possibility of controlling the mental forces of visualization and dreaming. Some suggest that until we are able to take command of our thoughts we are "like small puddles isolated from the great ocean."

If we take Jung's theory about the collective unconscious seriously, then when we are introduced to an ancient idea perhaps we understand it easily. In the *Upanishads*, the 6,000-year-old oral tradition from India, the original Sanskrit word *cakra* was a metaphor for the sun. It denotes an eternal cycle called the *kalacakra*, or circle of time, which also represents the celestial order and balance of the universe. We could call this cycle *eternal life force*. Later, the chakras were interpreted as wheels and more recently compared to computer discs, CDs, and DVDs that record and store information. Many people report they only sense the aura and chakras, and others say they can actually see them. Although the aura and chakras are not visible to most people, thousands of books, tapes, classes, and Internet sites are readily available on these ideas. In the past, we did not have CAT or PET scans or MRIs to see what we can now see in the body or brain; nor could we perform tests to reveal DNA. Perhaps in the future we will have a machine that can measure the external auric field and internal chakra system. In the meantime, some scholars reject Kirlian photography as pseudoscience in spite of the fact that it appears to capture an indication of color around both people and plants under certain conditions; others accept it as an actual recording of the biofields surrounding the body.

ENERGY SENSATIONS

People who make time to focus inward report that they become aware of bodily sensations as they pay attention and notice feelings of stimuli that can be quite subtle. Others understand chakras as a spinning vortex of energy. Some people report that they see energy running throughout various tubes of the body and theorize that this energetic current is a combination of both mental and physical aspects. Some believe chakras are centers of activity for reception, assimilation, and transmission of all of earth's energetic forces. In this way, the chakras are assumed to be chambers with a specific purpose of accumulating and disseminating information throughout the endocrine system. Others contend the chakras are not physical entities but rather they are similar to emotions and ideas. They cannot be viewed like physical objects, although they have a strong effect upon the body. Although chakras cannot currently be measured, some medical personnel recognize the correlation with the spine and internal organs as highlighted earlier. Many interested in this field maintain that we grow and change and interact with the world through these systems.

Many techniques are available to illuminate the connections of the chakras with the auric field. The sixth sense is an extrasensory way of knowing. It is possible to have a moment of insight at any time that allows us to gain a new understanding about self and others. Many people tell about sudden insights or occurrences that produce deeper, intuitive understanding. Several mental visualizations can enhance extrasensory perception. The desire to understand the eternal life force or how the cycle of life works is one motivation for beginning a daily practice such as the mental one that follows.

EXPERIENCING COLOR AND LIGHT

In addition to colors associated within the body, some people see or feel color emanate from the biofield. Barbara Brennan and Valerie Hunt have shown the human energy field to include electrostatic, magnetic, electromagnetic, sonic, thermal, and visual components. These fields behave as particulate and have fluidlike motion, similar to water and air currents that become visible to the human eye under certain conditions. All colors have a vibration, and they produce similar responses for most people. One model suggests that **red** generates creative thinking and short-term energy. **Yellow** and **orange** relate to physical work and positive moods. **Green** increases productivity and long-term energy. **Blue** is relaxing and promotes deep thinking. **Purple** is a tranquilizing color and shades of **pink** are restful and calming.

   Learning about the element of the colors may help to highlight your mood or set an intention. Adding the colors to our thinking process as described above can also be effortless and provide healing benefits. Other ways of adding color are to choose clothing of a specific color or to create a particular atmosphere when decorating a home or business.

   The exercise that follows includes imagining a specific color and concept for each of the seven main chakras from bottom to top. It is a compilation of ideas from several different authors and teachers. The colors correspond to the colors of the rainbow: red, orange, yellow, green, blue, indigo, and violet. It might be useful to have a friend read it aloud slowly, or record it in your own voice and then listen, therefore involving more senses. To maximize this practice, visualize the color while at the same time bringing your attention to the area of the body that corresponds with each chakra.

   The best way to sense the lower chakras is to bend the knees, keeping the feet flat, about shoulder width apart. This can be done while sitting or lying down, as well as while standing. An important step to bringing the entire system into balance is to take a deep breath and elongate the spine. Afterwards, it might be useful to draw a simple body and color it in with the colors that you imagine.

Begin to focus your attention on your toes, the balls of your feet, and then your heels. Let your awareness travel up through your legs. As you extend upward, as if reaching for the sky, breathe in deeply and become aware of the space between your ears at the top of the spinal column. From here, as you exhale slowly, send your attention down the spinal cord to the tailbone. Allow your awareness to extend below the tip of the spine as if a root is growing down, deep into the earth. Tilt the pelvis slightly backward and sense a third leg extending from your tailbone, making the spinal column even longer.

   The root chakra, beginning at the base of the spine and extending through the feet, represents the element of earth, self-preservation, and the fact that we have a physical body. **Red** *is the color of blood when it is exposed to oxygen and it represents life and survival. This lowest chakra reminds us that we have a home base as a foundation from which to build. This base or root connects with gravity to keep us grounded to the magnetic field of the Earth. Although the first chakra represents survival and connection, it is usually not the one of which we are most aware.*

Take a deep breath into the area below the navel. The second sacral chakra, represents the element of water. This sexual chakra often calls our attention because we have a need for elimination and a motivation for activity and creativity. It is an area of self-gratification and emotional identity. **Orange** is the color to visualize as you move your awareness up from the base into the pelvic area. Imagine the pelvis filling up with a watery orange liquid, paying attention to the fact that your reproductive organs are located in the same area as the urinary tract, anus, colon, and intestines, as well as the penis or vagina. Remember that in order to create, we must also release. Male or female, young or old, this law does not change. The vital life force of sexual drive is more than our capability to bring forth new life, it is also the impulse to create new thoughts or ideas, new music or art, new ways to experience connections in the world. Our capacities to want and to accept change are important aspects of the second chakra. Slowly move your hips from side to side, and up and down.

The third chakra, called solar plexus, is the central energy source, represented by fire, which both shifts and regulates the body's energy. All balance begins in this area. Take a deep breath as you imagine **yellow** radiating both into and away from the navel, where we were connected via the umbilical cord to our mother. The human cord is dangerously long, and although it was essential to our survival it could also be a threat. Beginning with the birth process, we learn navigation skills and make use of our internal guidance system. We experience "as above, so below;" we are the connection between earth and sky. Gut reactions, or burning sensations, represent self-definition through empowerment and independence. This center of action represents vitality, spontaneity, purpose, strength of will, ego identity, self-esteem and power. Residing here are the kidneys that filter waste from the body, and the adrenal glands that handle stress and warn us when we are in danger.

Moving attention to the sternum or breastbone, the fourth chakra represents self-acceptance, love, and relationships. Focus on the area where blood flows through the heart to the veins and arteries, and air is pumped in and out through the lungs. We need the element of air to live. Visualize **green**, which represents the exchange of oxygen with vegetation. We cannot survive without the trees and grass, plants and flowers; they are an intrinsic part of our life support system. Place your attention in the middle of the seven chakras. The heart chakra also includes the arms and hands and the sense of touch. This chakra provides meaning *for life when we feel appreciation, compassion, gratitude, peace, and understanding. In addition, the stomach and upper digestive system reside between the heart and the throat. This area of social identity represents the integration of opposites—male-female, day-night, ego-separateness, and unity. When there are no blockages or leaks, the flow of energy is unwavering and we experience stability as it becomes integrated.*

*As we continue up to the neck and shoulder area, the fifth chakra connects to the digestive system. Let out the sound of a deep sigh as you visualize **bright blue**, like the sky on a sunny day. Let your sound resonate the clarity and harmony of clear self-expression. The vibration of the throat charka corresponds to our ability to communicate. Find a place where you are able to express with words and sounds the feelings of your heart in connection with the thoughts in your head. Our opinions and beliefs need to be spoken and heard. Our tone of voice often reflects our emotional mood. Be aware that communication can be harmonious or harsh as you notice the tension and release the breath with a sigh. The fifth chakra encompasses the complexity of both speaking and hearing, as well as the origination of tasting and smelling. The smell of food often makes us hungry, or we see something and then we want to taste it. This area includes the perceptual and communication system and creative identity. BREATHE in and out, and feel the release through the exhale. Use your sounds to express your desires. Allow original expressions of art, words, and music to call your attention to that fact that we are not separate from the unity of creation. Most species use sound as a way to communicate needs. As you take another deep, deep breath, know that everything that exists is a part of the unified, universal whole.*

*As your eyes drift back into your head, be aware of the possibility of dreaming, imagining, visioning, planning for the future, and reflecting on the past. Become even more sensitive as you visualize the **dark indigo** or **navy blue** of a clear night sky. Let the sparkle of stars wash over the area of your brow. Remember the elements of light are suggestions for feeling the energy of each chakra. The sixth chakra represents our imagination as well as the ability to think logically and process information. Our visual sense is usually the strongest sense. While your eyes are closed, notice the other senses: hear, smell, taste, touch. The third eye is known as the seat of intuition and home of psychic abilities. BREATHE out as if you could release the breath from your forehead and take time to look into the future. Imagine your desires.*

The Path of Love

Remember: "The faults you find in others may often be your own."
Alvera Robinson

Learning to Love yourself is the greatest gift of all. Everyone worth having around will be delighted, because the more you appreciate yourself, the more others can appreciate you.

The Seven Chakras

7th	Crown Violet	Connection to the Creator (source) Consciousness, Understanding, Awareness	I Know I Belong
6th	Third Eye Indigo Blue	Vision-Concepts-Ideals Projection-Light-Thoughts-Memories	I See Intuition
5th	Throat Sky Blue	Tone of Voice-Communication-Sounds Self-Expression **See Below**	I Speak I Hear
4th	Heart Green	Openness-Acceptance-Feelings Air -- Compassion, Relationships	I Love
3rd	Solar Plexus Yellow	Horizontal & Vertical Connection Fire -- Energy, Power, Transformation	I Will I Act
2nd	Below Naval Orange	Sexual-Creativity-Reproduction Water -- Pleasure, Movement, Elimination	I Want I Feel
1st	Root Red	Survival, Security, Grounding, Solidity Connection to Mother Earth (Source)	I Have I Am Here

There is no separation between above and below, the energy must flow in both directions, neither is higher nor lower.

**One: Oooo as in home
Two: U as in rule
Three: Ah as in Father
Four: Ay as in play
Five: Ee as in free
Six: Mm as in hum
Seven: Ng as in sing

Summary of Visualization.

*Begin to perceive energy coming or going through the crown chakra, at the top of the head. Allow it to lead to increased self-knowledge and conscious awareness of what some refer to as a higher power or spiritual connection. The seventh color is usually noted as **violet**, **purple**, or **lavender**, but some people describe the cord they see or feel emanating from the top of the head as **white**, which is the combination of all colors; others see it as **silver** or **gold**. Tuning into this color frequency can be imagined as a beautiful shimmering light pulsating so fast . . . it looks like thousands of golden threads . . . that surround the entire body. Allow the color to flow out of the top of your head and around the outside of your body, flowing back into the soles of your feet as you continue to breathe slowly and deeply. Press your feet down, connecting the threads from the soles, through your body, up to the crown, taking time for gradual fading of the light. Come back into the room feeling fully present in this moment, here and now.*

EXPANDING INTUITION

Many people cultivate this kind of guided imagery or creative visualization and discuss its benefits. Some report that the complexity of these threads represents their relationship to the creator or Great Spirit, divine mind, or universal identity, God/Goddess, or whatever phrase may express the idea that they are connected in a way that acknowledges that we are more than earthy flesh and blood, bones and muscles. Others explain the threads as the cycle of life, the eternal life force, or the order and balance of the universe. Many have found that connection to awareness is no more difficult than paying attention to our digestion process after eating certain foods.

What is our reaction to food that we might consider heavy or light? Some of our strongest preferences are around food. *How do we respond to food we like or do not like?* Just as we notice we have a desire for a sweet, spicy, or salty taste, most people can attain awareness through this experience of noticing their internal systems and focusing on bodily sensations. Every cell of the body is a connection point that receives, organizes, and assimilates information. The body's mind contains intuitive knowledge from the past that can provide direction for the future when we allow that information to come through.

As outlined in chapters 1 and 2, the throat area, which includes the nose and sinuses as well as the taste buds, provides an example. When we are having any sensation or problem in the nose or throat, we might benefit by slowing down, tuning into the intuitive sixth sense, and asking: "*What is it I am not saying? What do I want or need that I am not asking for? Am I withholding anything?*" or "*Did I speak out of turn? Have I harmed someone with my words?*"

By doing this, we can connect to the message the body is attempting to relay. Another example for observing the sensations in the body happens when our heart is beating fast and we are out of breath, or if we are holding our breath. In both circumstances, our tendency is to calm down and bring ourselves back to a normal state, where we are unaware of beating or breathing. However, when we exercise, we intend the heart rate to increase and breathing to deepen in order to provide more oxygen. We allow it to happen without questioning because we know we are doing something beneficial. When we sit quietly, resting or meditating, the heart also slows down and the breath becomes shallow, the entire system is able to recharge; this also happens when we sleep. Most of us learn to observe and control these changes without too much effort.

Regardless of how you visualize the auras and chakras, what matters most is that you take time to focus your thoughts. Think about sending whatever color you choose up and down as well as in and out of the body. Whenever possible take a minute to introduce this part of self to self and see what happens. Remember that experiencing the aura and chakras is about discovering our own Truth, not about being told what is true.

CONSTRUCTING REALITY

In many circles, people have accepted the idea that our thoughts create our health and experience through words. They also agree that feeling the movement of energy is beyond words. These experiences are sometimes labeled *psychic* or *paranormal*. Holistic practitioners teach various ways to get in touch with and balance the body's internal systems. Those who incorporate color, as suggested above, find this addition accelerates healing.

In 1978, Richard Gordon popularized a massage technique known as *polarity*, which assists the flow of energy through the body. Recently, he introduced Quantum Touch as a hands-on healing modality that also involves the activation of energy.[2] Gordon postulates that "all healing is self-healing" and that anyone can learn Quantum Touch, which is similar to Therapeutic or Healing Touch and Reiki. Often these techniques do not involve actual touching, but rather the hands hover over the energy body or biofield of yourself or others. This kind touch is said to ignite the body's healing response and to relieve pain. These procedures also include setting intention, breathing techniques, and focusing on bodily sensations. They can complement, or in some cases eliminate, the need for prescription medication, alcohol, or other drugs such as nicotine and caffeine that dull the senses. In addition, if these techniques are practiced on a regular daily basis, they often become a way to avoid illness and achieve an overall sense of well-being that improves intimacy.

Being healthy involves giving our attention to the flow of vital energy throughout the body and feeling pleasurable and possibly erotic sensations. Often we interpret movement within the chakra system as sexual arousal, and we translate this pleasurable feeling as a drive for sex. Just because we feel alive does not mean we must have sex, although there is nothing wrong with being sexual in the proper time and place. The life force can feel similar to either "falling in love" or being "engrossed in rage." Many people report feeling energy running up and down when raging mad or sexually aroused. More often than not, it is inappropriate to act on this rage or arousal. Sometimes we can instinctively move this energetic sensation up from the lower chakras into the heart area where we experience caring and compassion. In some cases, if there is dislike for the other person, the sensation spontaneously moves toward the throat chakra and something harsh or hateful is said. Frequently, we project the negative feelings onto ourself because of our reaction to the rage or arousal. Instead, if we can focus on the third eye and visualize possible future outcomes and perhaps begin humming or moaning, we can produce a different vibration throughout the body. Some people are capable of sublimating rage or sexual yearning into creative projects; for others the same thoughts and feelings can manifest as harmful addictions. When we activate energy, there is often a *felt-sense* of connection or rejection that moves us beyond the drive for sex. Some note feeling a gentle flow like a warm stream within the body. Others compare it to the visceral stirring we experience during an amazing sunrise, magnificent sunset, or hearing a piece of music that touches the heart.

This kind of effortless connection is beyond the tangible reality of what we see, hear, smell, taste, and touch. Some express this moment of awareness as peace, harmony, or love. This connection with the vital life force is said to manifest in a moment of awareness. It might occur in times of conflict or when we are at peace—suddenly an intuitive response in our body's mind calls our attention to our surroundings in a way that we were not previously aware. Often people experience the oneness and unity that is possible when we see our self as one little part of the larger wholeness of the universe. For many, this feeling of aliveness may transpire when we are in a natural setting, such as being outdoors in touch with the earth, plants, and trees, the ocean, a river or waterfall, a campfire, or volcano. It could also take place spontaneously in a car, on an airplane, train, or bus. It does not matter if we are alone or with a partner or a group of people; it just happens.

Thoughts of actively running energy involve erotic as well as familial and universal connections. As we gain understanding and awareness of our internal systems, we can achieve a higher quality of love energy. Different words describe this metaphysical experience of connection. Sometimes it is the union of the psyche with the physical—the connection of the body's mind with the emotional-spiritual aspect. It is part of the free-flowing process of thinking, discussed in chapter 8. It is part of a satisfying and healthy life. When we fully grasp how to move energy, we can learn from the sudden shifts, frustrations, and deceptions of the erotic impulse. Once we have taken the time to resolve the tensions left over from the crisis experienced during each developmental stage, we are able to generate the evolutionary awareness that brings about ego integrity without feelings of stagnation or despair. In order to achieve happiness, we must learn to release our lower, unaware self.

ᴄᴙ 10 ᴣᴩ

OVERFLOWING PLEASURE

Learning to slow down and breathe deeply are the first steps to achieving mindfulness. These steps open a gateway for extending joy and pleasure through the integration of spirituality into sexuality and exploring kundalini awakenings. Setting intentions and making time to cultivate pleasurable experiences is a magical path leading to personal growth.

ᴄ∞ᴑ

Have you ever noticed a very young baby's willingness to make eye contact? Small children know how to pleasure themselves and to please others. They know how to smile and do so automatically. From birth, we have an instinctual desire for silliness and game playing. Babies know how to focus and have fun, it just happens naturally. Eventually, stranger anxiety is a normal part of the developmental process. Spontaneity lessens as the body's mind contracts, expands, and creates defense mechanisms for protection from outside forces.

During our early teen years, many of us find pleasure participating in sports, discovering musical preferences, sharing video games, movies, books, cartoons or comics, joining groups, and exploring sexual feelings. As teens we often shop to look good not only for our own satisfaction but also to fit in with those we want to attract. Some of us experiment with drugs and alcohol. Many begin working and seek out others who are involved in aspects of life they want to learn more about. We are naturally inquisitive and ask countless questions. As we grow, we are supposed to stop playing and "act our age." In most cultures, older teens are encouraged to "settle down" and "get serious." At least this is what was encouraged in previous generations. With today's changing mores, many teens experiment with erotic expression younger than ever before. In the past, most religious practices only allowed sexual energy within a marriage contract.

In Freud's view, sexual longing was unacceptable and outside the strict moral code of his day. Therefore, most sexual acts were to be concealed and desire was experienced only at a *subliminal* or subconscious level. His teachings regarded sublimation of this desire as the defense mechanism that meant channeling unacceptable impulses into more suitable outlets. He implied that it was important to spend energy or vital life force on other creative endeavors and viewed sexual thoughts or emotions as inappropriate. In Jung's view, it was important to follow all desire as both a biological and psychological instinct. He found that longing and desire could lead to an opening of the collective unconscious or superconscious that he referred to as the soul. It is important to remember that during this period of history, most religions taught that it was necessary to save men's souls from damnation. However, women and slaves were often viewed as not having a soul.

Arguments against these teachings have helped many people to reconsider this limited way of thinking. Most healthy adults explore pleasurable experiences. In addition to following sexual urges, many find time to enjoy music and dancing, engage in playing sports, games, hobbies, and other leisure time activities like reading, watching sports, television, or movies. Some take a more active participatory role, while others become passive observers. In some cases, these activities provide joy and pleasure, for other people the same activity can cause stress, pain, and mental anguish. The required ingredients for sustained, balanced flow of vital life force energy can vary from one situation to another and from one stage of life to the next. It is essential to know the range of choices available regarding the essential mix of these ingredients. This chapter outlines possible options for becoming more playful and cultivating happiness.

VARYING DEFINITIONS

People who perceive life as purposeful enjoy positive emotions. Several authors addressing peak performance, flux, and flow have popularized the concept of thinking with both sides of the brain in order to find happiness. Mihaly Csikszentmihalyi notes "twenty-three hundred years ago Aristotle concluded that, more than anything else, men and women seek happiness."[1] Tal Ben-Shahar, a popular professor at Harvard University, also quotes Aristotle, "Happiness is the meaning and purpose of life, the whole aim . . . of human existence." Ben-Shahar suggests we must learn to live for today *and* for tomorrow at the same time so that we can combine immediate personal needs with long-term goals. He points out that people can endure emotional pain and still be happy overall. A happy person will enjoy positive emotions when perceiving life as purposeful. However, Ben-Shahar also points out that happiness involves emotional discomfort and difficult experiences, and he reminds us that going through difficult times can expand our capacity for more lasting pleasure. [2]

On the other hand, William Mikulas defines the difference between happiness and pleasure as if happiness were long lasting, while pleasure is a more fleeting experience. But neither need to be short lived when the vital life force moves in a balanced flow. The components for maintaining flow are different for each of us. When we examine learned behaviors and beliefs from the past, we can release anything that may block us from overflowing with continual joy. Once again the key is balance between staying stuck in past discomforts and moving toward newfound pleasures in healthy and balanced ways.

Different cultures promote different belief systems regarding happiness and pleasure. One example is that some people believe it is important to conserve sexual energy, while others believe that frequent spending of this life force promotes vitality. Some societies cling to traditional conditioning that states that sexual standards must remain different for men and women. Most cultures maintain a subliminal message that it is acceptable for men to masturbate and explore various sexual practices, while they expect women to be chaste. But social mores are changing. Modern medical knowledge has demonstrated that optimal health includes the flow of sexual energy throughout the lifespan. At the same time, it is important to gain an understanding of how our nervous system influences our immune system as it processes thoughts and emotions regarding desire. When we understand how our beliefs affect our health, we will experience deeper and more meaningful pleasure.

PSYCHONEUROIMMUNOLOGY

In the 1970s, American neuroscientists Candace Pert and Michael Ruff contributed to the discovery of opiate receptors in the brain. A receptor is a molecule with an electrically active indentation that another molecule with a matching shape must fit into. They explain how the body's mind functions as a psychosomatic network of information molecules that control health and physiology. Their discoveries led to a greater understanding of how emotional communication works and their ideas support the fact that deep breathing can affect the state of mind that keeps us in or out of equilibrium.[3] According to the theory of psychoneuroimmunology, our susceptibility to the microorganisms of disease fluctuates with attitude and beliefs. External events can be judged as good or bad. Aside from inherited conditions, such as hemophilia and sickle-cell anemia, and illness caused by occupational disease or environmental factors, such as food poisoning or poisoning from pollutants, we have more control over our health and well-being than most of us believe.

The emerging field of *body psychotherapy* includes a variety of modalities that can support us in finding more joy and pleasure. We can explore these methods on our own or with the aid of a therapist, counselor, or other practitioner. The practices include careful listening to signals from the body. As we become still and quiet, and focus on our innermost sensations, we access the body's messages regarding old hurts. In this frame of mind, experiences and insights have the opportunity to surface as we process the information that enters our perceptual awareness.

Refer back to the circle drawings in chapter 5 to recall that our physical sense of perception and mental cognition are constantly active, along with emotional and spiritual components. When we balance physical and mental with emotional and spiritual facets, we are in a state of happiness, joy, and pleasure. If we focus on any one aspect of physical, mental, emotional, or spiritual expression over the other, we are out of alignment. Once this happens, we might feel distracted or overwhelmed. This out-of-balance signal calls us to pay attention to the warning signs. When we are in physical pain, or if we feel mentally confused, we should pause, ask the body what it needs, breathe, pay attention, listen, and return to the present moment with an increased sense of into-me-see.

CREATING OUR OWN EXPERIENCE

Western scientific technology has begun to observe how the brain processes both perceptual and cognitive information, while Eastern teachings continue to describe the same process in terms of vital life force moving up and down the spinal column and in and out of the body. In both cases, we are learning that inner reflection can eliminate the excessive or deficient energy that is often the root cause of illness and disease.

How do you respond to extreme emotions? Do you have mental or physical reactions to insults, put downs, or even compliments? If we feel intense pleasure and overjoyed, is this good?

Have you ever used the expression "I was beside myself" when either in joy or in pain? Or have you had the thought, "This is so good (or bad) I could die"? Stress can come in both positive and negative forms. For instance, falling in love or getting a new job can make us feel ecstatic as well as nervous. We often become anxious when we are being judged or evaluated. In many instances, this anxiety takes us out of the present moment. We are confused and disoriented and fail to do our best. If we are able to quickly recognize the need to move from the lower biological and behavioral levels, we can stop and take a deep breath. This provides time to take the necessary actions that allow us to reenter the flow by experimenting with practices and exercises that have the capacity to lift us to higher levels of awareness.

Throughout the ages, we have found numerous ways to pleasure our self and eliminate pain. The body is constantly taking in fuel provided by earth's natural resources. It is important to breathe fresh air, feel the sun, drink natural water, and eat healthy, organic foods. Most of us are invigorated out in nature, close to trees, mountains, the ocean, a river, creek, or stream, or when we make time to walk or dig in a garden and smell the flowers. Another kind of sensory stimulation occurs when we look at any form of art or beauty, or read, or listen to music, or watch TV, films, DVDs, or videos that we enjoy. Additionally, our connections with other people provide an energetic awakening. Every body produces an energy field that affects every other body we meet along the way.

The more we understand how the flow of energy moves between people and throughout the body's mind, the more we nourish our ability to find pleasure and have fun. Fun can be something as simple as taking a bath or shower, walking outdoors, or coming inside. All of these activities can change our mood and provide a feeling of connection. This connection is called *grounding*. Any forms of exercise including yoga, martial arts, tai chi, dancing, having sex, or getting a massage or other therapeutic intervention are all positive ways to become more grounded. Other options include eating, drinking, smoking, or taking prescription, over the counter, or recreational drugs. Negative consequences can result when anything is done to excess. It is important to develop moderation in everything, including moderation. If we enter a state of mind that allows us to observe what is going on inside the body's mind without judging or evaluating, we can overcome the part of ego that thrives on destructive behaviors and instead take control of our own internal circumstance. We create our experience by how we react internally to external stimulus.

SIMPLE REMEDIES

When we feel annoyed, or overwhelmed, we tend to react. For instance, we may automatically modify the vibration of the sounds around us by turning the volume up or down or by listening to a different type of music. We change the temperature by adjusting the thermostat or putting on or taking off clothes. We could also reach for an ice pack or heating pad. As we make these alterations, we might also notice smells that bother us; perhaps we could light incense or realize it is time to take out the old garbage.

Some people learn how to have more happiness and pleasure by simply sitting still on a regular basis. They focus their attention inward with no other intention than to stop *doing* and just *be*. Many religious and spiritual traditions advocate meditation, which requires the clearing out of all thoughts. Practices, such as creative visualization or focusing, unite the body's mind with the motivational spirit. Those who actively engage in various forms of meditation, sports, dance, or other mindful practices discover two important keys to health: (1) being in the present moment, and (2) awareness of energy flow. These two activities can eliminate negative energy, or increase positive energy. You can begin to tune in by asking, *"What is this body telling me?"* Recognize that any discomfort warns us to change actions, thoughts, and behaviors.

Many uncomplicated techniques increase mindfulness and change internal experiences. Some people practice fasting and celibacy to discover how mental thoughts affect the body. When we take action and begin to perform a different behavior in the present moment, it can provide an overall sense of pleasure and well-being that will often transcend, although not eliminate, the biological urges of hunger and sexual desire. In most cases, these practices eliminate many forms of aggression, proven by various experiments on Transcendental Meditation.[4]

MIND MEETS BODY

The acknowledgement that thoughts and feelings are interrelated can be traced back 5,000 years when Huang Ti, the Yellow Emperor of China, observed that frustration made people sick. He taught that those who seek to be healthy should investigate their wishes, desires, and ideas. People who follow their desires will flourish and prosper while others will perish. A quote from the canon of traditional Chinese medicine states: If chi flows, one is healthy, if chi is blocked, one is not healthy. Chinese medicine and holism advocate that a strong vital life force will keep illness away.[5]

Hippocrates, the Greek physician recognized as the father of Western medicine who lived from 460–370 B.C.E., postulated that it was necessary for doctors to "have knowledge of the whole of things." This idea was still in effect at the beginning of the nineteenth century when French physician Pierre Jean Georges Cabanis expounded on the concept that "strong passions" could have pathological consequences. He is quoted as saying: "Just as the stomach and intestines receive food and digest it, so the brain receives impressions, digests them, and has as its organic secretion, thought."[6]

In the middle of the twentieth century, Martha and Howard Lewis noted the "flowering" of the theory that germs caused disease. Human personality and emotional responses were tossed aside due to the increasing interest in specific microorganisms as the root of various diseases. The study of psychoneuroimmunology, body psychotherapy, and chakra therapy now reintegrates personality and emotional reactions into their theories. By engaging in mindfulness, prayer, meditation, creative visualization, or focusing, rather than quickly reaching for a remedy that stops the symptoms, these alternatives can promote health and provide long-lasting experiences of pleasure.

PRACTICAL EXERCISES

We cannot simply read about the somatic techniques and exercises introduced in this chapter in order to feel the results. Instead, they need to be directly experienced to derive maximum benefits. Otherwise, it is similar to describing what an orange or strawberry might taste like and then expecting to get the nutrition they provide from listening to the description.

One basic technique entails a body sweep where we imagine and feel the sensation of the vital life force moving up from the feet and the legs, through the torso, out and around the top of the head, then down the arms, and out the hands. To begin the process of focusing on creative visualization techniques, FIRST, notice if any part of the body is hurting, therefore calling your attention to that particular area. THEN, turn your thoughts to a space of healing. Ask yourself, *"What can I learn from the distress I am experiencing? What is my body trying to communicate?"* As we ask these questions and observe the body, remember to use the metaphors from the body dynamic figure in the first chapter.

Take in a deep breath and tighten each muscle to create even more tension throughout the body. Release each muscle as slowly as possible and experience the relaxation of tension in any area that was hurting.

The next exercise can change the flow of thinking:

Begin with a deep breath and imagine the electromagnetic field from the earth entering the body through your feet and up your legs, continuing into the base of your spine, and rising up through the body to the top of your head. Feel the support of this energy force, and allow it to hold you up as you exhale completely.

When we are able do this, we experience our legs as pillars that support us, as opposed to feeling as if our feet, ankles, and knees are constantly bearing the heaviness of our weight. It is an opportunity to let go of frustration from gravity's downward pull.

RAINBOW IMAGERY

Each color of the rainbow correlates with various aspects such as security (red), creativity (orange), power (yellow), love (green), communication (blue), imagination (indigo), and connection (violet). Feel free to substitute any pleasing color. The idea is to visualize a color to represent the attribute we want to attract. For instance, we might want to increase the feeling of security, creativity, power, love, communication, imagination, or connection when we notice we are lacking in that area at this particular point in time. To begin: a simple undemanding exercise:

Take a deep breath. Imagine any color flowing as a ray of light into or out of a particular area that might feel overactivated, strained, blocked, or in pain. End with another deep breath.

In addition to visualizing colors within specific areas of the body, consider that the auric field is also a boundary or border that serves to protect us. Some people view the aura as if it contains layers of rainbow colors around our body. In order to increase our recognition of this, the following exercise can be easily done while lying in bed when first waking up or before going to sleep.

Place your mental focus in the center of your left foot and mentally draw a line of color up the outside of the left leg and torso all the way to the armpit. From there trace down the inside of the left arm, around the hand (or each finger), up the outside of the left arm to the neck. Let your thoughts travel around the head, from left to right ear, then proceed to the right shoulder and down the right arm past the elbow to the wrist to the hand. Outline each finger if you have time, and then continue the

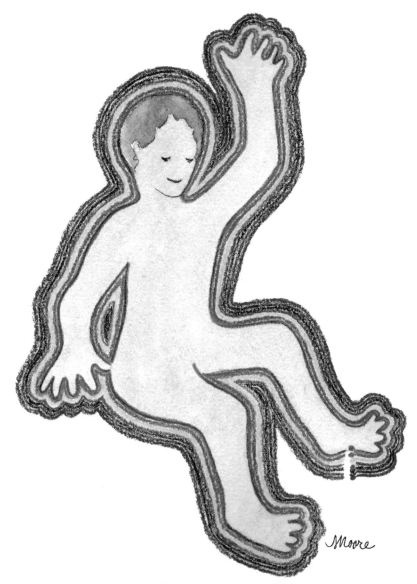

Trace and color this figure with rainbow colors beginning at the center of the left foot changing the color each time you come back to that point.

flow of attention back up the inside of the right arm to the armpit and down the right side of the body to the right foot. Mentally go across the sole of the right foot, up the inside of the right leg, imagining the soft, inner thighs of both legs, and then down the left leg, and back to the sole of the left foot. Each time your thoughts return to the left foot, begin again with a different color.

Any exercises similar to these are steps toward discovering the inner lover and becoming more integrated. After performing any of these exercises, notice if any sensations or emotions came up. Ask: *What was that like? Did you feel any particular rhythm or movement? Are you in a different state of mind or mood?*

PLEASURE PRESCRIPTION

No matter what our relationship is to the people around us, when we radiate happiness it is contagious; when we are sad or angry, others often match our mood. We need to be flexible about the flow of activities required by family and friends. Without a flexible flow, we revert to feeling as if we are operating at a loss. We feel deprivation. We are depressed or bored. When we look toward others for gratification they cannot or will not provide, we avoid reaching into our own depths to find satisfaction. Yet, it appears our destiny is to connect—to the earth and to each other. We need intimate, playful connections in order to survive. To become a worthy playmate, we need to tap the rich resources and opportunities available within us that provide for joy and pleasure. It is important that we learn to entertain ourselves without overconsuming. Hawaiian author Paul Pearsall, articulated *Five Factors of Fitness*:

1. *Food*, which includes eating and drinking in healthy ways.
2. *Flexibility* through exercise that not only increases stamina but also calms mental processing and allows for more options.
3. *Flow* refers to reducing stress, surrendering to the breath, and slowing down the heart rate and blood pressure as well as thoughts.
4. *Family*, meaning creating ties both emotional and spiritual, because healthy families provide transitional support from youth to old age. Pearsall thinks about family in a holistic way that includes the oceans, rivers, rocks, trees, plants, and all animals, including insects and creepy crawlies, as part of the whole.
5. *Fun*, which he says is not about trying to do it all or have it all but rather it is a state of awareness where we find our true nature in balanced pleasure.

For Pearsall, the purpose of all life is to find joy through living together with the wonderful gifts nature provides, without attempting to control, own, conquer, or even to protect the natural world. He finds there is something within all of us that remembers and longs to return to a paradise lost. His work suggests that we play in the splendor of daily existence by slowing down, being quiet, and letting this natural desire for paradise speak to us. According to Pearsall, and others who write about the experience of pleasure, once we learn to connect with our true inner nature, we find peace, contentment, and a deeper sense of compassion.[7] A sense of well-being ensues when the body's mental, emotional, and spiritual aspects come into alignment. We reap the benefits of internal empowerment when we gain mastery over our sixth sense of intuition and attain the skills of true intimacy. For pleasure to be more than a fleeting fancy, conscious awareness or mindfulness needs to become a daily discipline.

ISIS WHEEL

Gina Ogden outlines another model for creating pleasure and sustainable relationships. A sex therapist since the early 1970s, Dr. Ogden has compiled results from a survey received from thousands of women and men who answered questions and wrote essays regarding how they integrate spirituality into sexuality. Ogden developed a multidimensional model based on a Native American medicine wheel as the container for her research, which she calls the ISIS connection. The foundation of her model illuminates how the directions of north, east, south, and west correlate to spiritual, mental, physical, and emotional aspects of all partnerships. Ogden's research has concluded that many people navigate relationships only along the outer rim of the circle and enter into partnerships only through one portal, often the physical, although sometimes the mental or emotional. However, some connect primarily on a spiritual level. Ogden finds that when we are stuck in one of these aspects our experience of sexuality and all of life is limited, but when we incorporate all aspects, we can move into the heart of the circle at the center where transformation and true compassion occur.[8] These aspects extend into all areas of our lives such as enthusiastic connection to community, intellectual educational opportunities, physical health, and taking a stand on political platforms. When we explore happiness and pleasure and include all four quadrants, we increase emotional intelligence and generate an Integrated Self.

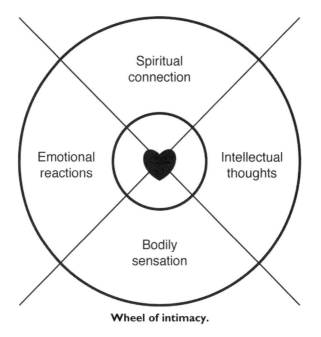

Wheel of intimacy.

An additional model might also highlight economical stability where expenses equal income, and partners agree that this element is also important to the relationship. The economic component of intimate partnerships can often cause as many problems as the sexual aspects. When we overspend or overuse any resource, we diminish our potential for happiness. Obtaining optimal healthy relationships and learning to love with compassion is not an easy task, but integration of all parts is well worth the effort.

KUNDALINI

As we progress on the path to conscious awareness and spiritual awakening through cultivating pleasure, we can also incorporate the images and feelings related to the themes represented by the seven chakras as previously mentioned, beginning with the root and moving upward: security, creativity, power, love, harmonious communication, imagination, and connection.

In doing this, we might experience a *kundalini awakening*. According to Hindu and Buddhist tantra traditions, Kundalini-Shakti is the

Kundalini Rising.

energizing potential of life. It is often represented as a serpent asleep at the base of the spine, which awakens and sends quivers up the spinal column similar to the sensation of an electrical current. The purpose of Kundalini, sometimes depicted as a brightly burning fire, is to energize, balance, and purify as the breath moves throughout the body.

Kundalini is a healing force, although like fire or electrical power that can be both useful and destructive, it might also feel like an unpleasant experience if it is unexpected or misunderstood. A kundalini awakening represents the movement of the creative life force and it is sometimes the outcome of an erotic encounter. But it can also be the result of celibacy or celebrating one's self through masturbation.

Anodea Judith relates that any mundane experience might trigger a reaction that feels as if hot energy is traveling upward and then out through the top of the head. "Kundalini is a condensed, primal force, similar to the potential energy found in matter. When released, it creates a vertical connection between each chakra by opening the subtle channels known as *nadis*, most specifically the central channel that moves up the spine."[9]

People who relate positive kundalini experiences say it is as if each area of the body is being ignited and brought into alignment, which results in feeling more balanced. Often because we are unaccustomed to being totally in balance this feeling can come as a complete surprise. At first it might feel overwhelming. If fire energy encounters a block or resistance while moving up the spine, feelings of contraction or too much expansive energy may occur. It is easier to control these feelings, and simply ride the wave, when one knows what to expect.

A kundalini awakening might be experienced as implosive rather than explosive. Some people describe the pleasure of this enhanced energy in motion as the opposite of the release caused by ejaculation, and they call this building of energy a *reverse orgasm*. The ability to move energy throughout the system allows us to discharge any aggressive or potentially unhealthy drives or motives.

Older books addressing kundalini warn that one should not attempt to cultivate this experience without a teacher, because a kundalini awakening may cause our energy flow to change too quickly. If we are not anticipating the possibility of a drastic change, the shift can produce heat, cold, tickling, or tingling, or spontaneous body movements. However, the resolution of these conditions can result in a pleasurable growth experience. Newer books promoting sexual ecstasy and hour-long orgasms suggest that "kundalini rising" is a positive goal to be achieved. If you attempt this awakening, it is essential to slow down and breathe. Under these circumstances, the quivering experience is not likely to feel shocking. Most practitioners report that energy orgasms provide a satisfactory sexual release, and often ejaculation or climax is no longer the end goal.

We can create a pleasurable kundalini experience through exploring our intuitive sense. If you desire to cultivate a kundalini awakening, it requires preparation such as developing the tools of introspection necessary to handle the feelings or thoughts that might arise. In most cases, kundalini awakening leads to a pleasurable experience. Nevertheless, if an awakening should occur that results in depression or a manic episode, it is better not to consult a practitioner in the Western therapeutic community. In many cases, it is difficult to communicate what is happening, and the incidence may be different for different people at different times. These experiences are sometimes diagnosed as psychotic, and often prescription drugs are offered in an attempt to control the feelings. It is not helpful to explain the occurrence to those who might hinder the process of inner growth. It is important to address the experience with a partner, friend, therapist, or Kundalini master, known as a *daka* or *dakini*, who is supportive of alternative and integrative healing.

EVERYDAY INTIMACY

Any of the practices mentioned in this chapter can open gateways beyond the biological, behavioral, and personal levels where we deepen relationships and achieve the tranquility of transcendence. Personal development may include the suggested relaxation exercises, and visualization, applying the pleasure principles, attending groups discussing the ISIS concepts, balancing time and energy budgets, or working with the subtle kundalini to enhance feelings of empowerment. All promote long-term happiness, pleasure, and contentment. Most people find attaining tranquility allows them to be free of endless cycles of repetitive projections and habits that do not promote peace, harmony, or vitality.

Over our lifespan, it is important to explore various methods to find one that works best at any given time. Only then can we experience more openness, passion, and intimacy. Only then can we move toward the brilliant, divine connections of inner peace and calm attained through intimate connections. The better we know our Integrated Self, the more we can release guilt, doubt, and shame about desire and pleasure and therefore enjoy the restorative aspects of love and sex in its many variations.

We can experience loving compassion in its restorative aspects and transcendent kundalini awakenings when we blend the boundary between what we perceive as reality and the mythical realm of imagination. Stories that blur the boundaries come in various shapes and sizes; for example: action adventures, science fiction, fairy tales, and myths that provide helpful insights to validate the social order and demonstrate ways to comprehend difficult concepts. Myths are magical stories about adventures in imaginary countries or universes that are intended to open us to the idea of mystery and at the same time reveal the nature of human beings. We can use them to make sense of the world and to provide commonalities from one era to another. Mythological stories manifest the collective unconscious and contain fundamental organizing principles.

II

CHANGING ROLES

When we desire to possess the beauty, characteristics, and qualities of someone we idealize, we may be projecting what we lack onto them. The integration of heart and mind is important in order to reinterpret traits previously defined as masculine and feminine. We move closer to an Integrated Self as we overcome various demons that haunt us in the illusionary concepts of what it means to be female or male.

The myth of Eros and Psyche is a popular story that originated in an era before people understood human emotions, and it illuminates the process of discovering your inner lover.[1] This particular story is one way to illustrate the internalized Eros as the spiritual, emotional aspect of personality and to better understand Psyche as the physical, mental expression. We can also view the mortal Psyche as a dimension of human consciousness and Eros as undeveloped feelings of warmth and affection. In addition, Psyche and Eros could represent the interplay between the body's lower, *doubting* mind and the higher, *encouraging* aspects. The tension between the physical-mental and emotional-spiritual leads to increased confidence and self-love. An interpretation of this myth can also be a valuable key for moving beyond internalized male-female roles.

These roles have the power to keep us acting as if we were separate egos in competition with each other, not just between men and women, but men with men, and women with women.

The story of Psyche and Eros illustrates the tests of transformation and determination that are necessary before we are able to enter healthy partnerships with others. Throughout our life, we must continuously practice the dance of trusting and doubting, withdrawing and yielding. One analysis of the myth provides a demonstration of how we move through Erikson's tensions created by autonomy, guilt, despair and depression, shame, initiative, industry, inferiority, identity, intimacy, generativity, stagnation, and integrity. Grasping knowledge of this information is one avenue for discovering the inner lover.

As the myth begins, the wealthy parents of a beautiful young maiden named Psyche consult an oracle to give them guidance because their attractive daughter has not found a husband. Most men are fearful of her magnificent beauty. Consulting the oracle is similar to visiting a for-tuneteller, and the oracle tells Psyche's parents that she must go to the top of a dangerous mountain where she is to marry a monster. At the time of the consultation, Aphrodite, the Olympian goddess of love also known as Venus, has become jealous of the beautiful Psyche. Aphrodite has demanded her young son Eros, or Cupid, to use his powerful golden arrows so that Psyche will fall in love with the ugliest man on earth. Ordinarily, Eros "strikes at whim and then abandons his subjects."[2] But when he sees Psyche, he disobeys his mother and falls in love with her. Psyche's family follows the oracle's orders and sends her to the top of the mountain where she enters a dark cave. There she finds herself sur-rounded by servants and all the riches of material wealth that anyone could possibly desire.

Eros is in the cave, but she cannot see him. He expresses his desire to be her lover. But because gods and mortals were not allowed marry, Eros instructs Psyche that it must be on the condition that Psyche would never actually see his face, and she must never tell anyone anything about him. Psyche agrees and he becomes a gentle, sensuous lover. When Psyche and Eros make love in the dark, they are both in a state of unawareness, but she follows his orders and obeys the rules because she understands his demand to be the will of the gods.

As the myth unfolds, her older, married sisters come to visit and they are jealous of the wealth that surrounds Psyche. She is tempted to tell them her life is not so great, since she is not allowed to actually see her lover. After her sisters' visit, Psyche feels imprisoned by being forced to stay in the dark and not being allowed to tell anyone what is happening to her; she decides she will overcome her lover's desire to not be seen. Psyche, who has become devoted to Eros, initiates growth by her desire to see him. She lights a candle to reveal his face, accidentally burning Eros with hot wax. His pride is hurt by her defiance and he returns to his mother. His leaving may represent how feelings of love can turn sour when trust is broken, and we often regress to an earlier stage of development when we are hurt or feel wronged in some way.[3]

Psyche is remorseful now that Eros is gone, and she pleads with Aphrodite for Eros to return. She instinctively seeks union and feels quite humble as she searches for Eros. Although Eros also desires to be reunited, Aphrodite is angry about her son's disobedience of her earlier demand, and she sets up a series of seemingly impossible tasks for Psyche to complete. As the Great Mother, Aphrodite has power over their destiny. First, Aphrodite demands Psyche to quickly sort a huge pile of grain and seeds. Psyche doubts that she will ever be able to complete this task in a short period, when trails of ants begin to help her. The ants represent industrious patience and persistence. By applying these values, she quickly gains the intelligence needed to sift, select, order, and evaluate—all tasks of formal operational thinking that must be achieved in order to communicate clearly before we are available for mature partnerships.

Psyche's second task is to gather some golden fleece from ferocious rams that are as strong and vicious as a major army. When presented with this challenge, Psyche begins to despair. Here the myth demonstrates that when we feel isolated from others, we tend to feel depressed and unlovable. As she looks at the impossibility of this task, the reeds of the river whisper to her that after the rams come to drink, she can easily retrieve wisps of their precious wool left behind in the rushes nearby. Psyche learns from the supple, flowing water plants to use an indirect approach as opposed to having a head-on confrontation. This lesson suggests learning to trust, waiting for things to change, taking only small steps, moving forward a little at a time.

Aphrodite assigns a third and even more difficult task: to obtain a flask of water from the treacherous Styx, river of hate, that separates the world of the living from the world of the dead. Achieving this seems impossible to Psyche for she has not yet learned to enter a deeper level of trust. Suddenly, an eagle appears and dives deep into the swirling water to fill the flask for her. The eagle might be viewed as a symbol of courage that exemplifies Psyche's power when the mind is aligned with love. As we dive deeper into self-love, we are able to access a sense of courage that lies dormant. The eagle might also symbolize our ability to tap into the flow as a way of thinking and a representation of the intuitive sixth sense.

Eros, who represents self-confidence, remains hidden to Psyche; however, it is as if an invisible thread of connection weaves them together, and their desire to be reunited supports her ability to accomplish the tasks. As she remembers the sensual feelings of love that she shared with Eros, Psyche grows stronger and wiser. She is able to take action and strive toward her goal to reunite with Eros. We can accomplish nothing if we are processing our thoughts only at the rational, analytical, or biological and behavioral levels as previously described. When we despair and doubt our ability to attract whatever it is we need, then we are not able to progress to a transcendent or superconscious level of knowing. This progression can only result from a continuing desire to give and receive love. Psyche's doubts are an important step toward growing awareness, but she must move beyond her doubtful mind and suicidal desires to embrace the confident inner lover, and then be ready to give and receive love.

THE STORY CONTINUES

Aphrodite cannot believe that this innocent mortal, who she thought was simply a pretty face, is able to accomplish these seemingly impossible tasks. The Great Mother devises a fourth increasingly difficult task. She sends Psyche deep into the underworld, which is full of deadly monsters, to obtain the secrets of youth and beauty from Persephone, who is trapped in Hades for one half of every year. Psyche could be consumed by the dark vortex of the underworld while she captures the box that holds Persephone's beauty secrets. Any one of us can be pulled into a depressing, even deadly, whirlpool of despair if we are continually faced with tasks beyond our current abilities. It is easy to become discouraged when it appears that we cannot succeed no matter how perfectly we affirm and visualize what we want or how hard we wish things were different.

Psyche is ready to give up, once again overcome with despair. Certain she will die, she climbs to the top of a high tower to have a last look at

earth. While in the tower Psyche's inner voice offers guidance for sur-
viving the perilous journey. She becomes aware of specific instructions
to overcome the demons that have the power to devour her. Psyche
must keep focused and not have pity for the various creatures she will
encounter. She is reminded that she must not yield to the feminine inclination to be so compassionate to the needs of others that she neglects
her own desires, and she must avoid the temptation to compare herself
to Persephone, who is even more beautiful than Psyche herself. To accomplish this task, Psyche must keep her balance between a healthy
desire for Eros and the suicidal pull to give up and die. Psyche's visit
to the tower, a structure erected by mortals, could be understood as a
representation of the wisdom of the current culture.

Psyche knows she will encounter the spirits of the dead during her
descent into Hades. This part of her journey represents a new dimension of awareness beyond the attraction to physical beauty. Renewed
strength stems from gaining balanced, emotional health. Psyche care-
fully follows the instructions she received while in the tower, and she is
able to obtain the box.

In spite of the fact that the jealous Aphrodite instructed Psyche not to
open the box, the curious young woman defies the Great Mother's command. Instead of finding beauty secrets, it is as if she reopened the box
of doubt and shame. This act puts her into a trancelike sleep, similar to
Sleeping Beauty or Snow White, when all of life is suddenly held in abey-
ance. This turn of events may symbolize the need to focus deeply in order to discover the essential power of inner beauty and the true essence
of self-love. Eros, once again in defiance of his mother, awakens Psyche.
Her perseverance has made her worthy and because she is in Hades, he
has the power to rescue her. Psyche and Eros are a demonstration of
defying parental control and overcoming outworn societal conventions.
Love has conquered the negative power of Aphrodite's jealousy. Encouragement and strength came from desiring the inner lover and triumph-
ing over the doubtful mind by shining the light of awareness.

CONTINUING INTERPRETATION

Another way of looking at this myth is to see that all forms of love symbolize more than a sensual game played out in the dark. Psyche was
persistent in her desire for a bond with her inner lover, represented by

Eros. This motivation overcomes the unenlightened command of the ego for self-love to remain hidden. Pathways to discovering the lover can only be found when we make time to identify our own desires and to truly love our innermost self. Taking steps toward self-love is essential before we attempt to establish partnerships with others. As we complete the various tasks placed before us, we mature and therefore become more willing and able to settle into love that transcends the ego. We birth an Integrated Self once we recognize that strength and wisdom come from within. Heart and mind mature through mutual desire and devotion. This perseverance for a relationship between the physical, mental, emotional, and spiritual aspects represents the necessary connections for creating social intelligence and loving compassion.

When mind and heart agree, the result is awareness of our higher power. In the myth, this connection becomes embodied by the birth of a daughter who is half mortal and half god. She is called *Hedone* in Greek or *Voluptas* in Latin, and she signifies the delights of joy and pleasure that are available when we are no longer ruled by a judging father god or jealous mother goddess. We open to blissful options when we let go of limited mental ideals and bodily emotions that desire physical beauty and drive us toward sexual experiences. Joy and pleasure represent the true love of mutual attraction. To achieve this, we must stop any illusions and projections that involve game playing. As we learn more skills regarding intuitive knowing, we move toward a greater capacity for into-me-see. Understanding the ISIS Wheel of Intimacy mentioned in the previous chapter is a demonstration of how to achieve new levels of union in various relationships. When any partnership remains in only one portal, rather than incorporating the spiritual, mental, physical, and emotional aspects, we miss opportunities to grow in each of these arenas. Physical aspects can simply include doing activities together.

GROWTH THROUGH AWARENESS

Another interpretation of this story focuses on personal growth if we use gender inclusive language rather than thinking about Psyche and Eros as female and male. In the ancient myth, intelligence or MIND was represented as feminine (Psyche), and the love or EMOTION as the masculine (Eros). Modern interpretations of heart and mind have twisted this perspective. In past centuries, the acceptable norm was that masculine meant more intelligent and less emotional, with a greater connection to the divine. Emotions were considered feminine traits and they were part of the unconscious mind that represented a lower state of being. Women were viewed as undeveloped and passive. Mental processing was in the realm of the more developed, active, and conscious masculine. People were either rational males or irrational females; there was nothing in between. In his writings and teaching, Jung argued against the current thinking of his time that women have no soul. The concept of being less than divine and having no soul was one justification for men's dominance over women, and although it may seem silly in retrospect, other groups were also denied civil rights for this same reason. This dualistic, either/or thinking established a basic precept of early psychological teachings.

A different interpretation regarding this standard was provided by one of Jung's outstanding students, Erich Neumann, who was best known for his theories on the changes that needed to take place in relation to the idea of men's domination. Neumann began to deconstruct the current thinking of the 1950s about the same time that television began its contributions to eventual change in how we view gender roles. Neumann, who often used Greek mythology as the base for his theories, practiced psychoanalysis in Israel. He is known for his philosophical and theological approach to therapeutic relationships, in contrast to the more clinical concerns that were based in England and the United States during this time. Although Jung and Neumann both wrote before the second wave of feminism, their work was instrumental in bringing about significant changes in gender roles.

Neumann's interpretation notes that from a symbolic Jungian perspective, Eros is Psyche's inner masculine side. Neumann's commentary recalls Jung's process of *individuation*, which describes what happens as we mature and move away from parental influence. This is the time when we become our own authority. For Jung, the immature man or woman identified with personal qualities that are symbolically related to specific gender stereotypes. Neumann takes this thinking a step further. He saw the tasks that Psyche, as mind, had to solve involved a component of relatedness. Relatedness was considered a female quality and independence was strictly in the masculine domain. Neumann understood both masculine and feminine attributes to be personifications of elements in the collective unconscious. Neumann notes that often the mind was in despair and not knowing what to do because it had lost sight of love. He points out that in the myth, the feminine unconscious gradually matured into an attitude of knowing and the conscious masculine became more aware of emotions. Relatedness is important because all forms of love outlined earlier can lead to a greater understanding of self.

INTEGRATION BEGINS

Eros and Psyche are attributes of the collective unconscious that contain combinations of both masculine and feminine characteristics. These characteristics have the potential to be constructed and developed in a variety of ways. Jung taught that early in life children construct a belief system about what it means to be male or female. He indicates that beliefs form as we observe everyday encounters with the opposite gender. Of course, gender roles were more rigid in his time than they are today, therefore the division of heart and mind was more obvious. When the head and heart are in opposition, it is difficult to tap the intuitive knowing required for healthy, intimate partnerships to manifest. When our mental and emotional systems are in balance, this union allows for the possibility of transcendent love that surpasses all fears. This is the desired outcome of emotional and social intelligence.

In most cultures, the first opportunity to intensify maturation and become a fully developed adult begins with an erotic encounter outside family boundaries. Jung and others have suggested that as men and women approach these relationships, we project our personal beliefs about the qualities of masculinity or femininity onto potential partners. Jung taught that men achieved fullness of self by confronting their irrational side personified by the intuitive feminine *anima* and that women, who were often more in touch with their intuitive side, became more rational and analytical as they come to understand their internal masculine *animus*.[4]

Jung realized it was necessary that we each develop all of our potentials. He taught that the best way to do this was to incorporate the unconscious influences of each gender into our conscious personality, and later developed what we now know as the Myers-Briggs Type Indicator (MBTI), which will be discussed later. He felt that too often we fail to recognize qualities that are symbolically the opposite of our birth gender and therefore limit our potential if we only develop those that match our biology. Jung speculated that men project the characteristics they desire onto one certain woman. In contrast, he found that many women projected the qualities they lacked onto most men, as if every male possessed what she most wanted for herself. He observed that men focused on finding the perfect female, while most women internalized that they were somehow less than all men, therefore lowering her self-esteem.

Thanks to Jung's insights, women's roles began to change. One of Jung's students, Demaris Wehr, named three masculine and feminine stereotypes to be challenged. She suggested that men needed to seek "unexplored depths of feeling, relationship, and sensitivity" and that women must enter the world of the "spirit, erudition, and the power of the word."[5] Since her writing, many opportunities have increased for women to participate in the world of spirit, education, and creativity. Beginning in the early 1970s, many more women realized the power of achieving a higher level of education, and many men learned to identify with feelings of sensitivity. Women found ways to articulate the power of the word as they created opportunities to publish their work and to enter professions such as law, medicine, and the ministry. This turnabout is a result of women, who were also mothers, attaining a higher level of education, which led to their sons relinquishing some of their power. Some women also became willing to join the military.

PARENTS ARE GODLIKE

Most of us begin life in the shadow of powerful Mother-Father archetypes, even when the father is absent or the mother is uninterested or vice versa. Children and teens often project onto their parents the struggle they must experience to become independent. Parents are surprised when they find themselves perceived by their children as either divine or demonic characters.

In the current culture in most developed societies, it is no longer generally acceptable that all women will simply follow men's lead, while the men provide for the women, as was the biological necessity in the past. Young women and men must now accept personal responsibility for all decisions and their outcomes. We take personal responsibility when we recognize that what is happening to us is no longer a function of strict parental or societal control or the arbitrary will of the gods. It has been a monumental step of development to realize that we are responsible for our own decision making and to understand the consequences of our actions.

In the past four decades, feminist scholarship has continuously questioned gender roles and self-actualization, and noted one basic difference between boys and girls who were raised with women as the primary caregivers. This statement sums up these findings: "The Girl baby realizes she is the same as the mother and easily develops a relational Self. The Boy baby notices he is different from mother, and easily becomes more individualized. As a result, Girls must spend the rest of their lives learning how to be separate individuals, and Boys must learn how to be in relationship." Almost forty years later, we may giggle at the truth of this statement, and hope some progress has been made. Although there are positive changes, they have created havoc because previous traditions around sexuality, marriage, divorce, and gender roles are now in constant upheaval. Because of current shifting roles in most cultures, stereotypical gender identities are no longer clearly defined.

CHILDREN ARE CHANGING

Only recently have we broken down masculine and feminine stereotypes by encouraging men to develop deep feelings, intimate relationships, and sensitivity, and allowing women to find the power of their words by accessing the worlds of spiritual and scientific education. This provides the opportunity to rethink the process of Psyche's development. It is useful to realize that it is co-dependent to look to someone else to bring us to fulfillment. The integration of heart and mind must first happen on an independent, intrapersonal level before true love and compassion can manifest on an interdependent, interpersonal level.

In mythological terms, integrating heart and mind is often described as being devoured by a monster, as an example, when Aphrodite sent Psyche into the underworld. If we are to become an Integrated Self, we must object to blind servitude of parental and cultural authority. This does not imply that mother or father, or other women or men, are monsters any more than our cultural conditioning is monstrous. It merely suggests that to find our own identity and fully individualize we must take the initiative to move beyond old-fashioned (monstrous) ways of thinking to make room for new thoughts and to understand new concepts.

YET ANOTHER INTERPRETATION

Much research in recent years has explained the limits and extremes of parental influence on personality. The Human Genome Project confirmed that the child's genetic makeup determines the nature of temperament. The fact remains that family and cultural influences, the nurturing aspect, also affect the outcome of personality. Returning to the myth, we can better understand how it illustrates this process of integration. Note that first it was necessary for the mind to refuse the heart's command to love blindly. When the psyche, our mental aspect, chooses to shine the light of love, the heroic journey begins. This journey includes coming to terms with the internalization of the masculine and feminine stereotypes and overcoming the demons in the quest for conscious development. The emotional aspect of love's command to remain in the embrace of darkness is an extension of the original unconscious state of unity that begins in the womb. In infancy, the mind (psyche) remains bound to the heart (eros) in the paradise of dark unconsciousness. As we mature and the mind awakens, original parental ties dissolve. For some, this causes feelings of separateness both from our parents and from what we understand to be the creator or any divine connection.

In the myth, Eros loses trust in Psyche, and he runs from her when she shines the light on their connection. Although this act brings the importance of love into the light, this illumination is followed by thoughts and feelings of guilt, doubt, shame, inferiority, and loneliness. The various tasks that Psyche accomplished provide examples of ways we develop emotional and social intelligence. The ants as patient teachers reflect the ability to sift, select, correlate, and evaluate; through them we can better understand Erikson's stage of industry versus inferiority. This skill of selectivity or discrimination allows us to make conscious choices about career, religion, and politics, as well as the decision of whom and how to love or not love. This is also an example of the tension around identity and role confusion, an illustration of the biological level of being, and overcoming the demons of fear and guilt.

In the second task, when Psyche must gather the Golden Fleece from the dangerous rams, Neumann sees the rams as the destructive power of the mechanistic death principle and the water reeds as the vegetative wisdom of growth. For Neumann, the feminine unconscious wisdom is to wait, therefore to avoid confronting the rams as masculine consciousness directly. Just as with the first task, Neumann sees the fulfillment of this task as the product of a fruitful contact between masculine and feminine, conscious and unconscious, the light with the dark. It is an illustration of resolving the tension of intimacy versus isolation, a balance of waiting and acting, stillness and activity. The activity taking action is an example of the behavioral level of being that allows us to move to the personal level when we can take power over the demons of shame and grief.

Neumann translates Psyche's third task as a quest for the vitality of life. Psyche has to catch some water (flow), which defies containment. He interprets the eagle that comes to Psyche's aid as a symbol characterizing maturity and self-actualization on the personal level. As we become individual vessels, our bodies provide specific form to the eternal movement of the life force. This means we need to encompass the powerful, vital life force which is neither masculine nor feminine. We often must release old ways of thinking before we are able to embrace the new. Neumann's view is that the first three tasks represent a confrontation with the negative masculine principle manifested as "masculine promiscuity" (seeds), "the deadly masculine" (rams), and the "uncontainable masculine" (stream of life). In each case, Psyche must overcome the negative or masculine potential, in order to integrate the positive or feminine aspects and overcome the demon of lies, illusion, and projections.

Most myths and fairy tales have three tasks, but in this case there was also a fourth. The number four is a symbol for wholeness in various numerology systems and provides meaning for the last task. Psyche must journey to the underworld and this time she is aided by a new structure of knowledge through the symbol of the tower, which represents the common, popular culture. Neumann believes that the strength Psyche accumulated by carrying out the first three tasks enabled her to face the most difficult task of all, a direct battle with suicidal thoughts. This journey into the darkness represents a struggle with the feminine principle embodied in the alliance of Aphrodite and Persephone who

personify beauty and motherhood, previously viewed as the sole requirements for feminine fulfillment. In the past, women were expected
to be beautiful, to be seen and not heard. In some cases, this continues
today. Many women feel they would rather be dead than show their age.
Some women, including mothers and daughters, often find themselves
competing over who is more beautiful. Hopefully this is changing as
more women accept themselves as intelligent, spiritual beings, as well as
physical, emotional beings. Psyche's completion of the various tasks was
a dramatic way of illustrating the dangers encountered in an attempt to
incorporate new dimensions and depths of compassion.

Only when the integration of the body's mind with the emotional,
spiritual aspects is complete we can overcome the demon of illusion
that portrays tangible, objective reality as the only reality. When we
substitute energy, as the vital life force connecting through the upper
and lower chakras, we can remove judgment of positive-negative gender
concepts. This allows everyone to embrace the sixth sense of intuitive
knowing that leads to emotional and social well-being. The birth of the
daughter at the end of the myth is often interpreted as "the birth of
the divine child," which in Jungian terms is the fruit of becoming an
individual. The fact that she was named Hedone or Voluptas, meaning
pleasure or *joy*, represents the connection of a mystical union far beyond the illusion that only what we see, hear, smell, taste, or touch is all
that exists. We can understand this union as the evolution of conscious
awareness. We speed up this evolutionary process when both men and
women set intentions and commit their attractions to include all four
quadrants while creating healthy and balanced understanding in every
aspect of all partnerships.

ตะ 12 ๘

OPENING CONNECTIONS

Taking time to reflect on the various tensions from each developmental stage provides an opening where a mature Integrated Self can emerge. Limited thinking is the root of dependence. Eastern ways of looking at health and well-being can help us eliminate addictions, depression, and feelings of oppression. Releasing worn-out negative patterns brings freedom, joy, and pleasure.

***

Myths have the power to reveal the energetic tensions that move amid the various gods. Simultaneously these same tensions can influence the people who read them today. The potentially playful and powerful synthesis of ideas found in ancient myths is often subdued when a more analytical mode of thinking takes over. As the myth of Psyche and Eros reveals the connection between the vital life force of the body (eros) and the linear mind (psyche), it can also illustrate the energetic union between the lower and the higher chakras. According to most authors, the higher chakras represent abstract, liberating thoughts and the lower chakras embody manifestation on this plane of existence. As our internal systems become integrated, the balance of power can shift. When this happens the higher chakras work in conjunction with the lower chakras to create success and harmony.

The practice of discovering the lover within includes observing our body's mind through the senses. As we become aware of how consciously seeing, hearing, smelling, tasting, and touching improves our well-being, we are able to attain a higher level of overall health. As we become willing to eliminate substances that cause illness and thoughts and attitudes that are not for the highest good, the sixth intuitive sense motivates the inner healer. This means the body's mind attains feelings of wholeness. On the other hand, there are times perscription drugs and surgery are required, along with a positive attitude, to attain the desired outcome. And in yet other cases, the illness leads to inevitable death no matter which system of healing has been activated. The fact of life is that we all eventually die. An Integrated Self knows this and does whatever it takes to create a life that is as full and fruitful as possible.

OBSERVATION IS THE KEY TO BALANCE

Early developmental psychologists, such as Freud and Jean Piaget, observed healthy children advancing through age-related phases. Erikson's work added adult stages. Later, Maslow and Mikulas proposed ideas not related to age but based on fulfillment of a need or acquisition of a skill. These theories are useful to understanding that we are dynamic and ever-changing beings moving from birth to death. When we consider nurture and nature as constant components of outer and inner influences, we have the opportunity to connect and balance physical-mental and emotional-spiritual aspects. If we include the idea that each organ system within the body is located in an area designated by a particular chakra, we can grasp how this symbol system might be descriptive of what happens when the body's mind is out of balance.

Holistic modalities, including meridian-based therapies, have uncovered that many mental and physical disorders originate from previous trauma. Integrative approaches outline healing practices that address the client or patient's entire life story. Most authors who embrace chakra work describe how blocks or leaks in the flow between each chakra may affect our personal cycles and influence our partnerships with others. Some practitioners who believe in reincarnation consider the possibility that we may have carried the trauma from one lifetime to the next, but a discussion of this is not necessary in the elementary understanding of how these systems work.

To better understand the integration of Eastern and Western thought, we again look to imbalances or traumas that correspond to an age-related developmental stage. Some authors compare each chakra to a seven-year cycle that has a particular theme. These themes begin during a cycle, but often they are not completed during these specific seven years. This model is flexible and the pattern is not the same for everyone, especially children and teens who mature more rapidly or those who lag behind. Many people do not fit any standard pattern due to circumstances far beyond their control. Therefore, the outline that follows does not imply that we move through these issues in this exact order. Often the correlation with the corresponding chakra overlaps with the next because we are continuously encountering the issue presented, until we are willing and able to let go of any tension or trauma. Sometimes a secondary trauma can occur when something happens to someone close to us. For instance, if a child has an accident, this will cause a traumatic response for the caregiver.

GAINING CONTROL

Most theories of holism include the notion that nonresolution of stress and tension will produce an illness or discomfort later in life. Illness and disease manifest as physical aches and pains, emotional depression, or spiritual frustration. Body-centered methods of understanding illness apply the suggestion that a primary pattern, or center of attention, is present during each stage of growth. This center links to our sense of personal identity. Anodea Judith and others have found that healing through increased awareness of the aura and chakra systems can reverse mental anxiety and physical symptoms. Some find this connection also leads to longevity.

Our body's mind and emotional spirit require constant renewal in order to thrive. Every crossroad throughout our lifespan presents an opportunity for change. Some cultures view these crossroads as *rites of passage*. As an example, one day Caroline Myss was teaching about tribal cultures when she had a flash of intuitive knowing that revealed a correlation of the chakras with the Catholic sacraments and the Jewish Tree of Life.[1] Her intuitions have provided new insights into the mysticism of Western religious beliefs and their possible integration with Eastern systems. These interesting and complicated explanations are beyond the scope necessary for the basic understanding of the physical, mental, spiritual, and emotional connections presented in this model but might prove useful in taking your understanding a step further. The underpinnings of Myss' interpretations are included in the following age-related explanations. It is important to note that as conscious evolution is progressing these propositions that relate to the expansion or contraction of each chakra may occur at earlier or later in life.

IN THE BEGINNING

The newborn starts out merged with her or his mother and gradually becomes a separate self. From birth to age seven, we become oriented to time and space. The first (root) chakra is the foundation of *physical identity and self-preservation.* It involves concerns of survival, security, fear, and trust. Myss sees the energy content as tribal power, which archetypically denotes group identity, group force, group willpower, and belief patterns beyond those of the family. Loyalty, honor, and justice are part of this tribal consciousness. First chakra energy can manifest in our need for logic, order, and structure. Stability most often originates in the family unit and early social environments. The work of the first chakra is to record physical data at face value. The young child's brain produces literal perceptions until we are able to construct metaphors of explanation such as those used in the defense mechanisms previously described. As we mature, it is important to reevaluate and reframe what may or may not have happened to us as children. This is a necessary step when we tune into our body's mind in order to comprehend the simple fact that our physical biology is dynamic and constantly changing. But if we pretend to be ignorant of this progression of biological changes and have a static mindset that ignores the fact that we begin to age from the moment we are born, the resulting physical changes become an unnecessary cause of distress. As an example, we must accept that we cannot perform the same physical activities as we progress through these seven-year cycles. On the other hand, it is possible that thoughts and emotions create somatic illness that could be avoided.

In this model, second chakra concerns are *emotional identity and self-gratification*. Freud placed oral, anal, and genital phases in the first seven years and called ages seven to fourteen the *period of latency* where normally there is little interest in sexual desire outside the familial bond. We now know that thoughts and feelings related to sex and lust are active during these years. Most children utilize masturbation, self-pleasuring, or self-soothing activities to apply the pleasure principle of maximizing satisfaction and reducing pain. Erikson's tensions regarding doubt, shame, and guilt are active during this stage. Healthy development means we learn the importance of having our needs for independence met in interdependent ways. As the second chakra becomes activated, we desire to control our physical environment. It represents striving toward an autonomous, dynamic, integrated self. All attachments, both positive and negative, link to the second chakra.

During the first fourteen years, other people become the center of attention. Interactions with authority figures begin to control our lives. The depth of impact varies from family to family. Between ages five to fourteen, children form attachment bonds that extend beyond the first caregivers, who in many cases are women. For instance, father figures and grandparents become important. Other caregivers also have an effect on the child's life, which later impacts the understanding of gender roles. Healthy children become more independent, taking initiative and being industrious, but feelings of inferiority can also begin at this time. This is the age when most bullying occurs and shame can become overwhelming. Operant conditioning is at its peak and consequences are effective in controlling behavior. Many teachers report that complex theories and questions of boredom also begin at this time as well as the challenge of managing both creative energy and erotic relationships. The power of choice resides in this area of the body close to the reproductive and elimination organs, reminding us that in order to produce, we must also eliminate. This reminder highlights the importance of letting go of old clutter in order to bring newness and aliveness into our lives.

From ages fourteen to twenty-one, personal power and self-esteem call our attention, as well as questions about earning money. Strong confrontational issues of *ego identity and self-definition* surround the third chakra. Known as the *hara, tanteim*, or *solar plexus*, this gravitational center of the body is located in the area of the navel. It is a central point of balance, the place of will. During this period of life, we bond with peers, risking failure and incompetence while hoping to achieve personal identity. This is when most of us begin to separate from our family. We must find our place in the larger world, which includes decisions about occupation, religion, politics, and the development of a personal philosophy. Concrete operational skills and moral development come into play during this time period. Freud labeled this the phallic stage. Attention turns toward questions of gender identity and sexual orientation. The third chakra is said to mediate between the primarily external characteristics displayed in the first and second chakras and the internalized awakening of individual consciousness. In the third chakra, the center of attention shifts from how we relate to those around us to how we relate to our self. We often ignore or overly exaggerate the ideal of self-love during this period. The decisions we make as we move into adulthood affect the rest of our lives. Whether or not to become a parent is one of the most important decisions we must make, yet random sexual urges often influence this important decision. Ages sixteen to thirty-six are main childbearing years, although some women produce children when they are younger, older, or not at all, and some men are able to impregnate indefinitely.

By ages twenty-one to twenty-eight the most challenging issues are *social identity and self-acceptance*. This is the transitional age of becoming a mature adult. We are aware of the emotional power of the fourth chakra in the area of the heart and lungs. As children most of us react to situations with a full range of emotions: love, hope, despair, hate, envy, jealousy, and fear, but as adults we are now challenged to mask these emotions and to avoid the demons. At this age, most societies expect people to generate an emotional climate of confidence, steadiness, and compassion. During this time, the power of love in all of its forms is introduced as we make decisions about bonding with a particular partner and establish our philosophy about marriage and children. Whether we choose one or many partners, it is important for an Integrated Self to establish intimacy with friends and family rather than becoming isolated and indifferent to those who were previously closest to us. Simultaneously, we are working on issues of understanding, empathy, and generosity, including both giving and receiving. The fourth chakra resonates with the emotional, feeling perceptions that determine the quality of lives much more than the mental, thinking perceptions.

Many people from age twenty-eight to thirty-five focus on inner work. *Creative identity and self-expression* become the centers of attention in this fifth, throat chakra. For many, art and music become important, and we are more aware of aesthetic values. Communications and creativity take the forefront, as most of us seek success in our career and desire to establish a home base. During this period, we grow closer to long-term friends beyond family, and we become more transparent as we achieve a greater sense of self. The throat represents the center of choice and consequence. We gain an understanding of receptivity and reciprocity, and learn to surrender as we both talk and listen. The location of the throat chakra lies between the emotional and the mental aspects. Mental energy provides power to participate in the external world, and emotional energy powers our personal domain. If heart and mind do not communicate, one will dominate the other, causing fear, mistrust, shame, doubt, guilt, inferiority, confusion, isolation, stagnation and despair which can result in not being able to speak our truth. This in turn results in a loss of integrity, which may influence the way we act and react toward others. Myss has found that one of our greatest fears is that we will have no authority or power of choice within our tribe or within our personal and professional partnerships. Knowing this presents an opportunity to be responsive rather than reactive, which means that we pause and think about a deliberate response rather than having a hasty, automatic reaction. Every choice we make, every thought and feeling we have, is an act of power that has biological, environmental, social, personal, and global consequences, whether we express them outwardly through words and behaviors or simply turn inward. Conscious evolution begins as soon as we recognize this potential. Therefore, it is essential that we take personal responsibility for our thoughts as well as our behaviors as early in the life cycle as possible.

From age thirty-five to forty-two the main focal point is the sixth chakra, the third eye, the power of mind, the seat of *archetypal identity and self-reflection*. This center links to our reasoning ability, intelligence, and psychological characteristics. In many cases, psychic powers and the sixth sense of intuition become most fully attuned at this point. A unique combination of facts, fears, personal experiences, and memories are continually active within the body's mind and emotional spirit. Many people wonder if there is another incarnation beyond this lifetime or if it is simply the awakening of superconsciousness. As the third eye opens, some people report clairvoyant seeing or visions. Most people become more introspective as we examine what we know and what we believe to be true. During this period, we often pay more attention to our dreams and questions of personal reality; by doing this we activate lessons that can lead to greater wisdom. The mental center of the third eye calls us to confront our shadow side and its attributes as we learn about detachment. We acknowledge that most of what happens to us is not a personal confrontation. Myss describes this opening as a time when we realize that there is neither one person nor a group of people who will determine our life's path.[2] When unexpected change happens, we recognize through symbolic insight and an impersonal mind that a larger dynamic appears to move us along the path. Erikson's word for this is *generativity*. This suggests a vision that relates to supporting future generations. In a sustainable ecological climate, young adults take responsibility not only for their own children and grandchildren but also for the next seven generations. When the third eye opens, we move toward loving compassion with those we do not even know, such as in xenia and agape types of love.

The crown or seventh chakra opens to *universal identity and self-knowledge*. This opening often follows major life changes that may occur between the ages of forty-two to forty-nine. This is a period when many seek a more direct connection to the creator or universal source. In Erikson's words, we avoid despair and find ego-integrity through acceptance of self and others. Many healthy adults attain a transpersonal or superconscious level of knowing that occurs as crown chakra opens to connect. As this is accomplished, we feel fulfilled and ready to complete the cycle, allowing our spiritual nature to become an integral part of our life. Although some people begin to worry about death at this point, it does not mean we are ready to die at age fifty; most are at the mid-point of lifespan. As we age, these cycles begin anew and repeat again and again.

BEFORE THE END OF LIFE

Libido, as the motivating life force, shifts its focal point during later life because there is no longer a preoccupation with questions regarding pregnancy. It is untrue that all people lose interest in sex as they get older. In most families, this is the time when adult children produce babies of their own and many become grandparents. In healthy, conscious aging, the erotic, creative energy becomes stronger when the drive for procreative, penetrative sex diminishes. Feelings of desire remain active and alive when we foster meaningful partnerships both with our selves and with others. When our energy moves throughout the body's mind with conscious activity and mindfulness, we are capable of experiencing the flow of vital life force until we die, although for some this is not true due to physical limitations or medical intervention. If creative energy is not moving, the resulting problems produce a lesser quality of life, yet many people choose to control other symptoms with a combination of prescription drugs that may be responsible for the loss of vitality. To avoid many physical, mental, and emotional problems, it is important to recognize our need for happiness and pleasure throughout the lifespan. The earlier we begin to follow through on fantasies and ideas, the sooner we will manifest success and see the results of our dreams coming true.

The Path of Manifestation is revealed when we activate energy from the higher to lower chakras, as opposed to moving vital life force through the Path of Liberation, in which the flow is seen as traveling upward.[3] Any project we undertake begins with an idea. Ideas form in the crown area above the head where we connect with the collective unconscious or superconscious. For instance, we get the idea that we want to search for a new job or begin a course of study. Now that we have the initial idea, we begin to visualize possibilities from the area of the third eye. We have many choices to make our idea reality. We begin to explore prospective jobs or courses of study to see what may be available. We might read about various colleges or research a university. We think about a visit to a particular school or job location. Then, we start to talk about the many courses of study or jobs that are available. We could schedule time with a counselor to explore the variety of offerings. We might actually make an appointment with prospective employers or have conversations with friends. This is throat chakra activity.

Next, the idea moves into the area of the heart. Here we sort out our wants and needs, our desires and skills. What is it we love to do? What will make our heart sing? We connect our passion with our words and continue to visualize the possible action steps. The potential for our idea becomes clear. The next step involves activity in the power center of the solar plexus. Here is where we check our gut feelings and reactions to the research we are doing. This area represents will power and we make the actual decision to move forward or not.

Once we decide to go after specific aspects of our idea, we need creativity to know which action steps to take. This entails planning time, spending resources, and moving our energy forward from the previous place of comfort. Making changes in our daily routines involve the creative, flowing attributes of the second chakra. Finally, the project takes root and eventually it can manifest on the physical plane. It is no longer simply an idea. We enroll in a class or send out our resume and actually give notice to our employer or let others know we are moving forward. All of these are first chakra, survival activities.

THE SEARCH FOR SUCCESS

When we reach our goals we are happy, and achieve peace of mind. Every stage of life requires that effort be put into the quest for joy and satisfaction. Victor Frankl's *Man's Search for Meaning*, written in 1956 after his release from a prison camp, remains one of the best examples of finding peace in tough times. The twenty-first century has found several authors asking; "What is happiness? Why do we avoid or overindulge in pleasure?" Provocative books such as Riane Eisler's *Sacred Pleasure* suggest people have systematically been discouraged from seeking pleasure for centuries; but this is changing as the next generation becomes aware of this basic biological need. Gina Ogden, who developed the ISIS Wheel, reminds us in *Return of Desire* that in order to know true happiness and pleasure, it is necessary to engage the mental, emotional, and spiritual along with the physical portions of the vital life force. They support the concept that pleasure will never be found solely in the drive for sex, the satisfaction of hunger, or being aggressive; we also require a sense of accomplishment and empowerment that goes far beyond sensual stimulation.

William Mikulas defines *pleasure* as a short-lived experience due to an enjoyable event or activity and *happiness* as long-term satisfaction with life. He suggests that all four levels of being must be engaged in having a purpose for living. *Biological* happiness begins when endorphins activate the pleasure areas of the brain. This includes Freud's pleasure principle regarding the drive to maximize pleasure and minimize tension. Those who enjoy the art of tattooing and/or piercing, branding, or cutting say they experience pain as a pleasurable stress reducer. This is also true for people who engage in acts that include playing with bondage and discipline, dominance, and submission, slave and master, often referred to as BDSM. At the biological level, Mikulas suggests that pleasure and happiness are largely homeostatic and hedonistic, meaning that we choose activities to feel balanced for our own gratification. We base happiness on an individualized experience of bodily, erotic expression and find feelings of contentment and satisfaction in that way.

At the *behavioral* level of being, maximizing the reinforcement of awards and minimizing punishment define happiness. This includes the intensity of the pain-pleasure spectrum but particularly relates to the social reinforcement of acceptance. Some children are said to have developmental delays that could be alleviated by working with the body's mind. Common sources of happiness can include rewarding tasks and enjoyable leisure time activities and hobbies, as well as agreeable and fulfilling sexual and nonsexual partnerships. At the *personal* level, depression can occur when we have unrealistic goals and expectations for our self or others. Mikulas proposes that in order to promote happiness it is important to recognize four interrelated attitudes:

- First, attainment of an affective, satisfying reality principle. This is similar to Freud's notion of needing to restrain natural instincts in order to maintain personal safety and facilitate interaction with others.
- Second, constructive mental associations or metaphors that include a sense of optimism, a healthy self-concept, and high self-esteem.
- Third, the realization that we are capable of influencing the world in a desired direction. This includes understanding our locus of control, defining feelings of mastery, and realizing that everything we do has a powerful effect.
- Fourth, we need to incorporate supportive and nurturing interactions with family, friends, and co-workers into our lives.

This brings us to the *transpersonal* level, where some people experience peace of mind, innate delight, and bliss consciousness because of what they refer to as a religious experience. Stanislav Grof writes about nonordinary states of consciousness.[4] He and others find that non-consensual reality can occur as a result of using substances such as LSD and marijuana. In addition, a drug called *ecstasy* is said to open the heart and provide the same feelings. According to writers such as

Jack Kornfield, Ken Keyes Jr., and Alan Watts, peace of mind can also occur when we disengage from the melodrama of our personal reality, reduce related attachments, and cultivate unconditional acceptance of whatever is going on around us. This means detachment from attempting to control others. Attachment and dependence on others also takes away from self-reliance, which is often what happens in cases of mental and emotional illness.

We integrate independence when we slow down, observe our thoughts, and gain inner control. As we gravitate toward the transpersonal level and take time for quiet reflection, we can achieve inner peace of mind.

However, in many cases when various external vibrations bombard us, we reach for legal or illegal substances rather than taking advantage of the great reservoir of resources available within. Dulling physical and mental sensations can lead to various forms of addiction and feelings of oppression and victimization.[5] To be truly free, we must not be attached or overly reliant on anything. Overeating, as well as alcohol, tobacco, and prescription or over-the-counter drugs, all suppress the body's feedback mechanism loop. This includes overindulging in nicotine and marijuana, as well as chocolate or caffeine, an ingredient found in many drinks such as tea, coffee, and energy boosters. Once we are able to reach the *transcendent* or superconscious level, we are able to perceive and appreciate all elements of life equally. We cease to judge things as "good or bad" and easily maintain moderation in all of our activities and behaviors.

Balance needs to be cultivated and nurtured in every aspect in order to attain greater *equanimity*. For instance, we need balance in the amount of sleep we get, the nourishment we eat and drink, the quantity of work, play, and exercise, time spent alone and with friends and family. Balance is also the key mechanism for working with the aura and chakra systems as a path to successful pleasure and happiness. Mikulas points out that pleasure contributes to happiness, but it seldom works to find happiness by primarily seeking pleasure.

When we have a balanced state of mind, pleasure lasts longer and therefore creates happiness. Inner control provides opportunities for personal growth and conscious evolution. Self-actualization and transcendence require stability as we gain knowledge of our intuitive sense. As we evolve, we attain lasting inner peace. We are less influenced by outer circumstances. We can find happiness and pleasure when there is balance in the upper and lower chakra system, and we take advantage of the gifts of nature such as the sun, ocean, lakes, rivers, trees, and plants as a way to refresh our personal energy field.

Most teachers mentioned throughout this book suggest that alignment and balance can happen quickly on all levels, when we simply take a deep breath, set an intention to hold awareness of clearing the chakras of any leaks or blockages, and cleansing the aura of various energetic forces. Using the colors of the rainbow as outlined earlier is especially helpful. This need not take longer than brushing our teeth or taking a shower; however, it must be done as often as we brush our teeth or shower. Components for achieving balance and stability include keeping the past in perspective to gain an understanding of the future. This means paying attention to the present moment and staying in the now.

Input from all of our senses in the form of pleasing light, color, sound, smells, and tastes of nutritional elements, and the feel of various textures all become major factors in the creation of joy when combined with mindfulness and meditation. Vibrations are components of healing modalities in many cultures from around the world and because they produce results the Western health care model is beginning to acknowledge them as part of the integrative medicine of the future. By opening to all of our senses, gaining control of what is happening around us, and taking time to go within, most people can access the innate delight, bliss consciousness, and experience of ecstasy. The good vibrations of pleasure, happiness, joy, and satisfaction are within the reach of an Integrated Self. They are our birthright!

~13~

BLENDING GENDERS

Men and women are both affected by the popular culture that surrounds us. To be empowered, we must recognize how cultural attitudes regarding gender influence our personal growth so that we do not get lost in the complicated labyrinth of another person's characteristics or requirements about who or how we "should" be.

⟨∞⟩

Throughout history, the birthright of boys and girls has not been equal. For centuries, men have controlled women in various ways. Traditional cultures clearly defined gender roles. When the written word became the method through which we learn and pass on information, women became the property of men, and men created laws that allowed them to have a strong financial hold over women. In recent history, women and men are finding ways to end the war between the sexes and the division of the masculine-feminine split. Becoming more in tune with intuitive knowing has increased our ability to gain greater emotional intelligence and, therefore, to create more balanced partnerships and intimate relations with each other.

During the suffrage movement of the 1920s, women began to meet in order to talk about their roles in the larger society outside of the home.

When Alfred Kinsey first released *Sexual Behavior in the Human Female* in 1953, many people were offended by his highlighting the behaviors of their mothers, sisters, or even grandmothers. No one wanted to know what was happening with women's libido, and few people talked about homosexuality or questions regarding masculinity or femininity. In the late 1950s, scholars were just beginning to discuss women's issues, gender roles, and concerns regarding sexual orientation and gender identity. Most women had limited public roles, and men seldom participated in housework and the raising of children. Only a few women, such as Queen Elizabeth and Indira Gandhi, held positions of power. Therefore, it was difficult for previous generations to even imagine what it meant for women to become capable of reaching their highest potential as fully functioning human beings, not to mention as sexual beings. Other than a few educated white men and a very few, women, most people stayed within strict gender roles. This continues to be as difficult for most men as it is for women.

In 1954, Christine Jorgensen became the first American to have a sex change operation, and others followed—both male to female (MtoF) and female to male (FtoM). More knowledge about sexual orientation has contributed to some people exploring *gender identity*. John Money, a medical psychologist who died in 2006, first suggested a distinction between biological *sex* and gender identity.[1] When someone has uncertainty about her or his gender identity, it is separate from sexual orientation. We now recognize these as two distinct, freestanding categories.

Brave individuals, who do not feel at home in their own bodies and explore the possibility of changing gender through medical intervention, have raised questions regarding what it means to be a "real" man or woman. There is no clear understanding about the difference between biologically based gender differences and those constructed by learned behavior. Identity, like personality, is eventually self-discovered. Every society, and each family within each culture, has a particular historical background that dictates how boys and girls should be raised, and most express expectations regarding behaviors. For instance, some families still believe girls "should be seen and not heard" and that "a woman's place is in the home." Other families teach that boys must be strong and never cry or show any emotions. Many children receive mixed messages, which leave them confused throughout their entire lives.[2]

ROLE MODELS

Any statement about gender differences is always a generality. All people possess attributes designated as masculine or feminine, but there is a difference in degree and balance regarding how people demonstrate these characteristics. The field of gender studies highlights that there are more similarities in some cases and more differences in others. Examples of this are Gabrielle "Coco" Chanel, a dress designer at the turn of the twentieth century, and David Bowie in his Ziggy Stardust performance days. As people began to ask about rights and responsibilities in general, they also questioned appearances and privileges that come with simply looking and/or dressing in certain ways. As television and movies became part of everyone's experience, they portrayed an assortment of cultural stereotypes on the subject of what it means to be male or female.

A paradigm shift began when mass media started to portray role models with a variety of qualities for men and women through both realistic actors and animation. Characters played a broad range of roles beyond what anyone witnessed in his or her own neighborhood. This has meant that since the advent of television in the early 1950s, children have been exposed to a full array of possibilities for observing women and men in various settings, including situation comedies, reality and talk shows, and cartoons. This exposure led to an era of unisex preferences in ways to act and dress. Men and women were striving for equality, and suddenly everyone was wearing tee-shirts, jeans, and sneakers.

TIMES ARE CHANGING

The civil rights activism of the 1960s and simultaneous technological revolution paved the way for consumerism to flourish. During this period, the first oral contraceptives or birth control pills became available. Wives and mothers continued to fight for the right to participate equally in all levels of the work force, and to be equal partners in relationships. Women's willingness to work outside the home benefited the manufacturing of goods. In many households, the wages of both husband and wife were necessary to buy a single-family house with a garage, and soon these homes had more than one car and a television

in every room. Women were now able to gain credit in their own names
and therefore have greater access to material wealth. The divorce rate
soared and women's liberation led to the ideals of feminism, which
held that everyone should have equal rights. The battle of the sexes was
in full swing. A great divide became evident between being feminine
and becoming a feminist. The struggle for equality increased when a
few questioned the accepted paradigm of gender roles. Some people
became aware of the detrimental influence that attitudes of inequality
had on children's development. Consumerism intended to exploit sexuality continues to drive the market. If we do not drive the right kind
of car, use the right skin product, or consume the right beverage, we
will not be seen as powerful, sexy, or successful. This kind of advertise-
ment leaves many wondering what it actually means to be a man or a
woman.

Cultivation of personal masculine and feminine traits is important.
But some fail to achieve this sense of integration. In 1974, Sandra Bem
challenged ideal traits that limit people to an either/or choice with
contradictory qualities.[3] She noted that some people are androgynous,
meaning they present a genderless blend of male and female characteristics that do not fit into any prescribed mold. Previously, you were
male or female, gay or straight, with nothing in between. Acceptance of
gender difference began within the lesbian, gay, and bisexual community. They were the first to embrace those who cross-dress and desire to
present as *gender queer*. When we view the full spectrum of humanity,
we can plainly see evidence of masculine females or feminine males. Today there is a greater occurrence of transsexual or transgender people.
However, gender differences also occur among those who identify as
heterosexual or asexual.

EQUAL RIGHTS FOR ALL?

Up until the 1970s, women were seldom allowed to wear pants in public; today men still have a limited selection of colors and styles available. Perhaps we need to embrace the concept of *Passionate Politics*
as suggested by bell hooks who defines feminism as "the movement to
end the oppression of both men and women." She affirms that we must
transform the enemy within before we can confront the enemy outside.

She names the enemy as sexist thought, which occurs when either men or women act, think, or feel superior to the other.[4]

Women and men have made great strides in the direction of gender equity, but these strides must give us the strength to go further.

Do we define women or men by the clothes they wear? How do we contribute to the division of masculine and feminine in the way we dress and relate to each other?

A thinly veiled investment remains within state laws and how corporations benefit from the regulation of gender. The fashion and beauty industries are significant factors in the recognition of equality between genders. Unisex clothes make us all appear more equal. Some styles accentuate differences, such as short skirts and high heels, which have come back into fashion. Successful men are still required to wear tightly buttoned shirts and ties that resemble nooses around their necks. This makes Psyche's last task regarding "finding the box that represents beauty" still relevant today. It will be interesting to see how things change, as more women become political figures, and men allow themselves to be more comfortable in the way they dress.

CONSTRUCTION OF GENDER

To demonstrate how gender is constructed, William Mikulas applies an established definition of culture that assumes women and men differ in perceptions, values, styles of communication, and approaches to working and playing. According to this definition, women and men have separate cultures. Since the 1960s there has been tremendous change due to the fact that women demanded access to higher education, and some gained positions of influence in most professions, as well as in the political arena. Women have become more visible in the media. Those who are public figures demonstrate that not all women have the same values or approaches to work and play. Just like men, women possess a continuum of communication and problem-solving skills. Women have a broad range in expression of emotions. The more we learn about the great spectrum of humanity that exists around the world, the more we recognize many variations in the characteristics of women and men alike.

Today, when we observe people in various settings, we see that both men and women utilize a variety of strategies for problem solving, building friendships, expressing emotions, and initiating and demonstrating expectations in romantic relationships. In other words, we can observe a spectrum of behaviors because both men and women now have the freedom to communicate and build partnerships with people of both genders. People approach work and play differently, and both men and women apply a variety of strategies for problem solving and expressing emotions.

The second wave of feminism continues to provide conferences and other opportunities where women form circles to focus on raising the low self-esteem that occurs due to cultural and societal conditioning. In the aftermath of the women's liberation movement, men also began to gather in encounter groups that promote healing by providing enthusiastic feedback to each other. These groups encourage men to be more in touch with their feelings, therefore allowing them to be "in touch" with one another's thoughts and feelings as well as sharing hugs. Physical touch between men is very much the societal norm in many cultures. Same-gender groups produce dedicated friendships, partnerships, and relationships where participants help each other to see the projection of shadow more clearly. This kind of deep intimacy and sharing has never before been encouraged.

THE BATTLE CONTINUES

Although structures regarding gender and relationships have become less rigid, people still have strong opinions and take sides on issues large and small. It is worth noting that when it comes to gender presentation, the amount of violence really escalates in attacks against individuals who cross-dress. People who struggle with identity issues or who simply dress as they please are seven to sixteen times more likely to be harassed and murdered than the average American.[5]

In our society, men do not wear skirts. If they appear in a skirt where this is not the cultural tradition, it is assumed they are acting out a feminine role; however, if a woman wears pants, no one thinks she wants to be a man.[6] This change in attitude has created a debate about the way women dress. Some men insist that if a woman wears a short skirt or a low-cut blouse or walks a certain way, she is too provocative and "asking for it." People are often confused about how appropriate sexual advances should be initiated. A healthy sexual encounter is not forced in any way. Sexual partnerships should include the entire physical, mental, spiritual, and emotional aspects of both people. This is true for homosexuals and heterosexuals, as well as bisexuals and transgender people. Sexual activity is best when it is a shared, consensual experience. The goal of any relationship should be to strengthen loving connections. To become a fully Integrated Self, the internal anima and animus need to be in balance.

No one knows exactly how many children are born with ambiguous genitalia, previously called *hermaphrodites*. No concrete boundaries have been established regarding *intersexed conditions*, therefore it remains surrounded with secrecy and deception. The advent of the Internet has made it possible for people who formerly had to contend with the lonely consequences of this condition to be able to educate themselves and to connect with one another. It is now estimated that one in 2,000 children, or five children per day, are born in the United States with visibly intersexed genitalia; this may mean they have some aspect of both male and female, or what the doctors see as ambiguous, which just means that this person does not fit the medical textbook models. Others have invisible mixed chromosome conditions or various hormonal imbalances.[7]

Medical technology regarding sex reassignment through hormone therapy or surgical procedures has evolved so that it is now possible to match how someone feels on the inside with the outward presentation of characteristic traits regarding masculinity and femininity. Most people never entertain a thought about their gender identity, just as the majority never questions their own sexual orientation, but for the minorities who do, it is important to respect their right to choose.

Or is it?

The answer to this question is important in any discussion of self-love. In a perfect world, we would all embrace *agape* and share love unconditionally. When we love everyone without judgment, we free up energy that would otherwise go toward protection from those we fear, simply because we perceive them as different or wrong. One aspect of gaining full intuitive knowing and emotional intelligence is an open, aware mind that accepts and appreciates differences. In order to love all aspects of

186

ourself, we must fully acknowledge all aspects of others. Hate or prejudice that we hold inside hurts us as much as when we direct it outward. For instance, Jerry Falwell is a preacher with many judgments; he boldly says he hates gay behavior and teaches that we do not have to approve of another's behavior to be willing to extend love and good will toward them. But he and many other church leaders fight hard against any kind of lesbian or gay rights, including gay marriage. When those in favor of these initiatives fight back, act in a hate-filled manner, and do not project love, then the vicious circle never ends.

By integrating the shadow of our own anima and animus, we begin to observe that men and women are equally capable of tapping into the intuitive knowing of the sixth sense. We are all a part of a *universal collective*, no matter how rich or poor, large or small, or masculine or feminine we appear. Although we do not always approve of everyone's behavior, we can still extend love and good will. When we are not projecting love, we are often judging and condemning others. Acceptance of difference is one path to peace on earth. Evolving into conscious awareness, both as a universal collective and as individuals, is an aspect of this path. Encounters with other people and their ideas constantly influence our own gender identity and our understanding of sexual attractions.

Fully functioning, mature adults allow for all possible variations of self-actualization and integration. This is something to strive for as we expand our capacity for intimacy through intuition. At the same time, it is also necessary to be aware of our own personal boundaries and the limitations of our tolerance. Only then can we move toward acceptance of those who are different from us and eventually reach the transcendent levels suggested by Maslow and Mikulas, where we recognize that we are all part of the same whole of humanity. This includes the ability to love without judging, and to fill our heart with compassion for those who are different from us.

CHANGING LEVELS

Letting go of childhood assumptions regarding the influence others have over us represents a shift from lower chakra attractions to the genuine love said to be found through the higher chakras. When healthy teenagers focus on the various aspects of love—agape, philia, eros, storge, and xenia—they develop a variety of meaningful partnerships with people they choose, who may be the same or opposite gender. This is very different from the recent past when we expected young adults to find one partnership to last for their entire life while forsaking all others. The public façade of most cultures assumes that neither partner will ever have another romantic relationship, or even a friendship, with anyone of the opposite sex.

We can follow this strain of thinking in order to further express the workings of our internal systems. Around the age of fourteen, we mature from the biological level of the first and second lower chakras to the behavioral level represented by the solar plexus, the third chakra power center. This indicates a change from infantile fascination to conscious loving. For many, the first pull of sexual attraction is to the opposite gender. But it often happens that our first crush is with someone of the same gender. In either case, it is likely the person we are attracted to has a more developed anima or animus than ours.

Connection begins in the fourth and fifth chakra, in the area of the heart and throat, from ages fifteen to twenty-eight, when as teens and young adults we awaken to both the conscious and unconscious factors of what it means to be male or female. We are now fully able to express true emotions, articulate our thoughts, ask questions, and formulate answers. When we begin to think about and plan for the future, the visionary imagination of the sixth chakra or third eye becomes involved. Through trial and error, we define the types of partnerships that are most important to us.

This shift from lower chakra stimulus to upper chakra integration is another opportunity to recognize how sex drive is different from the movement of the energetic vital life force. For example, as these feelings of love energy move up the spine, from the lower chakras to the powerful solar plexus and heart, both men and women begin to recognize that there is more to relationships than the rise and fall of sexual desire. On the other hand, sexual desire is also an important element in mature adult relationships in both opposite and same-sex unions. We strengthen the link between love for self and love for others as personal identity becomes stronger and the roles of women and men become equalized.

MASCULINE AND FEMININE ARCHETYPES

Years after Jung mentioned archetypes describing masculine and feminine attributes, they remain shrouded in personal opinion and cultural values, and this makes them difficult to define or analyze. Christine Herold notes that like subatomic particles, "They can be known only by the traces of their effects in the observer's mind."[8] Projections of the anima and animus create an illusion of understanding, which can mask the fluid nature of men and women. Another analyst, Demaris Wehr, a self-described feminist, acknowledges, "What Jung called the 'feminine' has pointed to what is lacking, undervalued, misunderstood, and feared [in women.]"[9]

Wehr and Herold, among others, are updating the understanding of gender as a spectrum rather than a dualistic opposition. Herold finds that making connections to collective unconscious symbols can "lead us into planes of awareness that draw us away from individual psychology and a sociological understanding of individuation." In her experience, this awareness can lead "to direct encounters with levels of reality offering spiritual awakening or enlightenment." For her this happens through visionary analysis, which "requires unlearning the programmed rationalistic response to language and reclamation of the mystical power of symbols."

Symbols, like myths, can involve all of the senses and resonate in the intuitive systems. Some forms of symbolism include looking at or drawing a mandala or viewing an icon; the sounds of a drum beating, repeating a mantra, or listening to piece of music; the taste of a special food; a certain smell; or the meaning behind a gentle touch. Perhaps symbols aid us in becoming more aware of our humanity and our divinity, regardless of gender, rather than feeling separate. Feelings of separateness and isolation associated with being *either* a man or a woman most frequently occur when we are stuck in strict gender roles and relationship paradigms that no longer serve to bring us together. Becoming aware involves releasing old ways of thinking.

HOPE FOR THE FUTURE

Many new ways are serving to bring us into wholeness or the oneness of being. The goal of most therapy is to be in touch with our highest or spiritual self. Long-term analysis, as prescribed by Freud, is no longer necessary to aid the process of individualization, which means, becoming a separate individual Integrated Self. We can do this by harnessing the experiences and memories from the past to create a vision of our individual, as well as collective, future. Currently, mixed gender groups are gaining popularity. Women and men assist each other toward an understanding of the various aspects of love and affectionate touch. Examples include workshops promoted by the Human Awareness Institute (HAI), tantric circles, and cuddle parties. In addition, many places of worship have begun to emphasize the necessity for women and men, across the spectrum of gender identity and sexual orientation, to come together in order to better understand the differences and similarities that exist among and between all people. Old fashioned, fundamentalist thinking is terrorizing. It is a means of separating people. Hopefully, the election of President Barrack Hussein Obama has begun to change this. Perhaps this is a time the United Nations will become more effective and those who really need to be connected will find peace with one another.

We are more fully conscious and aware when we embrace the importance of joining the mental and physical, mechanical brain-body with the emotional transcendent-superconscious. As an example, the practice of Taoism requires unlearning the programmed, rationalistic response to language and reclaiming the mystical power of symbols. The following story tells of a Hunchback Woman who found conscious awareness, sometimes called enlightenment. When asked where she learned what she knows, the woman answers:

> I have learned it from the son of Ink-writing, the son of Ink-writing learned from the grandson of Chanting-recitation, the grandson of Chanting-recitation from Clear-understanding, Clear-understanding from Quiet-affirmation, Quiet-affirmation learned from Immediate-experience, Immediate-experience from Dramatic-expression, Dramatic-expression from Dark-obscurity, Dark-obscurity from Mysterious-void, and Mysterious-void from Beginning-of-no-beginning.[10]

This short tale, which quickly covers generations of learning and unlearning, expresses profound metaphors for intimate connection, as well as demonstrating that we move both backward and forward in time. The words formed by Ink-writing are only the beginning. Or are they the end result of learning? *What does your intuition tell you?*

Take the opportunity to stop silently processing the words written here and speak them out loud or begin chanting and singing them. This will provide the direct experience of creating sounds with our voice, or we can tap out the rhythm by chapping our hands, drumming, or softly hitting a part of our body. We can stop thinking about this altogether and simply imagine the colors of the rainbow entering through each chakra. We can outline our auric field with rays of light. Or we can do nothing. Stop reading. Take the risk. See what happens.

❧ 14 ❧

EMBRACING SHADOW

Jung defined the shadow as the negative side of the personality. He saw the shadow as the sum of qualities we keep hidden. When we become aware of personality traits that are insufficiently developed, we have an opportunity to tap into our intuitive sixth sense. Learning about unconscious projections from our parents frees us to explore a gender spectrum that will benefit all of us, as well as to experience the self-love that can lead to deeper and more meaningful intimate encounters.

❧❧❧

Union of the heart and mind is essential to fully understand the symbolic meaning of the shadow. When we oppose the shadow, we can become polarized and out of balance. Many of us have an innate desire to gain an understanding of the shadow side of our personality. This desire causes us to seek answers in order to reclaim personality characteristics we may have rejected. Often when we project shadow qualities onto others, they respond with criticism that we do not agree with. If we allow others to point out what they view as our shortcomings, there is much to gain. For example, we may resist instinctual spontaneity and playfulness, which results in cutting ourselves off from the possibility of wholeness. Or, we may think we never get angry while we constantly enact a passive stubbornness. We may say we are not needy as we subtly manipulate our self into the center of attention. This behavior does not serve our own best interests, nor that of the collective.

To become more integrated, we might try body-centered therapies such as Hakomi, Emotional Freedom Technique (EFT) or Eye Movement Desensitization & Reprocessing (EMDR). Old hurts and traumas do not die, instead they continuously influence our behavior as we develop coping and defense mechanisms. Any form of denial requires the expenditure of energy. Denying the shadow can sabotage relationships as well as career goals, and sometimes it will lead to compulsive activities and risk-taking behavior. Often, the shadow will pop up in dreams. We learn about shadow through reflection, especially in a group where we receive feedback on the symbolism that we might not be able to see on our own. It is through this feedback that any secondary traumas can be released. We can also engage in processes such as "The Journey" or "The Work" or any other popular personal growth workshops currently available.

LIBERATION TOOLS

We each manifest a *persona*, or mask, that we present to the world as our individual personality. It is similar to what Freud referred to as the ego in that it also becomes a mediator as we adapt to our physical environment. Both persona and ego aid in the navigation of various social circumstances, and they enable us to play specific roles. The shadow-side of personality refers to character traits, both strengths and weaknesses, not yet acknowledged. Personality and ego are a blend of three aspects as outlined in chapter 5:

1. the continuously perceptive, conscious body,
2. the cognitive thoughts and memories of the subconscious,
3. the judgments and evaluations of the superconscious mind.

The ego's role as the gatekeeper constantly determines which perceptions, thoughts, feelings, and memories will enter awareness, and the persona determines what "face" we present to the outer world. A greater continuity of our identity can be achieved when the ego is not busily comparing itself to others, or defending itself from others. This continuity in turn becomes an Integrated Self.

In these circle illustrations, mind, body, and spirit can also represent a branch of social psychology called Transactional Analysis (TA). Eric Berne presented the idea that within the each of us there is a Parent, Adult, and Child persona constantly present. The judgmental Parent (P) is similar to the superconscious level; the Adult (A) responds from the conscious perceptive body; while the Child (C) holds the memories. Unfortunately, it appears to be part of the human condition that many of us remember hurts more than joys. This is true for both men and women. The exercises suggested throughout this book are a means to overcome these traumas of childhood wounding, and to become more sensitive to the needs of others, which in turn increases our own happiness.

A blend of individuality and communal thinking is most effective for the highest good of all concerned. To achieve this blend, the first step is to stop and recognize the emotional response within the body. When

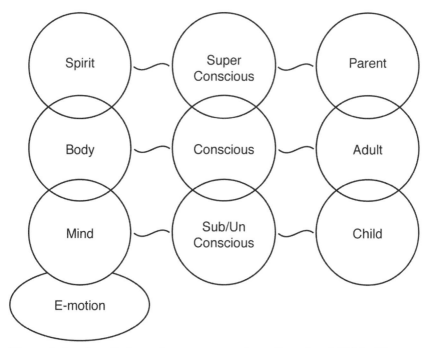

These circles show that we always carry our Inner Parent and Child with us as we become Adults.

we pay attention to any physical sensations that occur in the area of each particular gland and organ, we can notice any response metaphor in the corresponding chakra. This kind of noticing takes practice. Once we become familiar with observing the internal physical response, we can usually make quick, and eventually automatic adjustments to our behavior in any situation. At least, we can return to the person who offended us or someone we might have offended, and say, "You know after thinking about that exchange we had earlier and how I responded, I would like to help us see it from a different perspective." This type of interchange usually leads to improved intimacy on every level. It only takes one person to begin to use a style such as this, or to engage in a more formal nonviolent communication (NVC).

In many cases, we are caught in a maze of codependency when we are busy tracking the other person rather than discovering our own character traits. Too often, personal interests that existed outside of a new relationship are ignored because one partner becomes completely absorbed in the other; sometimes in not very agreeable ways. With progressive maturity and understanding, we can embrace the shadow and integrate differing personality styles, perhaps even experience compersion, the joy that occurs when someone you love is also experiencing joy. One possibility for the further exploration of intimacy comes when we engage deeply with more than one person rather than having surface encounters. This engagement is not necessarily of a sexual nature, but rather an opportunity to become transparent while maintaining primary partnerships. Many people are conditioned to focus only on one partner or friendship, and ignore others. As we master running energy, as outlined in previous chapters, we will be able to enjoy deep encounters, and learn more about the shadow, without a need to become sexual. This type of personal expansion is an example of true intimacy.

SHADOW WORK

In their popular anthology, *Meeting the Shadow*, Connie Zweig and Jeremiah Abrams coined the term shadow-work to refer to "the continuing effort to develop a creative relationship with the shadow."[1] They see the shadow as a psychic immune system that defines the ego as separate from everything else. They claim that all the feelings and capacities rejected by the ego, and exiled into the shadow, contribute to the hidden power of the dark side of human nature. Their hope is that those who actively participate in shadow-work will refrain from adding personal darkness to the density of the collective shadow. Many progressive people consider the idea of a collective shadow as old-fashioned and conformist. They feel that we must retain a strong sense of individuality at all costs. Others entertain the idea that we are all part of an interconnected universe, and that our individual lives make a difference in the overall evolutionary process of human nature. Discovering where you stand on this spectrum is part of developing a personal philosophy and therefore actively engaging in the process of evolution.

Liz Greene, a contemporary British analyst and astrologer, points to the paradoxical nature of the shadow as both "the container of darkness and the beacon pointing toward the light."[2] This means understanding the shadow as a way to move from the darkness to the light. Jung noted the importance of the shadow by pointing out that it "only becomes dangerous when our conscious attention to it is hopelessly wrong."[3] In other words, if we deny the shadow and fail to illuminate its traits, it will continue to haunt us. At this point in history, we are in the process of eliminating negative associations that regard certain personality traits as exclusively masculine or feminine. Constrictions on the capabilities of both men and women limit choices. We are beginning to recognize gender identity as a spectrum that includes a wide variety of roles for everyone.

Erich Neumann first introduced the idea that young adults project characteristics and tensions onto their parents. This is a natural part of the journey to become an individual and separate from parental and cultural influence. He noted that as we mature, we are able to modify our personality characteristics. In doing this, the person becomes separate from the collective. This process occurs in the development of both the human race and individual human beings. This is another way of saying we must find peace within ourselves in order to cultivate healthy relationships and peace-filled partnerships with other nations. Those who angrily oppose legislation reform without proposing viable solutions are an example of non-productive anger rather than those who work toward change outside the political system.

CHANGING ARCHETYPES

Throughout his writing, Neumann used the terms *masculine* and *feminine* not as personal sex-linked characteristics, but as symbolic expressions. He saw every individual as a psychological hybrid with traits that were archetypal and therefore transpersonal. He pointed out that a complication often occurs in healthy gender development when the child overly identifies with the masculine or feminine side of what Neumann called the "symbolic principle of opposites."[4] This complication occurs when we think that only men or only women are capable of displaying certain characteristics. When this happens, it violates the integrity or integral wholeness of our personality. Neumann points out that the anima and animus draw their power from the collective unconscious, but individual experiences also have their influence.

It is important not to lose sight that the traits any one person portrays must be a mixture of masculine and feminine aspects. Therefore, to expand our ideas regarding gender and intimacy, we need to consider three components of what it means to become a balanced, Integrated Self:

1. an inclination toward imagining gender possibilities,
2. awareness of the images and symbols of feminine and masculine that are culturally transmitted throughout history in mythology, art, movies, fairy tales, and religion,
3. personal experiences with people of various gender identities.

In addition to observing masculine and feminine characteristics as components of personality and gender identity, we also develop a preferred style of relating. Jung acknowledged that most of us have a complexity comparable to a gem with many facets. When we take time to learn about various personality traits, and cultivate the conscious realization that is necessary before getting involved with others, we can uncover unconscious motives and therefore alleviate the pain caused by failed relationships. Furthermore, if we open our hearts and minds to the possibilities of loving with open arms, we will find additional opportunities for personal growth and sustained pleasure.

PERSONALITY TRAITS

As a young man, Jung set out to gather information about how people make decisions. In his search to understand core mental functions, he studied the *I Ching*, a Chinese divination tool, and realized that several traits shaped an individual's personality and style of relating. He outlined three sets of contrasting characteristics:

1. Introversion and Extroversion
2. Thinking and Feeling
3. Intuitive and Sensate

As a brief introduction, *Introverts* and *Extroverts* gain energy and spend their life force very differently. Introverts are usually quiet, and find their energy depleted when they are surrounded too much of the time by other people. They tend to have an internal locus of control and internalize problems. Extroverts are more outgoing and therefore energized when around people. They have a more external locus of control, which means they often blame others for their problems. *Thinkers* process information analytically. We often observe these people as being "in their heads." *Feelers* are more sensitive to the kinesthetic response in their bodies, and they often describe their responses as "gut feelings." *Intuitives* are more in touch with the inner knowing of the sixth sense, and *Sensates* believe that if you cannot see it, hear it, smell it, taste it, or touch it—then IT does not exist. Sensates require proof beyond a reasonable doubt, whereas Intuitives are willing to consider many possibilities.

As the controversies that led to the Second World War escalated, Katherine Cook Briggs had the idea that a psychological testing instrument, based on these characteristics, might provide a foundation for appreciating and understanding human differences. She suggested that looking at these personality traits might be a means to solve some of the problems that resulted from Hitler's reign of terror. However, it was not until after the Vietnam War that this idea was expanded. Briggs worked with her daughter, Isabel Briggs Myers, to design a standardized measurement that would determine the extent of how these specific characteristics are displayed or acted out within an individual.

As the two women researched and developed the Myers-Briggs Type Indicator (MBTI), they added a fourth dimension that focused on how people deal with the outer world. They determined that some people have an orientation toward orderliness and decisiveness. These people prefer more planning and structure. They named this trait *Judgmental*, and the opposite *Perceptive*. Perceptive people gravitate toward continually gathering new information and going with the flow as they keep their options open, always looking for additional opportunities. Judgmental people prefer closure and often desire to know the outcome even before it is possible to discern. Most of us are not at the extreme of any of these traits. Again, balance is the key.

An appreciation of these eight categories enables us to relate more easily to those who use different modalities in their everyday tasks. When all eight characteristics are taken into consideration, the combinations become very complex. In 1978, Keirsey and Bates's practical book, *Please Understand Me*, brought the MBTI to a larger audience, and now thousands of books and workshops explain and promote understanding of these various traits. Based on this information we can better understand our own personality, as well as that of others. Although our responses to the questions on the type indicator might vary under different circumstances, we can still learn what effect our behavior may have on others. Using this insight is a great way to increase intimacy.

Often we are annoyed by those traits that are opposite from our own preferred style because they cause conflict. When we are able to notice how our own energy levels differ in various situations, we can then develop a greater sensitivity through our sixth sense of intuitive knowing. The knowledge that these opposite characteristics exist has saved marriages and partnerships where it appeared impossible to work through issues, because the parties involved were unable to communicate. Learning to talk about the personality traits, rather than gender differences, contributed to questioning preordained gender roles and looking at the similarities between masculine and feminine behavior across possibilities.

The Enneagram is another personality typing system that aids in opening our sixth sense and increasing intimacy. This Sufi teaching, first brought to the West by Oscar Ichazo, identifies nine specific defenses that can either hide or reveal the shadow. The Enneagram teaches, in a way very similar to Freud and Erikson, that character traits develop early in life in order to help us survive. Too often they later become limiting habits. It is important to note when negative traits dominate our personality. In order to overcome our shortcomings, we first need to admit that we are ready and willing to change. When we use detached self-observation and internal reflection to provide insight, we become capable of detecting and understanding the various messages these tools provide. If we have awareness of this, we are more able to bring our actions and reactions into a balanced and open range of behaviors. Balance and integration are key components to how people process information.

Through learning about and observing the mental processing tools that are most comfortable for us, we can understand how others might use the same tools differently. Before we "type" others, it is very important to gain knowledge of the tendencies and subtleties of our own defense mechanisms and coping skills. When we learn how characteristics different from our own manifest in others, then, in all forms of love, we can move beyond tolerance to new levels of acceptance of the relationships that are all around us. Once we achieve this, we often find deeper meaning and compassion in all of our partnerships.

THE MARRIAGE CONTRACT

The most complex partnerships involving the shadow occur when we experience erotic desire. Jung described the ideal of being in love and looking toward marriage as a state of complete harmony. He extolled marriage as a great happiness of one heart and one soul, and described it as a return to the original condition of "unconscious oneness." When he was first writing in 1925, deep emotional intimacy and sexual connections were to occur only within the marriage contract. Later, Jung wrote about marriage as the communion with life that obliterates and consumes everything individual. He observed that there is no birth of consciousness without pain, and that many marriages fail to develop because they cannot withstand the crises.

Jung found that the physical consciousness of the body pressed forward while the mental unconscious lagged behind. In many cases, the strength and inner resolve needed for intimacy could not be tapped, causing disunity. This disunity caused discontent, and, therefore, discomfort. Since most of us are not conscious of the real reason for the discontent, we project it upon others. This projection of the shadow too often results in a critical atmosphere, which Jung felt was necessary for conscious realization. He saw that union with others contained the power that led to greater self-actualization and transcendence.

As Jung began his writing on marriage, he agreed with Freud that most motivations derived from parental influences on the relationship of the young man to his mother and of the girl to her father. He suggested that the strength of the bond between these pairs unconsciously influenced the choice of a future partner, either positively or negatively. This influence often becomes a determining factor in the choices we make. In many cases, parents are unaware of their own internal motives, and as a result, they produce the worst results in their children. Some parents thwart themselves with artificial motives concerning what it takes to raise an emotionally healthy child, and then they pass their frustrations on to their children. When this happens, young adults often remain unconsciously driven in a direction intended to compensate for everything left unfulfilled in the lives of their parents. Unfulfilled wishes are unconsciously passed on to their children's children, unless this cycle is broken.

The myth of Eros and Psyche reminds us that it is important to overcome parental and societal controls. This is similar to the biblical portrayal of Adam and Eve. Both the myth and the bible demonstrate the necessity of establishing a grown-up relationship rather than remaining in the dark, unconscious paradise of the parental womb. When we fail to establish independence, we cannot move forward. Two influential, contemporary authors from the Christian tradition Scott Peck and Matthew Fox question the need for suffering as we struggle for conscious evolution. Their work supplies the historical context to how thoughts on this topic have evolved. Hindu and Buddhist literature is also a good resource for connecting to the idea of struggle while attempting to become non-attached when confronting the shadow side of personality.

Is struggling necessary, or can we evolve easily without having to suffer?

The Taoist yin-yang symbol reminds us that the darkness cannot exist without the light, nor the light without the darkness. In the same way, joy cannot be known without sorrow, the masculine cannot exist without the feminine and vice-versa. As we reach for the transcendent level or the highest rung of self-actualization, we begin to recognize how we attract people who embody our rejected shadow. Personality traits that we ignore in our selves often become clear in characteristics of our mates, bosses, co-workers, friends, neighbors, or even our own children. When we admire or criticize someone who expresses our shadow, it is an attempt to negate the source of our own discomfort. If we deny any aspect of our personality, the shadow serves as a defense mechanism. If we pay attention, and embrace the shadow quality, it will bring us out of our comfort zone into greater mindfulness.

As we develop the fullness of our personalities, through embracing the shadow, it is possible to evolve with less suffering and without a struggle. We do this when we identify the positive characteristics within ourselves that we choose to enhance, while at the same time recognizing the need to diminish the opposite traits. One example is the desire to become more open and loving, rather than closed and fearful. This involves applying the lessons learned from Erikson's stages of development. Once we become more trusting and autonomous, we must also take initiative to be more industrious. Only then can we establish an individual identity, separate from our parents and societal controls, move from role confusion into intimacy with people or projects that allow for generativity and ego integrity.

Embracing the shadow empowers us to become separate individuals who are self-actualizing while reaching for the transcendent, superconscious level that takes the collective into consideration. As we embrace the shadow through working with the inner systems of the body's mind, we can move beyond projections to a more conscious evolution. We must take a stand, not only as individuals in opposition to our parents, but also to become more aware of the future of the environment, the planet and all people. When we experience inner peace, we can expect peace on earth.

ALTERNATIVES TO MARRIAGE

In Jung's early practice of psychoanalysis, a marriage contract was the only choice sanctioned for personal development. In spite of this, Jung had several affairs during his long marriage to Emma Jung. The first was a sexual relationship with a former patient named Sabina Spielrein. Frank McLynn has written that Jung was a womanizer who developed deep interaction with his patients, including Toni Wolff, who was his mistress for twenty years. She frequently spent time with both Karl and Emma at their home. Both Emma and Toni eventually became analysts in their own right. Perhaps the different personalities of Jung's various relationships provided his insights into the concept of the anima and animus.[5]

Conventional roles for most men and women were common throughout the fifties when Jung was at the height of his career. Scholars began to discuss personality traits, women's issues, and customs regarding sexual orientation and gender identity. Many had questions regarding masculine and feminine traits. The civil rights movement of the sixties, which challenged race relations, also included acknowledgement of lesbians and gay men. The blossoming sexual revolution helped expand possibilities beyond casual sexual encounters and fostered deep connections with people of the same and opposite gender. During this period of sexual promiscuity, partially due to increased availability of birth control, many people, gay and straight, considered marriage and exclusivity unimportant. Ideas regarding *intimacy* took on a broader meaning and choices that appeared simple in the past became much more complicated.

Easy divorces and the acceptance of single parenting have modified the concept of long-term commitments previously regulated by traditional customs and prejudices. Many unhappy couples no longer stay together for the sake of their children. Single parenting and blending of gender roles have made it more difficult to define how the unconscious motivations of our parents, or their parents' parents, might influence the choices we make in the future. On the other hand, as children we still need a secure setting in which to thrive. And, in order to understand how we make choices, we need to examine the underlying ties to our upbringing.

Harville Hendrix, author of a series of books and workshops called *Getting the Love You Want* and *Keeping the Love You Find*, has popularized many of Jung's ideas. Hendrix recognized that when choosing partners, we are unconsciously attracted to traits that we either missed or loved in our caregivers. Concerning what he named *Imago Relationships*, Hendrix illuminates that we are attracted to partners whose personalities trigger aspects of childhood hurts that we react to in a negative way. Once we are ready and willing to face and heal these old wounds, we eventually develop additional choices about how to respond. Teachings such as these have a continuing influence as each generation becomes more aware of the impositions that occur when people remain in a marriage where both partners are miserable. We can break the negative cycle when we recognize particular traits that we appreciate or despise in either one of our parents or grandparents.

We are more likely to choose a partner with the characteristics we admire and avoid people with the traits that we dislike once we become more conscious. However if we are adopted or barely spend time with one parent, our choices become more difficult because we know less of our inherited shadow. If we have parents who are withholding, or who spend little time on personal development and block any form of intimacy, we must make a greater effort to understand inborn temperament and personality. Or if our parents are constantly changing and renewing themselves, then we must strive to understand "who we are" and take time to understand how they have evolved.

The generation who came of age in the sixties created a revolution against parental and societal control in regard to civil rights, women's rights, the rights of the disabled, and any right that blocked personal freedom. Many people feel this rebellion has undermined "family values," causing these values to be completely lost. Others find the freedoms gained to be a valuable step in the evolution of conscious awareness and mindfulness. These issues represent hot political topics that affect our intrapersonal growth as well as our interpersonal partnerships. As we define where we stand on these moral questions, we nurture the self-awareness, motivation, empathy, and mood management that are necessary ingredients to developing greater emotional and social intelligence.

CULTURAL REVOLUTION

Acknowledgment of women's ways of knowing began to honor intuition as well as more rational, analytical thinking. The movement for women's liberation was spearheaded by Betty Friedan who wrote the landmark book *The Feminine Mystique*. In 1966, Friedan helped found the National Organization for Women (NOW). One of NOW's most visible public actions was the Women's Strike for Equality held on August 26, 1970 in cities around the country. In New York, tens of thousands of women marched down Fifth Avenue with Friedan in the lead. These rebellious actions were a catalyst for changing roles for some women, and in turn, spawned a similar change for American men. This resulted in people from different backgrounds to have expanded opportunities in the workplace. For example, it became acceptable for men to become nurses, teachers, childcare workers, or airline stewards. At the same time, women became police officers, firefighters, professors, doctors, ministers, and lawyers. Eventually, more women entered politics and became lawmakers and judges. Additionally, both men and women began to share their emotions in a way that had not previously occurred in recorded history.

During the 1970s, the Human Awareness Institute (HAI), Shalom Mountain, Esalen Institute, and various encounter groups across the country, initiated circles where the sharing of emotions also included sharing of intimate touch regardless of gender. These movements have allowed people to tap more deeply into the intuitive knowledge provided by the sixth sense, rather than continuing to compare or defend masculine and feminine personality traits. Delving deeper into the full spectrum of human nature has provided additional opportunities for true intimacy with both self and others.

In 1974, Betty Dodson brought female masturbation out of the closet with a book and series of workshops that allowed women to explore their own pleasure.[6] Later the same year, Dell Williams created the first mail order catalog and shop exclusively devoted to the idea that women could take responsibility for their own sexual nature as a nurturing force in their lives. Williams designed a boutique called Eve's Garden in New York City as a place for women to celebrate and honor sexual desire.[7] Other examples of this cultural change include the Sweet Medicine Sun Dance Path of the Deer Tribe, which is a modern day representative of native sexuality that has evolved over thousands of years. Polyfidelity Education Productions (PEP) is now known as Loving More, Network for a New Culture, and Radical Honesty are other groups of this movement toward increased transparency and expanding intimacy include Radical Honesty and Network PEP.

The fields of motivational, transpersonal, and depth psychology grew from the ideals that personal growth through mindfulness, and the use of visualization, can become an antidote to anxiety, depression, divorce, and post-traumatic stress disorders (PTSD). Their methods require that we cultivate insight and intuition. Today, personal coaches and counselors aid clients in recognizing their shadow side, and developing emotional and social intelligence. Group dynamics, workshops, and other personal growth opportunities have made long-term analysis less necessary. Many psychiatrists have become more cautious about writing prescriptions that too often cause additional damage. Hopefully, a reformed universal health care plan for the United States will include the costs of promoting mental as well as physical health, so that modalities such as marriage counseling, meditation classes, and massage therapy will also be covered by insurance.

THE INNER LOVER

Letting go of the shadow and exploring the depths of our own desire and pleasure allows us to embrace an inner lover, which can lead to more happiness and greater pleasure. Our needs, wants, and desires are then able to manifest as we set clear goals. We become an organized, even if ever changing, Integrated Self when we connect the body's mind with emotion and spirit. The stronger we become as individuals, the less likely we are to be codependent and lose our self in the labyrinth of others. On the other hand, if we never make a long-term commitment to anyone, simply for the sake of remaining independent, then we miss a great opportunity for personal growth, full self-actualization, and transcendence into the bliss-filled state of superconscious that can lead to glorious kundalini experiences and extended orgasmic states of mind. It is possible to have orgasmic experiences without becoming sexually involved when we engage the entire human dynamic of the mental, physical, emotional, and spiritual quadrants. We can celebrate the fact of having more choices about life styles and opportunities for personal growth than previous generations.

Knowledge of our internal thinking process is essential when we desire to change our behavior. Listening to the body, integrating different modes of thinking, learning to observe logical, analytical, and flow thought processes all help to develop intuitive knowing. Continuously confronting past tensions, as soon as they show up can produce harmony both internally and externally. Our personality becomes the expression of the inner union of psyche and eros. When we embrace the intuitive, emotional, and erotic aspects of our biological and behavioral levels, we resolve feelings of dissonance that can lead to poor health and disease. As we become aware of how the tension from each developmental stage can interfere with our day-to-day activity, we can stop hurts remaining from childhood and adolescence from interrupting the expansion of intimacy in all of our partnerships. Once we are no longer pulled in opposite directions, then we are able to move to the transcendent and superconscious levels. When this happens we attain loving compassion for self and others, and find true peace of mind.

15

CREATING FOCUS

It is a great and surprising discovery when we find that what we had supposed to be the final peak is nothing but the first step in a very long climb.

—Jung[1]

As we allow ourselves to experience new sensitivities and sensual awareness, we begin to see the world differently. We are able to pay attention to things that may have previously appeared unimportant or even nonexistent. As we grow in awareness of the subtle energy fields around us, we listen to our intuitive sixth sense. We can use dreams and other divination tools as gateways to illuminate similarities rather than accentuate differences.

The energy field that makes up the mental, physical, and emotional aspects of human dynamics is revealed when we slow down, pay attention, and gain the ability to increase our emotional and social IQ. We begin to listen to our intuitive side, tapping into our superconscious and recognizing that we know things without knowing how we know. Phrases like "She had bad vibes" or "The energy was great" become part of ordinary vocabulary. We are able to tell when someone is staring at us, or we have a gut-level feeling that something is about to happen. During an argument we might feel as if we were slapped with words, or punched in the belly, when there is actually no physical contact. We may encounter an incident that feels as if a thick, gooey substance is being poured over us that might be too hot or too cold. At other times, we may experience being surrounded with light and bathed in a sea of sweetness, feeling blessed and lighthearted.

All of these occurrences have a component of reality in our energy field. Once we realize that although the world appears to be made up of solid, concrete objects, it is actually permeated with and surrounded by a fluid radiant energy, constantly moving, constantly changing like the ocean. The docu-movie called *What the Bleep Do We Know?* attempts to illustrate these ideas, as it playfully shows how separate aspects of self become part of a greater whole. Becoming part of the concept of holism is what many of us strive for as a way of experiencing more intimacy and having a greater sense of health and well-being.

In *Social Intelligence*, Daniel Goleman tells us that we are "wired to connect," meaning we are designed for sociability and that we are constantly engaged in a "neural ballet" where social interactions drive emotions. Medical and psychological science are now able to measure the effect of this drive through observing maps of the brain that record and regulate interpersonal dynamics. Our reactions to others and theirs to us have a far-reaching biological impact. Cascades of hormones are emitted that effect us as well as those around us.[2] Goleman has found that good relationships are like vitamins and bad ones are poisonous. We catch other people's emotions the same way as we catch a cold or flu. However, isolation and social stress can shorten our lives. If we are constantly in our car or connected to our phones, iPods, and computers, we are absorbed in a virtual reality that deadens us. We must pay attention to the real people who are close by, although in some cases, the phone and computer offer opportunities to connect that would otherwise be missed. The necessary key is once again balance.

SECURE ATTACHMENTS

Most intellectual development beginning at birth is modeled on observed behavior, which activates mirror neurons that become permanent folds in the gray matter of the brain. According to Goleman as we grow closer and more intimate with people, we not only observe their every move in the course of learning, we also become sensitive to their emotional state. When children are nurtured in a positive way, they form a secure base that allows them to know that all is well, similar to Erikson's basic sense of trust. When a secure base is formed a "looping" occurs in the body's mind that activates neurotransmitters, oxytocin, and endorphins, each adds a small bolt of pleasure to the feeling of being well-loved. Eventually, a tension is created between our need for security and our drive to explore away from the secure base. The result of balancing this tension forms a safe haven where we can easily return. This safe haven only develops when we can trust that people around us will do what they say they are going to do. As we mature, the more we follow through on promises we make to others, the more others will also follow through for us. This is a clear example of mutual dependence and reciprocity. The interdependent partnership that forms allows us to take the perspective of the other, which in turn promotes greater harmony through loving compassion.

Sometimes we need to look outside of current partnerships for insights as to why relationships feel imbalanced. Or we might seek coaching when everything is in order and we are ready to focus on our next goal. We often desire input from others to be held accountable and keep motivated. In addition to the many mental exercises mentioned throughout this book, other tools are easily available that tap our intuitive way of knowing such as consulting an oracle, astrological guides, a walk in a labyrinth, drawing a mandala, or interpreting dreams.

LOOKING FOR ANSWERS

Historical documentation demonstrates that people have always regarded prophecy or predictions as one way to find answers. Written records dating from 1830 B.C.E. indicate that the Egyptians, Greeks, Chinese, and Native Americans all looked to movements in the sky for a meaningful relationship to events on Earth. It is seldom revealed that the study of the stars and planets, known as astrology, later became the science of astronomy. During the Renaissance the field of physical science expanded and use of intuition contracted. Galileo and Copernicus risked their lives when telescopes were first invented. Once we learned that the world was not flat and that our planet circled around the sun, other seemingly outdated ideas were also disregarded. But some were preserved.

In Greek myths, priests or priestesses acted as oracles who imparted the response from a god to the human questioner. For all affairs of private and public life, people have often consulted oracles. The concept of gods becoming vocal is not confined to ancient times; medical intuitives, as well as hunters, consult what they refer to as *spirit guides*. Sometimes oracle is used to refer to the response; often dreams serve this purpose. Many people observe outward signs, such as the motion of objects dropped into a spring, the movement of birds, the rustle of leaves, or reading the dregs in the teacup. Currently experiments with subatomic particles and waves confirm that patterns are found everywhere, and some people have the gift to tap into them. Those who check in with these various tools believe intuitive awareness allows us to understand connections on the transpersonal level.

One example of using ancient wisdom is the *I Ching*, or *Book of Changes*, one of the oldest recorded sources for communicating with the collective unconscious or superconscious. The *I Ching* contains readings from standardized patterns found in nature that may have originally been designed to keep people in touch with the flow of universal life energy. According to Mary Clark:

> A person who consults the *I Ching* can expect to receive insights into the hidden energies and tendencies underlying the situation in question. The purpose of the oracle is to remind us that we are part of a bigger picture. Our concerns cannot be separate from the flow of life that surrounds us. By gaining insight into the larger patterns surrounding us, we can choose the path of least effort and greatest delight.[3]

Consulting oracles provide insights. Other tools for discerning archetypes and symbols include various tarot decks, the Kabalistic Tree of Life, and runes. The runes, a symbolic alphabet that dates back to the Neolithic period some 20,000 years ago, are one of the earliest attempts to record thoughts and language It appears that these tools were designed to aid conscious awareness. Using them can help us enter a state of wholeness that includes the practical, logical aspects, as well as honoring the creative, more playful, and pleasurable facets that are involved in developing intimacy and learning to love our self and others more completely.

CONNECTING SYSTEMS

Einstein once noted that human beings are a part of a whole, which he called *the universe* in order to denote the part that is limited in time and space. He commented that when we experience our thoughts and feelings as something separate from the rest, it is a kind of optical delusion. "This delusion is a kind of prison, restricting us to our personal desires and to affection for a few persons nearest to us. Our task must be to free ourselves from this prison by widening our circle of compassion to embrace all living creatures and the whole of nature in its beauty."[4]

Edgar Cayce, one of the early pioneers in the field of holism, noted the correlation between the chakras and the hormonal system. He was known as the "sleeping prophet" because he spoke while he was asleep and made suggestions to those who wrote to him regarding various ailments. Many of the remedies he suggested were proven to cure people and some are still used today. The Institute of Noetic Science (IONS) and a few other organizations including the International Society for the Study of Subtle Energies and Energy Medicine (ISSSEEM) have begun to document the outcomes of powerful healers who help people by using energy techniques. In many cases illness and disease are caused by unhealthy relationships. Many practitioners are able to experience the oneness and wholeness of the universe in ways that defy the current medical concepts of cause and effect. The work of these practitioners promotes therapeutic benefits that go deep and spread out to others in the surrounding energy field, therefore, having a positive effect on those who also experience the benefits that come from healthy partnerships.

Einstein's comment resonates with the Eros and Psyche myth and reminds us that people gather information both through the senses and through intuition, although many people show a preference for one or the other. According to information gathered from the Myers-Briggs Type Indicator (MBTI), in the past approximately 75 percent of the U.S. population was the sensing type who favored practical matters, with males and females equally represented. This is changing. More intuitive people, who prefer imaginary and abstract processing, are beginning to understand the importance of encompassing the full spectrum of dynamic personalities. Opening the vital flow of energy through our intuitive sixth sense will increase emotional and social intelligence. Using dreams and shadow work also helps to bring the masculine and feminine into balance.

THE BIGGER PICTURE

Dream work is one possible option for working toward personal and planetary growth. Sandor Ferenczi, a Hungarian contemporary of Freud and Jung, called dreams "the workshop of evolution." He commented that civilization is growing into a form that first takes shape in dreams.[5] Many dream specialists concur that we dream of matters that are beyond our ability to comprehend at our current stage of consciousness. However, we are learning that our waking imagination is able to tap into the same archetypes that are available when we are sleeping. This is why it is necessary to remember what we dream. The best way to facilitate recall is to have paper and pen next to the bed in order to write down the dream upon awakening.

Current psychologist Jeremy Taylor, author of several books and many workshops, estimates that he has worked with more than 100,000 dreams in his thirty-five-year career. Most deal with collective social issues, as well as intimate personal issues. Taylor finds that dreams work on several levels simultaneously, from employment to health to partnerships "to larger issues like nature, the cosmos, the divine, the whole psychic and spiritual evolution of human beings on this planet." Taylor states, "The health and harmony of the biosphere is absolutely essential to our personal health and harmony."[6]

Taylor's dream work recognizes that although technology has created the illusion that we are not connected with nature and the environment around us, while "the conscious mind functions as if this illusion was true, the unconscious knows better." He continues, "The reason we dream in symbols is that the symbol is simple enough on the surface to be grasped by the current state of consciousness, yet every symbol has multiple meanings, and serves as an invitation for consciousness to evolve and be understood at a deeper level."[7]

Dreams do not tell us what we already know; rather dreams invite us to go past what we know and have insight into the future, but it is often in the form of a riddle. Taylor finds most people are strong and resilient and that dream work is not likely to reveal any demons from the past or future information that we cannot handle. If we consciously accept that the figures in dreams are part of repressed aspects of our shadow, then we are able to discharge any self-deception and withdraw projections that we might make unto others.

Karl Jung theorized that the collective unconscious formed the foundation of our common humanity. He and others continue to teach that we are all part of one family. Often when we experience separation from this family, it is because we have suppressed normal feelings of aggression, jealously, and even hatred. Taylor suggests that when we deny these potentials in our self, we start to see them as the exclusive property of other people. When we believe that others who express these feelings are different from us, we begin to question their humanity. Taylor comments that this allows some people to speak casually about the *collateral damage of war* because they do not really believe the people who are being attacked and killed are suffering human beings.

Through his analysis of dreams in groups, Taylor has found that dreams become a tool for nonviolent political, social, and cultural change. Groups he has worked with demonstrate that sharing dream interpretation "sweeps prejudice aside and provides a place where anxieties can be relaxed, hostilities treated with good humor, and fears relieved through play." This playfulness can lead to individual feelings of pleasure and greater connections. Taylor reminds us that when speaking about the archetypes and personality traits, human beings are "predisposed to associate the direction *up* with light and goodness, and the direction *down* with dark, unconsciousness." It is important to recognize that the concept of *divine* or *brilliant* resides in both light and darkness; it is part of both masculine and feminine aspects found in all of us. We have the tools to learn to run energy down the spinal column in the path of manifestation as well as up in the path of liberation.

BODY, MIND, AND SPIRIT

We discover aspects of our own divinity as we explore the complexity of our personality and inner labyrinths. Knowledge of the aura and chakra systems is one of several paths that are helpful in this quest.

This knowledge can lead to using our internal systems to embrace the shadow. Similar to Psyche's descent into the underworld, it is necessary to welcome the shadow in order to reclaim the love of eros in our lives. It appears we must grapple with demons on our journey to become enlightened and whole. In order to overcome the demons of fear, shame, guilt, grief, dishonesty, and illusion, we must work through the tensions between:

- Trust and Mistrust
- Autonomy versus Doubt and Shame
- Initiative versus Guilt
- Accomplishment versus Inferiority
- Identity versus Role Confusion
- Intimacy versus Isolation
- Generativity versus Stagnation
- Ego Integrity versus Despair

When we become aware of the vital life force or libido running throughout the system, it creates a pathway for both liberation from the depths of sorrow and manifestation of our highest motives. Carolyn Myss and Norm Shealy remind us that what we refer to as chakras are a vital part of the whole system called the human body: "The chakra system is like a relay game with seven players constantly receiving identical information and responding to that information according to their particular skill."[8]

One Reiki master, Len Daly, sees the possibility of chakras as spinning wheels of information and a depository of memories that appear where each bone connects with a joint in the body and where every cell becomes the branch of a neuron. Therefore, the idea of checking in with the body is expanded to the cellular level. Doing the actual check-in is more important than learning any specific model for noticing what is going on. When we focus on the messages provided by the body's mind, take time to observe the resulting feelings, and then share these emotions with others around us, the quality of our relationships increases.

Most holistic healing practitioners incorporate these techniques in their work with the whole mental, physical, emotional, and spiritual system. Our internal systems are dynamic, constantly in flux and change in order to provide evolutionary growth. Intuitive knowing of these dynamics, including using dreams, nightmares, and other divination tools, provides guidance for releasing the blocks that separate us from healthy well-being and loving compassion.

AN IDEA WHOSE TIME HAS COME

The most recent discoveries of neuroscience show that dreams are simply activity in the brain during sleep with nothing mysterious about them. But the fact is that we dream and we learn. When we understand how we learn, we are better able to do the learning. Reflecting on messages received from both our brains and our hearts are valuable ways to explore e-motion.

Sharing our vital life force and "energy in motion" with others allows us to cooperate and communicate with confidence. Aspects of human dynamics on the mental and physical as well as emotional and spiritual levels of being become the traits of emotional and social intelligence. When our curiosity is sparked, we are motivated to set intentions about what we want to achieve and to find enough self-mastery that will carry us into the healthy relatedness that makes the manifestation of dreams possible. Using language to share our thoughts with others allows us to engage in ways that other species cannot. We have the ability to not only know what we are thinking but also to imagine what someone else might be thinking.

However, it is important not to make assumptions about their thoughts, but rather to take the time for the into-me-see that comes when both parties allow space for transparency and reciprocity. Finding clarity of purpose and achieving integration requires us to move from dramatic expression of our immediate experience to clear understanding and quiet affirmation. These acts can open us from dark obscurity and the mysterious void, full-circle back to the beginning of no-beginning. From this place of exploring personality traits and reflecting on dreams, it is important to utilize the information received. We can do this through contemplation of the colorful rainbow correlations mentioned throughout this book:

- Red for the base of security that establishes I AM HERE.
- Orange for the flow of creativity that cries out I FEEL, I WANT.

- Yellow, the strong power that declares I WILL ACT.
- Green, the necessity that longs for I WANT TO LOVE and BE LOVED.
- Blue, clarity in communication that affirms I SPEAK and I HEAR.
- Indigo, the value of imagination that allows I SEE and WANT TO BE SEEN.
- Violet for the reward of connections that KNOW I BELONG.

These are just a few of the many ways to understand the universe through our bodies and gain experiences that can provide intuitive insight into our next steps of loving compassion. Each step is a means toward joyful appreciation of our inextricable connection to past, present, and future. We all move at a steady pace from birth to death as time is measured in days and weeks, months and years. Both Eros and Thanatos are alive and well deep within our psyche. In spite of all of the evolutionary awareness provided by the many teachers promoting methods of personal growth, and the many tools available on our path to integration and wholeness, we cannot escape this one truth: Human beings may be born helpless, but we live within intimate relationships throughout our lives from when our eyes first open until they close.

NOTES

CHAPTER 1

1. www.funderstanding.com/eq.cfm

2. Sandra Seagal and her associates at Human Dynamics International have conducted continuing research since 1979 involving more than 80,000 people from twenty-five cultures, www.humandynamics.com

3. Martin Lowenthal, www.livinglifefully.com

4. Compersion was first coined by the Krista Community in the 1970s. See Tristan Taormino, *Opening Up: A Guide to Creating and Sustaining Open Relationships* (San Francisco: Cleis Press, 2008) for the best information regarding its use.

5. Arthur Jersild, www.livinglifefully.com

6. Ninety-seven different names are listed in J. White and S. Krippner, eds., *Future Science: Life Energies and the Physics of Paranormal Phenomena* (Garden City, NY: Anchor Books, 1977).

7. Biophysicist Beverly Rubik was instrumental in naming the biofield in 1994. She has published more than eighty papers on this topic and as time goes by her work is being acknowledged by a wider community.

8. See the Association for Comprehensive Energy Psychology (ACEP), www.energypsych.org

9. Karl Jung, *Aspects of the Masculine/Aspects of the Feminine*, trans. R. F. C. Hull (New York: MJF Books, 1989), 120.

CHAPTER 2

1. For example, American psychologist Rollo May, a popular author of more than thirty-six books.

2. Susan Hendricks and Clyde Hendricks, *Romantic Love* (Newbury Park, CA: Sage Publications, 1992).

3. To create a personalized food pyramid, go to www.mypyramid.gov.

4. Copyright © 2008. For more information about the Healthy Eating Pyramid, please see The Nutrition Source, Department of Nutrition, Harvard School of Public Health, www.thenutritionsource.org, and *Eat, Drink, and Be Healthy*, by Walter C. Willett, M.D. and Patrick J. Skerrett (2005), Free Press/Simon & Schuster Inc.

5. Linda Creed and Michael Masser, composers, "Greatest Love of All," 1977.

6. See www.TrueHealth.H2Origin.com.

CHAPTER 3

1. Englishman John Woodroffe translated at least twenty of Patanjali's earliest texts from approximately 200 B.C.E. under the pseudonym Arthur Avalon. *The Serpent Power* (1919) gave specific instructions to meditate on the area of the body that corresponds to each internal organ.

2. www.changezone.co.uk

3. Popularized by a documentary called *The Secret*, directed by Drew Heriot and Sean Byrne, Prime Time Productions, 2007.

4. www.worldchiropracticalliance.org/resources/greens/green5.htm

5. http://www.highchi.com/pdf/

6. *The Skeptic Dictionary*, www.skeptic.com

7. Morphogenetic fields are basically nonphysical blueprints that give birth to forms equivalent to an electromagnetic field.

8. Ken Wilbur, *Grace and Grit: Spirituality and Healing in the Life and Death of Treya Killam Wilber* (Boston: Shambhala, 1991), 158.

9. Quote from English physician Dr. Francis Peabody found on www.normshealy.com/

CHAPTER 4

1. www.iep.utm.edu/descmind.html

2. Barbara Brennan, *Hands of Light* (New York: Bantam Books, 1987), 35.

3. Richard Gerber, *Vibrational Medicine* (Santa Fe, NM: Bear & Co, 1988).

4. Altheia Foundation, http://www.holisticu.org/jack/.

5. Gerber, *Vibrational Medicine*, 372.

CHAPTER 5

1. Howard Gardner. *Frames of Mind: The Theory of Multiple Intelligences* (New York: Basic Books, 1983).
2. http://pinker.wjh.harvard.edu

CHAPTER 6

1. An organization called Loving More supports this kind of open and honest relationships. See www.lovemore.com for more information.
2. http://webspace.ship.edu/cgboer/jung.html
3. *Libido* in Latin means "desire, longing, fancy, lust, or rut." Although the adjective libidinous, meaning lustful, had been used in English for 500 years, libido only entered the language in 1913. http://www.medterms.com/script/
4. Thanatos might be poetically called the brother of Hypnos (Sleep) who goes kindly among the mortals. But Thanatos was a creature of bone-chilling darkness with a heart made of iron. When he takes hold, the world of light ceases to be. From on high, Helios (the Sun) never casts his light on Death. http://messagenet.com/myths/bios/thanatos.html#cite
5. http://changingminds.org/explanations/behaviors/coping/coping.htm
6. See Marnia Robinson for more on this at www.reuniting.info
7. In 1754, Horace Walpole named serendipity as a faculty possessed by the heroes of a fairy tale called *The Three Princes of Serendip.*

CHAPTER 7

1. In addition, Ron Kurtz created a form of body-centered psychotherapy, called *Hakomi*, based on assisted self-study to process and transform undigested experiences.
2. In 1966 James W. Prescott initiated research programs that documented how the failure of "Mother Love" in infant monkeys adversely affected the biological development of their brains. Funding for his research was withdrawn, but he continued to write about the importance of breast feeding.
3. Harry Harlow and R. Zimmerman, "Affectional Responses in the Infant Monkey," *Science* 130 (1959): 421–32. Harlow also published an article in 1966, "Learning to Love" in *American Scientist* 54, 244–72.
4. Tiffany Field, Philip M. McCabe, and Neil Schneiderman, eds., *Stress and Coping Across Development* (Hillsdale, N.J.: Lawrence Erlbaum Associates, 1985).

CHAPTER 8

1. Sigmund Freud, "A Difficulty in the Path of Psycho-Analysis," *The Standard Edition of the Complete Psychological Works of Sigmund Freud*, Vol. 17 (1917–1919), *An Infantile Neurosis and Other Works*, 135–44.

2. Directed by Frank Oz. Produced by Laura Ziskin and Bernie Williams, 1991.

CHAPTER 9

1. Michael Talbot, *Mysticism and the New Physics* (New York: Bantam Books, 1980), 152.

2. Richard Gordon, *Quantum Touch*. Berkeley, CA: North Atlantic Books, 1999.

CHAPTER 10

1. Mihaly Csikszentmihalyi, *Flow: The Psychology of Optimal Experience* (New York: HarperPerennial, 1991).

2. Tah Ben-Shahar, *Happier: Learn the Secrets to Daily Joy and Lasting Fulfillment* (New York: McGraw-Hill, 2007).

3. Candace Pert et al. "Localization of opiate receptor binding in presynaptic membranes of of rat brain." *Brain Research,* 1974, 70, 184–88.

4. More than 600 scientific studies verifying the wide-ranging benefits of meditation have been conducted at 250 independent universities and medical schools in thirty-three countries: See www.tm.org for more information.

5. Zeng Qingnan. *Qigong: Believe it or Not* (Bejing, China: Foreign Language Press, 1991).

6. www.spiritus-temporis.com/pierre-jean-george-cabanis/ 7.

7. Paul Pearsall, *The Pleasure Prescription* (Salt Lake City: Publishers Press, 1996).

8. Gina Ogden, *The Heart and Soul of Sex* (Boston: Shambhala, 2006).

9. Anodea Judith, *Eastern Body, Western Mind* (Berkeley, CA: Celestial Arts, 2004), 452.

CHAPTER 11

1. Valerie Harms, *Inner Lover* (Boston & London: Shambhala, 1992).

2. Harms, *Inner Lover.*

3. Erich Neumann, *Amor and Psyche, The Psychic Development of the Feminine* (Princeton, NJ: Princeton University Press, 1956).

4. Note these stereotypes were never true for everyone. Depending on parental and other cultural influences, some boys have always been more in touch with their intuitive aspects and some girls with rational thinking. This internal concept of gender identity has little to do with later sexual orientation. However, this issue was not part of what Jung was taking into consideration at the time of his writing.

5. Demetris Wehr, *Jung & Feminism: Liberating Archetypes* (Boston: Beacon Press, 1987), 66–67.

CHAPTER 12

1. Caroline Myss, *Anatomy of the Spirit: Seven Stages of Power and Healing* (New York: Harmony Books, 1996).

2. Caroline Myss, *Sacred Contracts: Awakening Your Divine Potential* (New York: Random House, 2003).

3. Lion Goodman and Anodea Judith, *Creation is Ecstacy! The Spiritual Technology of Manifestation Through the Chakras* (Self-Published, 2008).

4. This is evidenced by the promotion of Viagra and other similar drugs. See *Time* magazine, "Sexual Healing" by Alice Park, January 19, 2004.

5. The controversial documentary *What the Bleep Do We (K)now*, dirs. William Arntz and Betsy Chasse (2004), aptly illustrates this concept.

CHAPTER 13

1. John Money, *Lovemaps: Clinical Concepts of Sexual/erotic Health and Pathology, Paraphilia, and Gender Transposition of Childhood, Adolescence, and Maturity*. (New York: Irvington, 1986).

2. An excellent book that addresses this issue is *Raising Cain: Protecting the Emotional Life of Boys* by Dan Kindlon and Michael Tompson (New York: Ballantine Books, 2000). Another is *The Identity Work Book*.

3. Sandra Bem, "The Measure of Psychological Androgyny," *Journal of Clinical Psychology* 42 (1974): 155–62.

4. bell hooks, *Feminism is for Everybody: Passionate Politics* (Cambridge, MA: South End Press, 2000).

5. According to Dean Spade, Sylvia Rivera Law Project, the number is seven, but the number is sixteen according to Marcus Arana, discrimination investigator with the San Francisco Human Rights Commission.

6. www.skirtcafe.org.

7. Gender Identity Disorder (GID) is a new addition to the *Diagnostic and Statistical Manual* (DSM-IV) that provides for insurance reimbursement, and in several parts of the United States it has been added to anti-discrimination and hate-crime laws.

8. http://www.thejungiansociety.org/Jung%20Society/Conferences/Conference-2003/Post-Jungian-Critical-Manifesto.html

9. Demaris Wehr, *Jung and Feminism: Liberating Archetypes* (Boston: Beacon Press, 1987), 113–14.

10. As quoted by Christine Herold from Chuang Tzu, *Inner Chapters*, trans. Gia-Fu Feng and Jane English (New York: Vintage Books, 1974), 126.

CHAPTER 14

1. Connie Zweig and J. Abrams, *Meeting the Shadow* (New York: Tarcher/Putnum, 1991), xxv.

2. Zweig and Abrams, *Meeting the Shadow*, xxiv.

3. Zweig and Abrams, *Meeting the Shadow*, xxiv.

4. Neumann, Erich. *The Origins and History of Consciousness*. New York: Routledge and Kegan Paul, 1949, 42.

5. Jung actually must have begun thinking about this quite early because in a letter to Freud dated January 30, 1910, Jung wrote: "The prerequisite for a good marriage, it seems to me, is the license to be unfaithful" (W. McGuire, ed. 1974), *The Freud/Jung Letters: Correspondence between Sigmund Freud and C G Jung* (R. Manheim & R F C Hull, Trans, Princeton University Press, p. 289).

6. Betty Dodson, *Sex for One: The Joy of Selfloving* (New York: Random House, 1983) was first self-published as *Liberating Masturbation* in 1974, and later as *Selflove and Orgasm.*

7. Dell Williams with Lynn Venucci, *Revolution in the Garden* (Hong Kong: Silverback Books, Inc. 2002).

CHAPTER 15

1. Karl Gustav Jung, *Aspects of the Feminine*. Trans. R F C Hull (Routledge, 1986), 42.

2. Richard Davidson, director of the Laboratory for Affective Neuroscience at University of Wisconsin, found in Goleman, *Social Intelligence*, 83.

3. Mary Clark, *I Ching* (Dorset & Boston: Element Books Ltd., 1998), 1.

4. www.wisdomquotes.com/000762.html (May 1, 2009).

5. Karen Karvonen, "Last Night I Had the Strangest Dream," *Sun* 363 (March 2006): 5–13.

6. Jeremy Taylor, *Where People Fly and Water Runs Uphill* (New York: Warner Books, 1992),

7. Carolyn Myss and C. Norman Shealy, *The Creation of Health* (New York: Random House, 1988), 93.

8. Personal conversation, April 2009.

RESOURCES AND REFERENCES

Ackerman, Diane. *A Natural History of the Senses*. New York: Vintage Books, 1990.

———. *A Natural History of Love*. New York: Random House, 1994.

Ainsworth, Mary. "Object Relations, Dependency, and Attachment: A Theoretical Review of the Infant Mother Relationship," *Child Development* 40 (1968): 969–1025.

Amen, Daniel G. *Sex on the Brain*: 12 Lessons to Enhance Your Love Life. New York: Bantam Books, 2007.

Anapol, Deborah. *Responsible Nonmomogamy: The Quest for Sustainable Intimate Relationships*. San Rafael, CA: IntiNet Resource Center, 1991.

Arntz, William, B., and M. Vicente Chasse. *What the Bleep Do We Know?* Deerfield, FL: Health Communications, 2006.

Aron, Elaine N. *The Highly Sensitive Person*. New York: Random House, 1996.

Arrien, Angeles, *The Four-Fold Way: Walking the Paths of the Warrior, Teacher, Healer, and Visionary*. San Francisco: HarperSanFrancisco, 1993.

Avalon, Arthur [John Woodroffe], trans. and ed. *The Serpent Power: Being the Shat-Chakra-Nir̄ Pana and Pā Dukā-Panchaka, Two Works on Laya Yoga*. Madras, India: Ganesh & Co. 1919.

Bailey, Alice A. *Esoteric Healing*. New York: Lucis Publishing, 1953.

Ballentine, Rudy. *Radical Healing*. New York: Three Rivers Press, 1999.

———. *Diet and Nutrition*. Honesdale, PA: Himalayan International Institute, 1978.

Basant, Annie, with C. W. Leadbetter. *Thought-Forms*. New York: Theosophical Publishing Society, 1905.

Bays, Brandon. *The Journey*. London: Thorsons 1999.

Becker, Robert O., and Gary Selden. *The Body Electric*. New York: Morrow, 1985.

Berne, Eric. *Games People Play: Basic Handbook of Transactional Analysis*. New York: Grove Press, 1964.

Blakeslee, Sandra, and Matthew Blakeslee. *The Body has a Mind of its Own*. New York: Random House, 2007.

Blank, Joani. Ed. *First Person Sexual: Women & Men Write About Self-Pleasuring*. San Francisco: Down There Press, 1996.

Blavatsky, H. P. *The Secret Doctrine*, abridged and annotated by Michael Gomes. New York: Jeremy P. Tarcher/Penguin, 2009.

Blofield, John. *The Tantric Mysticism of Tibet*. New York: Dutton, 1974.

Bloomfield, H. *TM: Discovering Inner Energy and Overcoming Stress*. New York: Delacorte Press, 1975.

Bluestone, Sarvananda. *The World Dream Book*. Rochester, VT: Desti Books, 2002.

Blum, Deborah. *Sex on the Brain: The Biological Differences between Men and Women*. New York: Penguin, 1997.

Booth, W. C. "What is an Idea?" Pp. 49–52 in *Orientation to College*, 2nd ed., edited by E. Steltenpohl, J. Shipton, and S. Villines. Belmont, CA: Thomson/Wadsworth, 1992.

Bornstein, Kate. *My Gender Workbook: How to Become a Real Man, a Real Woman, the Real You, or Something Else Entirely*. New York: Routledge, 1997.

Borysenko, Joan. *Minding the Body, Mending the Mind*. New York: Bantam Books, 1987.

———. *Guilt is the Teacher, Love is the Lesson*. New York: Warner Books, 1990.

Bradshaw, John, E. *Healing the Shame that Binds You*. Deerfield Beach, FL: Health Communications. 1988.

Brantley, Jeffrey, and Wendy Millstine. *Five Good Minutes in Your Body*. Oakland, CA: New Harbinger Publications, 2009.

Braude, Ann. *Radical Spirits: Spiritualism and Women's Rights*. Boston: Beacon Press, 1989.

Brennan, Barbara Ann. *Hands of Light*. New York: Bantam Books, 1987.

Burton, R., and F. F. Arbuthnot. *The Kama Sutra of Vatsyayana*. New York: Putnum, 1963.

Buscaglia, Leo. *Living, Loving & Learning*. New York: Ballantine Books, 1982.

Byrne, Rhonda. *The Secret*. Hillsboro, OR: Beyond Words Publishing, 2006.

Capra, Frijof. *Tao of Physics*. Boston: Shambhala Books, 1975.

———. *The Turning Point: Science, Society, and the Rising Culture*. New York: Simon & Schuster, 1982.

———. *Uncommon Wisdom: Conversations with Remarkable People*. New York: Simon & Schuster, 1988.

———. *The Web of Life: A New Scientific Understanding of Living Systems*. New York: Anchor Books, 1996.

———. *The Hidden Connections: Integrating the Biological, Cognitive, and Social Dimensions of Life into a Science of Sustainability*. New York: Doubleday, 2002.

———. *The Science of Leonardo: Inside the Mind of the Great Genius of the Renaissance*. New York: Doubleday, 2007.

Capra, Frijof, and Charlene Spretnak. *Green Politics: The Global Promise*. New York: Dutton, 1984.

Capra, Frijof, and D. Steindl-Rast. *Belonging to the Universe: Explorations on the Frontiers of Science and Spirituality*. San Francisco: HarperSanFrancisco, 1991.

Carlson, Richard and Joseph Bailey. *Slowing Down to the Speed of Life: How to Create a More Peaceful, Simpler Life From the Inside Out*. San Francisco: HarperSanFrancisco, 1997.

Carrellas, Barbara. *Urban Tantra*. Berkeley, CA: Celestial Arts, 2007.

Casey, Karen. *Change Your Mind and Your Life Will Follow*. Boston: Conari Press, 2005.

Charles, Rachel. *Mind, Body, and Immunity*. London: Mandarin Books, 1990.

Chia, Mantak, and Maneewah Chia. *Healing Love through the Tao: Cultivating Female Sexual Energy*. Huntington. New York: Healing Tao Books, 1986.

Childre, Doc, and Howard Martin. *The Heart Math Solution*. San Francisco: HarperSanFrancisco, 1999.

———. *The HeartMath Solution: Proven Techniques for Developing Emotional Intelligence*. London: Piatkus, 1999.

Chopra, Deepak. *Perfect Health: The Complete Mind/Body Guide*, New York: Three Rivers Press, 1999.

Claremont de Castillejo, Irene. *Knowing Woman: A Feminine Psychology*. New York: Harper Colophon Books, 1973.

Comforti, Michael. *Field, Form and Fate*. Woodstock, CT: Spring Publications, 1997.

Covalt, Patricia. *What Smart Couples Know: The Secret to a Happy Relationship*. New York: American Management Assoc., 2007.

Crowley, Alex. *Eight Lectures on Yoga*. Phoenix, AZ: Falcon Press, 1985.

Dale, Stan. *Fantasies Can Set You Free*. Millbrae, CA: Celestial Arts, 1980.

———. *My Child, My Self*. San Mateo, CA: Human Awareness Publications, 1992.

Damasio, Antonio R. *Descartes' Error: Emotion, Reason and the Human Brain*. New York: G. P. Putnam's Sons, 1994.

———. *The Feeling of What Happens: Body and Emotion in the Making of Consciousness*. New York: Harcourt Brace, 1999.

Davidson, John. *The Web of Life: Life Force—The Energetic Constitution of Man and the NeuroEndocrine Connection*. Essex, UK: C. W. Daniel Co., 1988.

Dewey, Barbara. *As You Believe*. Ft. Wayne, IN: Knoll Publishing Co., 1985.

Dodson, Betty. *Orgasms for Two*. New York: Harmony Books, 2002.

Dolma, L. T. *Healing Mandalas*. London: Duncan Baird Publishers Ltd., 2008.

Dossey, Larry. *Space, Time and Medicine*. New York: Rutledge, 1982.

———. *Healing Words*. New York: HarperCollins, 1993.

———. *Reinventing Medicine: Beyond Body Mind to a New Era of Healing*. New York: HarperCollins, 1999.

Dunas, Felice. *Passion Play: Ancient Secrets for a Lifetime of Health and Happiness through Sensational Sex*. New York: Penguin, 1997.

Dunbar, Helen Flanders. *Emotions and Bodily Changes: A Survey of Literature on Psychosomatic Interrelationships, 1910–1933*. New York: Columbia University Press, 1935.

Dychtwald, Ken. *Bodymind*. Los Angeles, CA: Jeremy P. Tarcher, 1977.

Dyer, Wayne D. *The Power of Intention: Learning to Co-Create Your World Your Way*. Carlsbad, CA: Hay House, 2004.

Easton, Dossie, and Catherine Liszt. *The Ethical Slut: A Guide to Infinite Sexual Possibilities*. San Francisco: Greenery Press, 1997.

Eden, Donna, and David Feinstein. *Energy Medicine*. New York: Tarcher/Putnum, 1998.

Ehrenreich, Barbara, Elizabeth Hess, and Gloria Jacobs. *Remaking Love: The Feminization of Sex*. Garden City, New York: Anchor Press/Doubleday, 1986.

Eisler, Riane. *The Chalice & the Blade*. San Francisco: Harper & Row, 1987.

———. *Sacred Pleasures: Sex, Myth and the Power of the Body*. San Francisco: Harper-SanFrancisco, 1995.

———. *The Power of Partnership*. Novato, CA: New World Library, 2002.

Epstein, Mark. *Thoughts Without a Thinker*. New York: Basic Books, 1995.

Ferguson, Marilyn. *Aquarian Conspiracy*. Madison: University of Wisconsin Press, 1980.

Ferrer, Jorge N. *Revisioning Transpersonal Theory*. Albany: State University of New York Press, 2002.

Fetzer Foundation. *Energy Fields and Medicine: A Study of Device Technology Based on Acupuncture Meridians and Chi Energy*. Kalamazoo, MI: Fetzer Foundation, 1989.

Field, Tiffany. *Infants Born at Risk: Physiological, Perceptual, and Cognitive Processes*. New York: Grune and Stratton, 1983.

———. *Touch in Early Development*. New York: Lawrence Erlbaum Associates, 1995

———. *Touch*. Cambridge, MA: MIT Press, 2003.

Finger, Alan. *Chakra Yoga*. Boston: Shambhala, 2005.

Fisher, Helen. *Anatomy of Love*. New York: W. W. Norton & Co., 1992.

———. *Why We Love*. New York: Henry Holt & Co., 2004.

Fox, Matthew. *Original Blessing: A Primer in Creation Spirituality*. Sante Fe, NM: Bear and Company, 1983.

Frankl, Victor. *Man's Search For Meaning*. Boston: Beacon Press, 1956.

Friedan, Betty. The Feminine Mystique. New York: W. W. Norton, 1963.

Fromm, Erich. *The Revolution of Hope*. New York: Bantam Books, 1968.

———. *The Greatness and Limitations of Freud's Thought*. New York: Harper & Row, 1980.

Gallegos, Eligio S. *Animals of the Four Windows*. Santa Fe, NM: Moon Bear Press, 1992.

Gallo, Fred, and Harry Vincenzi. *Energy Tapping*. Oakland, CA: New Harbinger Publications, 2000.

Gawain, Shakti. *Creative Visualizations*. Berkeley, CA: Nataraj/New World Library, 1978.

Gendlin, Eugene. *Focusing*. New York: Bantam Books, 1978.

Gilligan, Carol. *In a Different Voice*. Cambridge, MA: Harvard University Press, 1982.

Goleman, Daniel. *Emotional Intelligence*. New York: Bantam Books, 1994.

———. *Social Intelligence*. New York: Bantam Books, 2006.

———. *Ecological Intelligence: How Knowing the Hidden Costs of What We Buy Changes Everything*. New York: Random House/Broadway Books, 2009.

Gordon, Richard. *Your Healing Hands: The Polarity Experience*. Berkeley, CA: North Atlantic Books, 1978.

———. *Quantum Touch*. Berkeley, CA: North Atlantic Books, 1999.

Gray, John. *Men are from Mars and Women are from Venus*. London: Thorsons, 1997.

———. *Men, Women, and Relationships*. New York: HarperCollins, 1993.

Greene, Eliot, and Barbara Goodrich-Dunn. *The Psychology of the Body*. Philadelphia: Lippincott, Williams & Wilkins, 2004.

Greenwell, Bonnie. *Energies of Transformation: A Guide to the Kundalini Process*. Saratoga, CA: Shakti River Press, 1990; Transformational Counseling Services, 1995.

Grof, Stanislav with Christine Grof. *Spiritual Emergency*. Los Angeles, CA Tarcher, 1991.

Grof, Stanislov with Hal Zina Bennett. *The Holotrophic Mind: Three Levels of Human Consciousness and How They Shape Our Lives*. San Francisco: HarperSanFrancisco, 1993.

Grun, Bernard. *The Timetables of History*. New York: Simon & Schuster, 1978.

Haddon, Gina. P. *Uniting Sex, Self and Spirit*. Norwick, CT: CT PLUS Publications, 1993.

Handlers, Laurie. *Sex & Happiness: The Tantic Laws of Intimacy*. Ocean Beach, NY: Butterfly Workshops Press, 2007.

Hanh, Tich Nhat. *The Miracle of Mindfulness*. Boston: Beacon Press, 1975.

Harrar, Sari, Julia VanTine, and Barbara Bartik. *Extraordinary Togetherness: A Woman's Guide to Love, Sex and Intimacy*. New York: St. Martin's Press. 1999.

Hay, Louise. *You Can Heal Your Life*. Carlsbad, CA: Hay House, 1994.

Helwig, Monika. *42 Indian Mandalas*. Alameda, CA: Hunter House, 2001.

Hendricks, Gay, and Katherine Hendricks. *At the Speed of Life*. New York: Bantam Books, 1993.

Hendrix, Harville. *Getting the Love You Want*. New York: Holt Publishing, 1988.

———. *Keeping the Love You Find*. New York: Simon & Schuster, 1992.

Hittleman, Richard. L. *The Yoga Way*. New York: Avon Books, 1968.

Horney, Karen. *Neurosis and Human Growth: The Struggle Toward Self Realization*. New York: Norton, 1950.

———. *The Neurotic Personality of Our Time*. New York: W. W. Norton & Co., 1937.

Houston, Jean. *The Possible Human*. Los Angeles: J. P. Tarcher, 1982.

Hover-Kramer, Dorothea. *Creative Energies*. New York: W.W. Norton, 2002.

Hunt, Valerie. *Infinite Mind: Science of Human Vibrations of Consciousness*. Malibu, CA: Malibu Press, 1989/1996.

Jaffe, D. T. *Healing From Within*. New York: Simon & Schuster, 1980.

James, William. *Varieties of Religious Experience*. Cambridge, MA: Harvard University Press, 1902.

Janov, Arthur. *The Primal Scream: Primal Therapy, The Cure for Neurosis*. New York: Putnum, 1970.

———. *The Primal Revolution*. Harleysville, PA: Abacus Press. 1975.

Jawer, Michael. *The Spiritual Anatomy of emotions: How Feelings Link the Braid, the Body and the Sixth Sense*. Rochester, VT: Inner Traditions: Park Street Press, 2002.

Judith, Anodea. *Wheels of Life*. St. Paul, MN: Llewellyn, 1987.

———. *The Truth About Chakras*. St. Paul, MN: Llewellyn, 1994.

———. *Principles of Mind-Body Integration: Therapeutic Techniques for Wholeness*. Unpublished workbook, 1998.

———. *Eastern Body, Western Mind*. Berkeley, CA: Celestial Arts, 2004.

———. *Waking the Global Heart: Humanity's Rite of Passage from the Love of Power to the Power of Love*. Santa Rosa, CA: Elite Books, 2006.

Judith, Anodea, and Selene Vega. *The Sevenfold Journey: Reclaiming Mind, Body & Spirit through the Chakras*. Freedom, CA: Crossing Press. 1993.

Kabat-Zinn, Jon. *The Miracle of Mindfulness.* Boston: Beacon Press, 1987.

———. *Full Catastrophe Living: Using the Wisdom of Your Body and Mind to Face Stress, Pain, and Illness.* New York: Delacorte Press, 1990.

———. *Wherever You Go, There You Are: Mindfulness Meditation in Everyday Life.* New York: Hyperion, 1994.

Kamm, Laura Alden. *Color Intuition.* Boulder, CO: Sounds True, 2008.

Keen, Sam. *Voices and Visions.* New York: Harper & Row, 1970.

Keleman, Stanley. *Human Ground/Sexuality, Self and Survival.* Thousand Oaks, CA: Center Press, 1971.

———. *Living Your Dying.* New York: Random House, 1974.

———. *Somatic Reality.* Thousand Oaks, CA: Center Press, 1979.

———. *Emotional Anatomy: The Structure of Experience.* Thousand Oaks, CA: Center Press, 1985.

———. *Embodying Experience: Forming a Personal Life.* Thousand Oaks, CA: Center Press, 1987.

———. *Patterns of Distress.* Thousand Oaks, CA: Center Press, 1989.

———. *Love: A Somatic View (Clinical Education in Somatic Process).* Thousand Oaks, CA: Center Press, 1994.

———. *Bonding.* Thousand Oaks, CA: Center Press, 1996.

Keller, Thomas C. *Pure Limitless Energy: How to Get & Keep It.* Los Angeles, CA: TK Quality Co., 1993.

Kelly, Matthew. *The Seven Levels of Intimacy.* New York: Fireside, 2005.

Keyes, Ken. Jr. *Handbook to Higher Consciousness.* Coos Bay, OR: Living Love Center, 1975.

———. *Conscious Person's Guide to Relationships.* Cool Bay, OR: Love Line Books, 1979.

———. *The One Hundredth Monkey.* Mill Valley, CA: Visions Books, 1984.

Kieffer, Gene, ed. *Kundalini for the New Age: Selected Writings of Gopi Krishna.* New York: Bantam Books, 1978–1988.

Kigma, Daphne Rose. *The Future of Love: The Power of the Soul in Intimate Relationships.* New York: Broadway Books, 2001.

Kilner, Walter J. *The Human Aura.* Secaucus, NJ: Citadel Press, 1965.

Kinsey, Alfred C., Wardell B. Pomeroy, and Clyde E. Martin. *Sexual Behavior in the Human Male.* Philadelphia: W. B. Saunders Company, 1948.

———. *Sexual Behavior in the Human Female.* Bloomington: Indiana University Press, 1998.

Kornfield, Jack. *A Path With Heart: A Guide Through the Perils and Promises of Spiritual Life.* New York: Bantam Books, 1993.

Kotulak, Ronald. *Inside the Brain: Revolutionary Discoveries of How the Mind Works.* Riverside, NJ: Andrews McMeel Publishing, 1997.

Krieger, Delores. *The Therapeutic Touch: How to Use Your Hands To Heal.* New York: Prentice Hall.

Krippner, Stanley, and Daniel Rubin, eds. *The Kirlian Aura: Photographing the Galaxies of Life.* Garden City, NY: Anchor Books, 1974.

Krishna, Gopi. *Living with Kundalini: The Evolutionary Energy in Man.* Boston: Shambhala, 1993.

Krishnamurti, Jidda. *You Are the World*. Wassenaar, Netherlands: Servire, 1972.

Kurianski, Judy. *The Complete Idiot's Guide to Tantric Sex*. Indianapolis, IN: Alpha Books, 2002.

Kurtz, Ron. *Body-Centered Psychotherapy*. Mendecino, CA: LifeRhythms, 1997.

Kuthumi, Djwal Kul. *The Human Aura*. Los Angeles: Summit University Press, 1962.

Lancaster, Roger. "The Trouble with Nature: Sex in Science and Popular Culture." Found in Adrian Brune, April 16, 2004, www.washblade.com/2004/4-16/news/national/antrho.cfm.

Lark, Susan. *Overcoming Chronic Fatigue: Effective Self-Help Options to Relieve the Fatigue Associated With Cfs, Candida, Allergies, Pms, Menopause, Anemia, Low Thyroid and Depression*. New York: McGrawHIll, 1996.

Leadbeater, C. W. "The Aura: An Enquiry into the Nature and Functions of the Luminous Mist Seen about Human and Other Bodies." *The Theosophist*, http://leadbeater.info/1895.

Lesser, Elizabeth. *The New American Spirituality*. New York: Random House, 1999.

Levine, Barbara. *Your Body Believes Every Word You Say*. Lower Lake, CA: Aslan, 1991.

Levine, Peter, with Ann Frederick. *Waking the Tiger, Healing Trauma: The Innate Capacity to Transform Overwhelming Experiences*. Berkeley, CA: North Atlantic Books, 1997.

Lewis, C. S. *The Four Loves*. New York: Harcourt Brace Jovanovich, 1960.

Lewis, Howard R., and Martha E. Lewis. *Psychosomatics: How Your Emotions Damage Your Health*. New York: Viking Press, 1972.

Lewis. T., F. Amini, and R. Lannon. *A General Theory of Love*. New York: Vantage Books/Random House, 2001.

Lilly, John. *Programming and Metaprogramming in the Human Biocomputer*. New York: Julian Press, 1972.

Lowen, Alexander. *The Voice of the Body*. Alachua, FL: Bioenergetic Press, 2005.

Magdalena, Ina. *Libido: Where Sex, Science and Spirit Meet*. Altona, Canada: Friesens, 2006.

Maines, Rachel. *Technology of Orgasm: "Hysteria," the Vibrator, and Women's Sexual Satisfaction*. Baltimore, MD: The Johns Hopkins University, 2001.

Mann, W. Edward. *Orgone, Reich and Eros: Wilhelm Reich's Theory of Life Energy*. New York: Simon & Schuster, 1973.

Mann, W. Edward, and Edward Hoffman. *The Man Who Dreamed of Tomorrow: A Conceptual Biography of Wilhelm Reich*. Los Angeles, CA: Crucible, 1990.

Marks, Linda. *Healing the War Between the Genders*. Boston: HeartPower Press, 2004.

Martine, Yvonne, and Linda Clark. *Health, Youth and Beauty through Color Breathing*. Millbrae, CA: Celestial Arts, 1976.

Maslow, Abraham H. *Motivation and Personality*. New York: Harper & Row Publishers, 1954.

——. *Religions, Values and Peak Experiences*. Columbus: University of Ohio Press, 1964.

May, Rollo, *Love and Will*. New York: W.W. Norton and Company, 1969.

Mazza, Joan. *Dreaming Your Real Self*. New York: Berkley Publishing Co., 1998.

McCallum, Ian. *Ecological Intelligence: Rediscovering Ourselves in Nature*. Boulder, CO: Fulcrum Publishing, 2008.

McGaugh, James L. *Memory and Emotion*. New York: Columbia University Press, 2003.

McLaren, Karla. *Your Aura and Your Chakras: The Owner's Manual*. York Beach, ME: S. Weiser, 1998.

——. *Emotional Genius: Discovering the Deepest Language of the Soul*. Columbia, CA: Laughing Tree Press, 2001.

McLynn, Frank. *Carl Gustav Jung*. New York: St. Martin's Press, 1996.

McTaggart, Lynn. *The Field: The Quest for the Secret Force of the Universe*. New York: HarperCollins, 2002.

——. *The Intention Experiment: Using Your Thoughts to Change Your Life and the World*. New York: Simon & Schuster, 2008.

Metzinger, Thomas. The Ego Tunnel: *The Science of the Mind and the Myth of the Self*. New York: Basic Books, 2009.

Michaels, Mark A., and Patrica Johnson. *The Essence of Tantric Sexuality*. Woodbury, MN: Llewellyn, 2006.

——. *Tantra for Erotic Empowerment*. Woodbury, MN: Llewellyn, 2008.

Mikulas, William L. *Integrative Helper*. Pacific Grove, CA: Brooks/Cole, 2002.

Moir, Anne, and David Jessel. *Brain Sex*. Delta, 1992.

Mountrose, Phillip, and Jane Mountrose. *Getting Thru to Your Emotions with EFT: Tap Into Your Hidden Potential with the Emotional Freedom Techniques*. Sacramento, CA: Holistic Communications, 1999.

Moustakas, Clark E. *Loneliness and Love*. Englewood Cliffs, NJ: Prentice-Hall, 1972.

Mumford, John [Swami Anandakapila Saraswati]. *Psychosomatic Yoga: A Guide to Eastern Path Techniques*. Wellingborough, UK: Aquarian Press, 1974.

——. *Sexual Occultism; The Sorcery of Love in Practice and Theory*. St. Paul, MN: Llewellyn Publications, 1975.

Nearing, Ryam. *Loving More: The Polyfidelity Primer*. Captain Hook, HI: PEP Publishing Co., 1992.

Nichols, Sallie. *Jung and the Tarot: An Archetypal Journey*. New York: Samuel Weiser, 1980.

Northrup, Christiane. *Mother-Daughter Wisdom: Creating a Legacy of Physical and Emotional Health*. New York: Bantam Books, 2005.

——. *Women's Bodies, Women's Wisdom: Creating Physical and Emotional Health and Healing*. New York: Bantam Books, 1994.

Odier, Daniel. *Desire: The Tantric Path to Awakening*. Rochester, VT: Inner Traditions International, 2001.

Ogden, Gina. *Woman Who Love Sex*. Boston: Shambhala. 1996.

——. *The Heart and Soul of Sex*. Boston: Shambhala, 2006.

——. *Return of Desire*. Boston: Shambhala, 2008.

Ornish, Dean. *Dr. Dean Ornish's Program for Reversing Heart Disease*. New York: Random House, 1991.

Ornstein, Robert. *The Evolution of Consciousness*. Upper Saddle River, NJ: Prentice Hall, 1991.

Orr, Leonard. *Physical Immortality: The Science of Everlasting Life*. Berkeley. CA: Celestial Arts, 1982.

———. *The Story of Rebirthing.* Staunton, VA: Inspiration University, 1990.

Orr, Leonard, with Sondra Ray. *Rebirthing in the New Age.* Bloomington, IN: Trafford Publishing, 2007.

Öz, Mehmet, and Michael Roizen. *YOU: The Owner's Manual: An Insider's Guide to the Body that Will Make You Healthier and Younger.* New York: Collins, 2005.

Öz, Mehmet, Ron Arias, and Dean Ornish, *Healing from the Heart: A Leading Surgeon Combines Eastern and Western Traditions to Create the Medicine of the Future.* New York: Collins, 1999.

Palmer, Helen. *The Enneagram.* New York: HarperCollins Publishers, 1991.

Parnell, Laurel *Transforming Trauma—EMDR: The Revolutionary New Therapy for Freeing the Mind, Clearing the Body, and Opening the Heart.* New York: W. W. Norton & Co., 1997.

Pearce, Joseph Chilton. *The Biology of Transcendence: A Blueprint of the Human Spirit.* Inner Traditions, VT: Park Street Press, 2002.

Pearce, Joseph Chilton, and Thom Hartmann, *The Crack in the Cosmic Egg: New Constructs of Mind and Reality.* Melbourne: Lyrebird Press Ltd., 1973.

Peck, M. Scott. *Road Less Traveled.* New York: Simon & Schuster, 1978.

Pelletier, Kenneth. *Mind as Healer, Mind as Slayer.* New York: Delta Books, 1977.

———. *Toward a Science of Consciousness.* New York: Delta Books, 1978.

Pert, Candace. *Everything You Need to Know to Find Go(o)d.* Carlsbad, CA: Hay House, 2006.

———. *Molecules of Emotion: The Science Behind Mind-Body Medicine.* New York: Simon & Schuster, 1977.

———. *Your Body is Your Subconscious Mind.* Audio recording. 2004.

Pierrakos, John C. *Core Energetics.* Mendocino, CA: LifeRhythm Publications, 1989.

———. *Eros, Love and Sexuality.* Mendocino, CA: LifeRhythm Publications, 1997.

Pinker, Steven. *The Blank Slate.* New York: Penquin, 2003.

Prescott, James W., Merrill S. Read, and David Baird Coursin, eds. *Brain Function and Malnutrition: Neuropsychological Methods of Assessment.* New York: Wiley, 1975.

Radha, Sivananda. *Kundalini Yoga for the West.* Boulder, CO: Shambhala Publications, Inc., 1978.

Rama, S., and S. Ajaya. *The Creative Use of Emotions.* Honesdale, PA: Himalayan Institute, 1988.

Reich, Peter. *A Book of Dreams.* New York: Harper & Row, 1973.

Reich, Wilhelm. *The Function of the Orgasm.* New York: Orgone Institute Press, 1942.

———. *The Bioelectric Investigation of Sexuality and Anxiety.* New York: Farrar, Straus & Giroux 1982.

Resnick, Stella. *The Pleasure Zone.* Berkeley, CA: Conari Press, 1997.

Riso, Don Richard. *Personality Types: Using the Enneagram for Self-Discovery.* Boston: Houghton Mifflin Company, 1987.

Robinson, Marina. *Peace Between the Sheets: Healing With Sexual Relationships.* Berkeley, CA: Frog Books, 2003.

Rosenberg, Marshall B. *Nonviolent Communication: A Language of Life*, 2nd ed. Encinitas, CA: Puddle Dancer Press, 2003.

Rossi, Ernest. *Mind-Body Therapy*. New York: W.W. Norton, 1968.

Rubin, Lillian B. *Intimate Strangers: Men and Women Together*. New York: Harper-Perennial, 1984.

——. *Erotic Wars: What Happened to the Sexual Revolution?* New York: Farrar, Straus & Giroux, Inc. 1990.

——. *60 and UP*. Boston: Beacon Press, 2007.

Savage, Linda E. *Reclaiming Goddess Sexuality: The Power of the Feminine Way*. Carlsbad, CA: Hay House, 1999.

Schaef, Anne Wilson. *Women's Reality*. New York: Harper & Row Publishers, 1981.

Scharmer, Otto. *Theory U: Leading from the Future as it Emerges*. Cambridge, MA: Society for Organizational Learning, 2007.

Schnarch, David Morris. *Constructing the Sexual Crucible: An Integration of Sexual and Marital Therapy*. New York: W. W. Norton, 1991; reissued as *Passionate Marriage: Love, Sex, and Intimacy in Emotionally Committed Relationships*. New York: W. W. Norton, 1997.

Schulz, Mona Lisa. *Awakening Intuition: Using Your Mind-Body Network for Insight and Healing*. New York: Harmony Books, 1998.

——. *Voluntary Controls*. New York: Dutton, 1978.

Scott, M. *Kundalini in the Physical World*. London: Routledge & Kegan Paul, 1983.

Seyle, Hans. *The Stress of Life*. New York: McGraw Hill, 1956.

——. *Stress Without Distress*. Philadelphia: Lippincott, 1974.

Schwarz, Jack. *Human Energy Systems*. New York: Dutton, 1980.

Shapiro, Francine, and Margot Silk Forrest. *EMDR: The Breakthrough Therapy for Overcoming Anxiety, Stress, and Trauma*. New York: Basic Books, 1988.

Sheldrake, Rupert. *A New Science of Life: The Hypothesis of Formative Causation*. Los Angeles: J.P. Tarcher; Boston: Houghton Mifflin, 1981.

——. *The Presence of the Past: Morphic Resonance and the Habits of Nature*. New York: Vintage Books, 1988.

——. *The Rebirth of Nature: The Greening of Science and God*. New York: Bantam Books, 1991.

Shlain, Leonard *The Alphabet versus the Goddess: Conflict Between Word and Image*. New York: Penguin Compass Group, 1998.

Shumsky, Susan. *Sexual Peace: Beyond the Dominator Virus*. Santa Fe, NM: Bear & Co, 1993.

——. *Exploring Chakras*. Franklin Lakes, NY: Career Press, 2003.

Siegal, Bernie S. *Love, Medicine and Miracles: Lessons Learned about Self-Healing from a Surgeon's Experience with Exceptional Patients*. New York: Harper & Row, 1986.

Sky, M. *Breathing: Expanding Your Power and Energy*. Santa Fe, NM: Bear & Co., 1990.

Somé, Sobonfu. *Spirit of Intimacy: Ancient Africa Teachings in the Ways of Relationships*. Berkeley, CA: Berkeley Hills Books, 1977.

Spiegelman, J. M. *Hinduism and Jungian Psychology*. Phoenix, AZ: Falcon Press, 1987.

Spitz, Renee. "Hospitalism" in *The Psychoanalytic Study of the Child*, vol. 1. New York: International Universities Press, 1954.

Stein, Diane. *Essential Reiki*. Freedom, CA: Crossing Press, 1995.

Stevens, Jon O. *Awareness: Exploring, Experimenting, Experiencing*. Moab, UT: Real People Press, 1974.

Talbot, Michael. *Beyond the Quantum*. New York: Macmillan, 1986.

——. *The Holographic Universe*. New York: HarperCollins Publishers, 1991.

Tanenbaum, Joe. *Male and Female Realities: Understanding the Opposite Sex*. Sonora, CA: Columbine Communications & Publications, 1990.

Tannen, Deborah. *You Just Don't Understand: Women and Men in Conversation*. New York: HarperCollins, 1990.

Tavris, Carol. *Anger: The Misunderstood Emotion*. New York: Simon & Schuster, 1982.

Taylor, Karen. *The Ethics of Caring: Honoring the Web of Life in Professional Relationships*. Santa Cruz, CA: Hanford Mead Publishers, 1995.

Terrell, Lisa. *Snow People World: Healthy and Happy Relationships*. Self-published, 2007.

Thie, John. *Touch for Health: A Practical Guide*. Marina del Ray, CA: Devorss & Co., 1973.

Thurston, Mark. *Synchronicity as Spiritual Guidance*. Virginia Beach, VA: ARE Press. 1977.

——. *Essential Edgar Cayce*. New York: Jeremy Tarcher, 2004.

Tolle, Eckert. *The Power of Now: A Guide to Spiritual Enlightenment*. New York: New World Library, 1999.

Watts, Alan. *Psychotherapy East and West*. New York: Random House, 1961.

——. *Man, Woman and Nature*. New York: Vintage, 1991.

——. *Nature, Man and Woman*. New York: Pantheon Books, 1958.

Weil, Andrew. *Spontaneous Healing*. New York: Fawcett Columbine, 1995.

——. *Roots of Healing: The New Medicine*. Carlsbad, Ca: Hay House, 1997.

——. *Eight Weeks to Optimum Health: A Proven Program for Taking Full Advantage of Your Body's Natural Healing Power*. New York: A.A. Knopf, 1997.

Weldwood, John, ed. *Awakening the Heart: East West Approaches to Psychotherpay and the Healing Relationship*. Boulder, CO: Shambhala, 1983.

——. *Challenge of the Heart: Love, Sex and Intimacy in Changing Times*. Boston: Shambhala, 1985.

White, John, and Stanley Krippner. *Future Science: Life Energies and the Physics of Paranormal Phenomena*. Garden City, NY: Anchor Books, 1977.

White, Ruth. *Working with Your Chakras*. York Beach, ME: Samuel Weiser, 1994.

Wilbur, Ken. *The Essential Wilber*. Boston & London: Shambhala, 1999.

Wing, R. L. *The I Ching Workbook*. New York: Doubleday & Co., 1979.

Winton-Henry, Cynthia, and Phil Porter. *What the Body Wants*. Kelowna, BC, Canada: Northstone Publishing, 2004.

Wydro, Ken. *Secrets Revealed: The Untold Story of Sigmund Freud and Carl Jung*. Staged Reading, August 11, 2006.

Yogananda, Paramahansa. *Autobiography of a Yogi*. New York: Philosophical Library, 1946.

Zukav, Gary. *The Dancing Wu-Li Masters*. New York: William Morrow, 1979.

——. *The Seat of the Soul*. New York: Simon & Schuster, 1990.

INDEX

ABOUT THE AUTHOR

Suzann Panek Robins currently lives in Denver, Colorado, after spending time in Vienna, Austria, researching the lives of Freud and Jung. The material for this book came together after many years of practicing and teaching tai chi and yoga. She is available to speak to audiences large and small about the material synthesized in this book. She can be reached at suzannrobins@gmail.com.

5/10